Cycling ·in· France

◆Tim Hughes◆

The Crowood Press

First published in 1996 by
The Crowood Press Ltd
Ramsbury, Marlborough
Wiltshire SN8 2HR

British Library Cataloguing-in-Publication Data
A catalogue record for this book is available from the British
Library

ISBN 1 85223 961 1

Picture Credits
All photographs and maps by Tim Hughes/Cyclographic

Printed and bound by Times Offset, Malaysia

Contents

Acknowledgements   4

Introduction   5

  1. About France   7

  2. Getting There   24

  3. Accommodation   30

  4. Places to Eat   34

  5. Touring Bikes   37

  6. Roads and Maps   42

  7. Cycling the French Way   50

  8. Cross-Channel Weekends   59

  9. Fairly Gentle France   67

 10. A Bit Hillier   90

 11. Moderate Mountains   108

 12. The High Mountains   128

Useful Books   159

Useful Organizations   161

Glossary of French Road Signs   163

Glossary of French Cycle Terms   165

Place Names Index   170

Subject Index   175

Acknowledgements

Once again I have to record my deep indebtedness to Jenny Ballinger (formerly Reason) for her unstinted help – some of it in very difficult circumstances – in researching many of the routes in this book, and to Johanna Cleary for her help with route research and her additional support in the long search for a publisher after the demise of the one that originally commissioned the work.

The following (in alphabetical order to avoid accusations of favouritism) were also companions on some of the fact-finding and route-prospecting trips. Their support and company proved invaluable: Heather Beeson, Ted Beeson, Simon Butcher, Pat Cooper, Karen Crombie, Gina Farmer, Debbie Garnett (now Butcher), Sue Hall, Chris Horsler, Roger Hughes, Richard Page, Chris Stevens and Caroline Young (now Holub). Wherever the words 'we' and 'us' crop up, it is not through any delusion of regal or even editorial grandeur – just a grateful acknowledgement that I was rarely alone on the road.

I should also like to put on record the inspiration of the late Mrs Catherine E. Wears-Taylor, who managed to convey a love of France and its language to a class of unruly 14-year-olds who probably never dreamed in those austere post-war days that they would one day actually visit the country. Finally, I owe much to the writers, photographers and publishers of those magnificent indigo and sepia photogravure magazines of the 1950s, *But-et-Club* and *Miroir-Sprint,* whose superb coverage of the Tour de France in the Alps and Pyrenees made me want to go and see the mountains for myself. Thank you all.

Introduction

France and the British Isles are close neighbours: the cliffs of Dover in Kent are barely 32km from Cap Gris Nez near Calais, each easily visible from the other across the Channel. This watery barrier opened up only some 8000 years ago, but ever since it has been a natural punctuation mark – sadly, some people make it a full stop.

Yet this narrow Channel is quick and easy to cross, hardly worth a comma. True, they do not speak English over there, but French is still the most common foreign language to be taught in UK schools, despite the ups and downs of Anglo-French relations over the centuries. France is naturally the first foreign country that most Britons visit, and many fall rapidly in love with the land and its culture.

For cycle tourists France has extra offerings. To begin with, it is a spacious country by European standards, two and a half times the size of the UK. As the population is roughly the same, there is a great deal more room and – given the superb network of minor roads – very much less traffic outside the towns and off the major routes. The range of landscape is immense, from leafy and domestic to glacier-topped high mountains, from the almost English north to the hot and Mediterranean south. About the only things that France lacks are real desert and a coastline to rival the grandeur of the west coasts of Ireland, Scotland and Wales.

Bikes have a particular place in French culture. The UK and France shared the early development of the bicycle but it was France that adopted cycling as a sport to the degree that cycling stars are national heroes and heroines. Meanwhile the bicycle itself has a special sentimental spot in French affections as *la petite reine* (the little queen). Finally, there is no better end-of-day complement to a cyclist's out-door appetite than superb food – and you have to look no farther than France's national art for that.

Cycle touring anywhere can stimulate all the senses; in France it can be a sensuous affair indeed. One of the delights of gentle cycling is the tremendous variety of scents that drift across your path. On these tours we met the sudden, resinous smell of pines in the heat of the Midi, the heady autumn waft of fermenting grapes in Champagne and the Beaujolais, the scent of spring flowers in the Alpine uplands, the aroma of herbs and lavender in a Provençal summer, the sharpness of wood smoke in a dozen forests. But of all of them, the abiding memory is the mouth-watering smell of lovingly crafted soups and sauces hanging in delicious, mingling pools across a myriad of villages and hamlets as the clock neared noon or on a still evening as dusk fell.

But surely there must be some blemish on this earthly paradise? Well, the French are fiercely proud of their country and its culture and achievements. The country that gave birth to Descartes – and which uses a great deal of unarguable logic in its everyday administration and affairs – also fostered Nicolas Chauvin: *chauvinisme* (my country, right or wrong) is quite definitely French. Even if they detest a particular government, the bureaucracy, or some other national irritant of the moment, the French reserve the right of criticism to themselves, defending the institutions fiercely against any foreign attack. The country sometimes behaves with an independence that can seem perverse and stubborn to outsiders.

The French firmly believe that theirs is the language in which all civilized discourse is conducted and the only one in which romance is even possible. They also tend to believe in their own ways of doing things and their own manufactures. Foreign-built cars, for example, are less common in France than in the UK, and there was a near explosion in the French cycling world when a French cycle manufacturer first dared to fit *Japanese* components.

Despite two centuries of *liberté, egalité, fraternité,* there is still some dichotomy between the richest and poorest parts of French society – the largely metropolitan haves and the rural have-nots. France has been in administration and outwardly perceived culture extremely Paris-centred, even if strong regional identity is now being reflected in regional government and institutions. Meanwhile, you should never forget – while noting the country's overall affluence and a welcome willingness to spend public money on projects for the public good – that a great deal of the picturesque character of remote rural France stems from the hard life followed by those working the land, now and over many centuries. Remember the debt you owe them as you watch the play of light and shade on the perfect sculpture of an Alpine meadow, stony-terraced vineyard, riverside orchard or olive grove.

The major part of this book covers specific – and unashamedly rural – routes in different parts of France, chosen to give not only a progress from easy to strenuous but to introduce you to some of the immense variety of the country's landscape. But they are only samples from an enormous whole, and your discovery of France should not end with them. I hope that these tours will be only a beginning, for the real object of this book is to help you to make friends, by bicycle, with a great and beautiful country and – by extension – with its people. If it succeeds in that, then it will have done what it set out to do, and you will have found for yourself that cycle touring in France can be inspiring, that it can be exciting – and above all that it can be fun. *Bonne route – et bon appetit!*

1
About France

France is roughly hexagonal and about 1,000km from corner to opposite corner – French TV, newspapers and magazines often refer to *la hexagone* when they mean mainland France. In general the north, west and north-east are flattish or rolling, while the centre (the Massif Central), the south-west (the Pyrenees) and the east (the Vosges, Jura and Alps) are where the mountains are. The Massif Central and the Alps are separated by the great cleft of the valley of the River Rhône, and the Jura from the Alps by Lac Leman (Lake Geneva). While the high mountains include many areas of igneous rocks such as granite – crystallized direct from the molten magma beneath the Earth's crust – or have been changed by exposure to high temperatures and pressures during the mountain-building process, a large part of upland and lowland France is limestone, and this imparts many of the features of the landscape. There is more detail on individual areas later in this chapter.

As mentioned earlier, France has for long been very centralized in its administration. Moves beginning as far back as the 1950s but finally implemented only in 1982 decentralized some aspects of government by establishing groupings of *départements* to form precisely defined regions, with regional capitals and some degree of autonomy. Now quite a few institutions, among them tourist boards, are arranged on a regional basis. The names of the old historical divisions of France – such as Aquitaine, Burgundy, Normandy, Picardie, Savoie, many of them originally independent kingdoms, dukedoms and the like – live on in some of these new regions. The map on page 8 shows these official administrative regions. More of the old names frequently crop up in general travel writing – much as in England we might refer to Wessex or the Cotswolds – the map on page 9 shows some of those.

For more local administration the country is divided into 93 départements (plus two more for Corsica), the rough equivalent of English counties. Most are named after natural physical features, often large rivers that flow through them, presumably to stave off local rivalries if the names of large towns and cities had been used instead when they were established nearly 200 years ago. These départements are numbered in alphabetical order from 01 for Ain to 89 for Yonne, with 90 to 95 used for more recent divisions. These numbers usefully form the first element of postcodes and the last element of car number plates, as well as being universally used as shorthand instead of the name. There are farther subdivisions down to *commune* level – roughly the equivalent of an English parish, but with rather more administrative powers.

WHEN TO VISIT

For the French, July and August are the traditional holiday months, with firms often shutting down from mid July to mid August, or for the whole of August. This means that the pressures on accommodation and travel are highest then, with chaos on many main roads when millions of Parisian holidaymakers seem to set off or return at once. Fortunately, these are perhaps the least pleasant months for cycling, particularly in the south where it can become uncomfortably hot – and I write as someone who likes it hot.

For the south, spring is superb, with temperatures from mid March often matching an English June and the spring blossom a bonus – ideal for an Easter break. As May progresses into June, the heat can become oppressive at low altitudes but it is very pleasant higher up, say at 1000 or 1500m. However, some of the highest mountain roads are still blocked by snow until the end of June or early July, though this varies with the severity of the preceding winter. With this proviso, and bearing in mind that some facilities such as restaurants, hotels and camp sites may not yet have opened, May and June are highly recommended.

Autumn, after the end of the August rush, is again a fine time, with virtually all the roads open, and autumn tints beginning quite early in the mountains. Some hotels and camp sites begin shutting up shop in mid September; in mountain areas many proprietors snatch their annual break in this gap between the summer and winter seasons.

Winter touring is not practical in much of France because of the cold weather. However, the west, which comes under the influence of the Atlantic, and regions bordering the Mediterranean can be suitable for cycling at almost any time.

Spring in the Tarn gorges. Spring is one of the best seasons for cycling in the southern half of France.

The official administrative regions of France.

THE REGIONS OF FRANCE

The official administrative regions are listed here in geographical order from west to east and north to south – as though you were working through them on the map like words on a page. After the name of the region are given the names of the départements it comprises and any of our routes in the region. There is more local detail in the route descriptions in later chapters.

Nord-Pas-de-Calais and Picardie

Départements 59-Nord, 62-Pas-de-Calais; 02-Aisne, 60-Oise, 80-Somme
Route Boulogne

These two northernmost regions run almost seamlessly into each other and

Some of the older divisions of France.

the lower Seine and, once more, are strongly reminiscent of southern England, but in this case of the patchwork of small fields, known in France as *bocage*. Here is a country of stock-raising and of course orchards, from which come cider and its distilled spirit calvados. Between Dieppe and Le Havre in the north-east the coast has some fine chalk cliffs, while to the west the coast of the Cotentin peninsula gives a foretaste of the ruggedness of Brittany.

Southern Normandy is quite hilly and in many ways reminiscent of the Forest of Dean. At the foot of the Cotentin peninsula lies the spectacularly sited Mont St Michel, crowned with its soaring cathedral. Bayeux, farther east, houses the famous Tapestry depicting William of Normandy's successful 1066 excursion, as well as another fine cathedral. Farms and villages are more humble, with thatch and cob walling common.

The Seine valley gives some fine

are – together with much of Normandy – the most English part of France. Not surprisingly, since until about 8000 years ago they were one, they share the downland landscapes of their English counterparts, though for the most part with fewer hedged fields so that the high-yielding arable land rolls to the horizon, interrupted only by small river valleys.

The regions are far less densely settled than nearby England, enhancing the feeling of open space. Easily accessible via Boulogne, Calais, Dunkerque and the Channel Tunnel, they also have a network of minor byroads and enough essentially Gallic atmosphere to make a fine introduction to leisurely cycle touring in France.

Basse-Normandie and Haute-Normandie

Départements 14-Calvados, 50-Manche, 61-Orne; 27-Eure, 76-Seine-Maritime
Route Cherbourg

These two regions span the winding valley of

Lush grazing and tree-lined streams – a Normandy landscape.

cycling, though it is hillier than you might expect, with bridges or ferries crossing many of the meanders. Like the two northern regions, Normandy offers enough Frenchness and enough variety to make a fine introductory tour in France. It is easily reached from southern England through the ports of Dieppe, Le Havre, Ouistreham (Caen), Cherbourg and St Malo. Boats from Ireland also cross to Cherbourg and Le Havre.

Île-de-France (Région Parisienne)

Départements 75-Paris, 77-Seine-et-Marne, 78-Yvelines, 91-Essonne, 92-Hauts-de-Seine, 93-Seine-St-Denis, 94-Val-de-Marne, 95-Val-d'Oise

This is a region where the population density approaches that of the UK. Over a fifth of the French working population lives in this 'island' between the valleys of the rivers Seine, Aisne, Oise and Marne, although it occupies an area of only a fiftieth of the whole country. France is still a very forested country – something like a quarter of it is woodland – and great forests such as Fontainebleau and Rambouillet surround the capital.

Affluent for many centuries, it is a region rich in architecture – even leaving aside the splendours of Paris – with such spectacular buildings as the cathedral at Chartres. As with any capital city, traffic is heavier in the immediate surrounds of Paris, but pleasant cycling country – not unlike the middle Thames Valley and its nearby hills in England – extends surprisingly close to the city. Paris can be reached by air from most foreign airports or by rail from London, while the region is a relatively short road distance from the ports of Dieppe and Le Havre.

Champagne-Ardenne

Départements 08-Ardennes, 10-Aube, 51-Marne, 52-Haute-Marne
Route Montagne de Reims

With this region, north-east of Paris, you begin to encounter the real wide-open cereal lands of France. The Paris basin is rather like an enlargement of the area surrounding London, with outward-facing chalk and limestone scarps. One of these, the Montagne de Reims, is the source of the grapes for the world's best-known sparkling wine, and provides

the setting for one of our routes. Stretching away from here are broad open farmlands merging into wooded areas, including the great forest of Argonne, with a number of natural ponds and artificial lakes. The whole makes very pleasant, if unspectacular, rolling cycling country but settlements – which means sources of food and accommodation – can be quite a long way apart.

To the north, the Ardennes département shares part of the character of the Belgian Ardennes and the German Eifel, heavily forested with mixed broad-leafed trees and conifers, dissected by deep river valleys. It is decidedly hilly. The region is quite a way inland – Reims is some 250km from the nearest Channel port, Dieppe – and is probably most easily reached via Paris or Amiens.

Lorraine and Alsace

Départements 54-Meurthe-et-Moselle, 55-Meuse, 57-Moselle, 88-Vosges; 67-Bas-Rhin, 68-Haut-Rhin

Merging with Champagne to the west, Lorraine is largely a transition zone of mixed farming (a landscape that Michelin dismisses as 'monotonous') between the plains and the mountains of the Vosges. Part of Lorraine, a band north from Nancy to the Luxembourg border and taking in Metz, was the cradle of French heavy metallurgical, chemical and engineering industry, though much of this has declined in recent decades, as elsewhere in Europe.

This is an area that has been fought over for centuries and there are many traces, war cemeteries and monuments (as indeed there are over most of northern France) to the First and Second World Wars. In the 1914–18 conflict, Verdun was the scene of terrible French losses in a campaign lasting a year and a half. This is commemorated in the sombre Voie Sacrée, with memorial kilometre stones and other markers, leading to the town, which lies on one of northern Europe's great rivers, the Meuse.

The Vosges are the northernmost of France's mountains, with the highest point the Grand Ballon towards the southern end at 1,424m. The northern section of the ridge is red sandstone, the southern part, including the rounded summits of the *ballons*, is granite, giving a variety of scenery. Numerous small roads and minor cols (and one or two not so minor) cross the range, and for part of the length there is a ridge road, the Route des Crêtes, which makes for some fine cycling at about 1000m. Roads also go to the top of the Grand Ballon, and almost to the tops of the Petit Ballon (1,267m) and the Ballon d'Alsace (1,250m, road height 1,178m), figuring from time to time and occasionally decisively on the route of the Tour de France.

The mountains are heavily wooded – except for the summits, which are mostly high-level pasture – with lakes nestling in many of the hollows. The rounded rather than rugged summits and the mixture of tree and pasture give the Vosges something of the appeal of the English counties of Shropshire and Herefordshire, on a scale approaching the Scottish Highlands. The Vosges are particularly attractive in spring (when snow may linger since the winters are frequently very hard) and autumn. The use of the mountains for downhill and extensive cross-country skiing in winter means that accommodation is plentiful.

The Vosges lie partly in the administrative region of Lorraine and partly in Alsace. True Alsace is the narrow strip between the mountains and the Rhine. It has a distinctly Germanic air and a Germanic local dialect. It is an area of orchards and vineyards, often with almost chocolate-box villages of black-and-white timber frame houses bedecked with flower baskets. Alsatian wines, virtually all varietal whites, also tend towards the Germanic in character, though they are noticeably drier.

You are most likely to reach Lorraine as part of an eastward traverse across northern France, although it is possible to fly or travel by rail to Nancy. The easiest access to the Vosges, again by rail or air, is by way of Strasbourg, the decidedly European city that is the capital of Alsace.

Bretagne *(Brittany)*

Départements   22-Côtes-du-Nord, 29-Finistère, 35-Ille-et-Vilaine, 56-Morbihan

Brittany is probably the part of France most visited by cyclists from the UK. Like Wales and Cornwall, it is part of Europe's Celtic fringe, having been populated in the fifth century by settlers from Cornwall. The Celtic language, Breton, is very similar to Welsh and is quite widely spoken and, give or take a few lls and k for c, place names look very Welsh or Cornish, with similar Celtic saints' names commemorated: Breton Langolen is obviously Llangollen (St Collen),

for example, while Kerhuel is recognizably Caerhywel.

The province is a great granite peninsula jutting into the Atlantic, with a rugged and very indented coastline that also shelters sandy bays and fishing harbours. Inland are the remains of the forests that once covered the area and broad tracts of heath and moorland relatively uncommon in the rest of France. With all this ruggedness it comes as something of a surprise that the highest point in Brittany, the Roc Trévezel, is only 384m – lower than the higher parts of much gentler Normandy. The region is rich in prehistoric remains, with the most spectacular the alignments of megaliths at Carnac. There is an abundance of minor roads, some of them quite hilly, and accommodation is plentiful. Brittany may be reached direct by sea from Plymouth or Cork to Roscoff, or from Portsmouth to St Malo, the attractive walled town that lies at the junction of Brittany and Normandy.

Pays de la Loire and Centre

Départements   44-Loire-Atlantique, 49-Maine-et-Loire, 53-Mayenne, 72-Sarthe, 85-Vendée; 18-Cher, 28-Eure-et-Loir, 36-Indre, 37-Indre-et-Loire, 42-Loir-et-Cher, 45-Loiret
Routes   Grande Brière, Alpes Mancelles, Châteaux to cave-dwellings

Between them, these two regions cover an enormous tract of gentle western and central France – and the division between the two and other adjoining regions is a little artificial in places. It came a something of a surprise to discover that our 'Alpes Mancelles' route was actually in the Loire region and not Normandy, and that the Brière route was not officially in southern Brittany.

To the north and east the regions are in effect one vast and rolling chalky plain, the source of much of France's grain crops with, as harvest approaches, rolling waves of gold as far as the eye can see, making the remnants of the avenues of trees that once lined most of France's main roads the more prominent. It is undoubtedly gentle country for cycling – but those broad horizons can take a long, long time to change. Settlements, too, are in places quite widely spaced, while accommodation and camp sites can be less abundant.

The valley of the River Loire, by contrast, has

Broad, lazy rivers, harmonious landscapes and towns – Chalon-sur-Saône (Burgundy).

Bourgogne *(Burgundy)*

Départements 21-Côte-d'Or, 58-Nièvre, 71-Saône-et-Loire, 89-Yonne
Routes Morvan, Beaujolais

Burgundy owes its unity as a separate region more to history than to any obvious geographical division, the Dukes of Burgundy having been powerful from mediaeval times. The area has many large and small tracts of woodland, which contrast sharply with the open plains to the west. The agriculture is very mixed – enhanced by the influence of European Union policy, which has tended to introduce fashions in sunflowers or oilseed rape in characteristic coloured patches. Burgundy also means wine, especially some of the world's great reds, and the eastern escarpment of Burgundy above the River Saône, the Côte d'Or, harbours some of the finest.

By contrast the area of the Morvan, granite

frequent woodlands and immense fertility, and is highly developed for visiting tourists. The valley is one of several to attract a 'garden' label, sometimes being known even as the 'garden of France' for its market-gardening produce. Loire wines, which cover a wide range of reds, rosés and whites, and some sparkling varieties, are world-famous. Our route in the area passes through some of the best-known *appellations*.

The welcoming nature of the valley led to its other claim to fame, its numerous exuberant and often ornate châteaux, built here in the Renaissance period of the sixteenth century. Many may be visited, though often the effect of the whole in its setting is more impressive. There is a maze of minor roads ideal for cycling. It is possible to fly to Nantes at the mouth of the Loire, though you may have to change aircraft. You can reach Orléans, Tours or Nantes by rail from Paris. One of the European Bike Express routes has drop-off points at Orléans and Tours.

A series of ridges and deep valleys – the Jura (Franche-Comté region).

as opposed to the limestone of the rest of the region, is almost austere. Its quite steeply rolling countryside makes for some exhilarating cycling, however, so we have a choice of two Burgundian routes, one in the forests of the Morvan, the other in the woods and vineyards of the Beaujolais. It is possible to travel by rail via Paris to Dijon and Chalon-sur-Saône, while the airport of the city of Lyon, which has direct flights from UK airports, is about 60 miles (100km) to the south. The European Bike Express sets down at Beaune and Mâcon.

Franche-Comté

Départements 25-Doubs, 70-Haute-Saône, 39-Jura, 90-Territoire-de-Belfort

The major part of this region is the French share of the mountains of the Jura – a succession of limestone ridges and valleys running roughly south-west to north-east from the valley of the Rhône to the Rhine, and shared with Switzerland. The highest point is the Crêt de la Neige, (1,723m) near the south-western tip, but the tops of many of the ridges are little lower, at around 1,200 to 1,400m. This is fine limestone country, with many cliffs and gorges. The pronounced south-west to north-east grain means that your cycling impressions of the Jura will vary markedly according to whether you are following this grain or attempting to cross it.

The area enjoys a high rainfall (and snowfall in winter), allowing beech and oak forests to flourish together with conifers, and supplying the many torrents and lakes. It is a very green countryside, with

The natural bridge of the Pont d' Arc over the River Ardèche.

nearly half of it tree-covered. As in Switzerland, the enforced indoor life during the harsh winters led to craft traditions of woodworking and clock-making. It is possible to reach Besançon, the regional capital, by rail from Paris, but the easiest direct entries to the Jura are via two Swiss airports, Basle and Geneva.

Poitou-Charentes

Départements 16-Charente, 17-Charente-Maritime, 79-Deux-Sèvres, 86-Vienne
Route Châteaux to cave-dwellings

Lying immediately south of the Loire valley and the Centre region, this transitional region, down to the estuary of the Gironde, faces the Atlantic to the west and the hills of the Limousin to the east. The coastal lands of the Vendée have two great marshes, the Marais Breton and the Marais Poitevin, as well as many smaller wetlands rich in wildlife and marshland flora. Inland there are broad areas of almost treeless farmland on the level limestone plateau.

Towards the south the vineyards of Cognac produce the raw material for the famous spirit. Near the coast there is a fine network of minor roads, and plenty of accommodation and camp sites. Some parts, including some of the offshore islands, are quite developed as holiday centres. Inland, however, in the more agricultural areas, roads and settlements are more sparse. To the south and west and the valley of the River Charente the country is more wooded and once more has a network of small roads. Poitiers and Angoulême can be reached by rail via Paris and it is possible to fly to Poitiers, though you will almost certainly have to change aircraft if flying from the UK. The European Bike Express also sets down at Poitiers.

Limousin

Départements 19-Corrèze, 23-Creuse, 87-Haute-Vienne
Route Haut Limousin

Limousin is here used for the country surrounding the ancient city of Limoges. It comprises the north-western foothills of the Massif Central, most of which lies in Auvergne. It is a pleasing mixture of meadows, forest and open heathland, the latter vivid with the yellow of broom and gorse in summer.

Our route based on the artificial Lac de Vassivière takes in a typical sample. The country is not highly developed for tourism – which is part of its attraction for quiet cycling – but we found adequate provision of accommodation and camp sites. Limoges can be reached by rail via Paris or you can fly there, with a change of aircraft if flying from the UK.

Auvergne

Départements 03-Allier, 15-Cantal, 43-Haute-Loire, 63-Puy-de-Dôme

This is the heart of the Massif Central, a largely volcanic mountain area, which despite its name lies in the south-east of the country. It is largely a rugged and open landscape, with one of the outstanding features the remarkable puys – steep, often almost conical volcanic hills. The most prominent is the Puy-de-Dôme, which dominates the regional capital, Clermont-Ferrand. The toll road up to its (1465m) summit is officially open to cyclists only one day a year for a special event or when the Tour de France goes up it.

There are plenty of other high roads, however, including the Col de la Croix Morand (1,401m) and the Col de la Crox Robert (1,426m) on the roads into the resort of Mont-Dore, from which it is possible to take a cable car to the highest point in Auvergne, the Puy de Sancy (1,885m). Farther south, two higher cols, the Pas de Peyrol (1,582m) and the Col de Redondet (1,531m) lie close under the summit of the second highest peak, Puy Mary.

At times the Auvergne offers a savage landscape on its bare uplands, tempered by green river valleys lower down. Another feature of the area is spas and hot springs. We once came across a piped spring by the side of the road – appropriately enough near Chaudes-Aigues, literally 'Hot Waters'. It bore no label except the warning '72°C'! Auvergnats, the inhabitants of the region, have a reputation for toughness, stubbornness (or tenacity, depending on your viewpoint) and bluntness. The roads too have an often deserved reputation for toughness; be prepared for some long and steady climbs.

Accommodation, camp sites and villages are patchily distributed – plentiful in some areas, sparse in others. You can reach Clermont-Ferrand by rail via Paris or you can fly there by changing aircraft.

One of European Bike Express routes also passes through Clermont-Ferrand.

Rhône-Alpes

Départements 01-Ain, 07-Ardèche, 26-Drôme, 38-Isère, 42-Loire, 69-Rhône, 73-Savoie, 74-Haute-Savoie
Routes Beaujolais, Vercors
Cols Aravis, Collet, Cormet de Roselend, Croix de Fer, Glandon, Glières, Iseran, Madeleine, Méraillet, Mollard, Crêt d'Oeillon, Romeyère, Rousset, Saisies

This very large region embraces an enormous range of scenery, from the flat bottom of the middle Rhône valley to the highest summits of the Alps (Mont Blanc is (4,807m) and even taking in the eastern flanks of the Massif Central. In this area the river valley is a vast communication corridor, with major roads and rail routes. It is also a fruitful area for viticulture and market gardening, and there are enough minor roads for the N7 and other busy main roads to be generally avoided.

In the part of the region lying to the west of the Rhône there is some fine cycling country in the département of the Ardèche. It is a quite hilly limestone area, but with some very well-graded climbs, and an intricate web of excellent cycling roads. The gorge of the River Ardèche, famed for its white-water canoeing, is quite spectacular in parts.

Between the Rhône and the high Alps lie some lower but still mountainous blocks, notably the Vercors, the setting for one of our routes, and the Chartreuse. Both these tower above the rapidly expanding and increasingly high-technology city of Grenoble. In the mountains you may have from time to time to follow main roads, although there are often minor alternatives and some very attractive cols on smaller mountain roads. Accommodation and camp sites are plentiful as tourism, summer and winter, is a thriving industry.

The entries for the various cols give more detail on the nature of the different mountain areas. You can reach the regional capital, Lyon, by rail via Paris or by air, including direct flights from UK airports. The airport at Grenoble also has some direct flights but is used mainly for winter skiing charters. The European Bike Express passes down the Rhône valley with a setting-down point near Lyon.

Aquitaine

Départements 24-Dordogne, 33-Gironde, 40-Landes, 47-Lot-et-Garonne, 64-Pyrénées-Atlantiques

The very large region of Aquitaine reaches from the western slopes of the Massif Central right to the Atlantic and the western end of the Pyrenees. As well as the immense plain of the Landes south and west of Bordeaux, it takes in another of the most popular areas for Britons in France – the Dordogne – and the Bordeaux wine areas.

The Dordogne is a very mellow area. Its mellow limestone buildings, mellow and mature agricultural landscapes and mellow broad-leafed woodlands are a bit of a home-from-home for Britons, but redolent overall of sunshine and warmth. Add the good living and it is no wonder that so many retire or settle here as well as swarming in for their holidays. Much of what is thought of as the Dordogne is in the département of Corrèze, but nevertheless is close to the River Dordogne. There are many hills but most are gently graded and, by French standards, not very long. This is very pleasant cycling country, not an area to hurry in. There are also many prehistoric remains and a number of very attractive towns and villages.

Farther south and west, flanking the rivers Dordogne and Garonne and the Gironde estuary and formed by the joining of the two, lie the celebrated vineyards of the Bordeaux appellations. Rivalry between Bordeaux and Burgundy in wine production has always been intense – textbooks give Bordeaux the edge but you will enjoy the experimentation necessary to form your own conclusion. South of Bordeaux lie the Landes, until the early twentieth century a grassy, rough-grazing prairie but now a pine forest forming a great triangle about 75 miles (120km) on each side. Views are limited; riding all day in a uniform forest can be quite frustrating. Roads are relatively sparse but there are number of cycle paths near the Atlantic coast, linking the resorts that have sprung up. Immediately inshore from the beach lie some of the most extensive sand dunes in Europe.

In the far south the region meets the western end of the chain of the Pyrenees in the Basque country, which is linguistically and culturally quite distinct. Basque is little related to any other European language and is spoken on both sides of the Spanish border. Basques in both countries look on themselves as Basques first, and French or Spanish a distant second.

It is possible to reach Bordeaux, the regional capital, and Biarritz by rail via Paris. You can fly direct to Bordeaux from some UK airports, and one European Bike Express route goes to Bordeaux.

Midi-Pyrénées

Départements   09-Ariège, 12-Aveyron, 31-Haute-Garonne, 32-Gers, 46-Lot, 65-Hautes-Pyrénées, 81-Tarn, 82-Tarn-et-Garonne
Routes   Quercy, Tarn Gorges
Cols   Cirque de Gavarnie, Hourquette d'Ancizan, Tourmalet

Like Aquitaine, this very large region stretches from the limestone country of the south-western parts of the Massif Central down to the Pyrenees. Once more

the boundary is a little artificial: for example the old province of Quercy, close in culture and geography to the Dordogne, comes in this region rather than Aquitaine. Equally arbitrarily, the Tarn gorges, the setting for three of our routes, lie in this region, while the adjacent Dourbie gorges are in another.

This is definitely southern country, with sun-blanched villages and the silence of the siesta in the early afternoon. As you approach the Pyrenees the country becomes at first steadily rolling and then noticeably hillier, and the Pyrenees stretch in a great wall ahead of you, rearing up from the rolling foothills. The highest peak in the range, the 3,404m Maladetta, lies just inside Spain and is over 1,400m lower than Mont Blanc in the Alps, but the Pyrenees form a continuous chain, remarkably uniform in height and stretching for nearly 400km. Though none of the roads go as high as the Alpine giants, there are still some very respectable cols, the highest wholly in France being the Col du Tourmalet (2,115m) The regional capital, Toulouse, may be reached by rail via Paris, or you can fly direct from some UK airports. The European Bike Express sets down at Carcassonne.

Languedoc-Roussillon

Départements   11-Aude, 30-Gard, 34-Hérault, 48-Lozère, 66-Pyrénées-Orientales
Routes   Camargue, Gorges of the Dourbie and Mont Aigoual, Tarn Gorges

The third of the large southern regions again stretches from the southern slopes of the Massif Central, here the granitic Cévennes, to the Pyrenees and east to the shores of the Mediterranean. As you travel east along the foothills of the Pyrenees there is a definite point, or at most a stretch of 10km, where the western, greener and more Atlantic-influenced vegetation gives way to the greyer and dustier greens of Mediterranean plants: olives, lavender, white oak and chalk-loving herbs. On the particular route we followed on one occasion, this demarcation was

France abounds in architectural surprises. This is the Abbaye St Michel above Prades in the Conflent in the eastern Pyrenees.

very sharp at the top of the little Col des Frères (1,253m) on the road between the towns of Quillan and Ax-les-Thermes – grey to the east, green to the west.

The hilly country of the Roussillon gives way to the flatter coastal plain as you approach the Mediterranean. The coast has been the site of substantial, if controlled, tourist development, and much of it is built up – a temple to the bronzed body. Inland there are many small roads and cols in the arid-looking hills, and plenty of interest. This is the region where most of France's everyday wine is produced, although some areas have now won appellation contrôlée status.

Languedoc was one of the regions of France most settled by the Romans, and there are many spectacular Roman remains, including the great amphitheatre at Nîmes and the awe-inspiring aqueduct of the Pont du Gard. Accommodation and camp sites are abundant.

South of the Roussillon lie the eastern Pyrenees. Like the western end, this area too has its own culture and language: Catalan spans the Spanish and French sides of the mountains. There are some fine, if strenuous, cycling roads and off-road tracks, particularly round the Catalans' sacred mountain, the 2,784m peak of the Canigou. Farther west lies Andorra, reached by high mountain passes from both France and Spain, the sole remnant of the separate small states that used to exist along the Pyrenees.

You can reach Nîmes, Montpellier, Carcassone and Perpignan by rail via Paris, fly direct to Montpellier in the summer season, or reach the area by the European Bike Express, which has drop-off points at Montpellier and Narbonne. The eastern Pyrenees are also easy to reach from the Spanish airport for the Costa Brava, Gerona.

Provence-Alpes-Côte d'Azur

Départements   04-Alpes-de-Haute-Provence, 05-Hautes-Alpes, 06-Alpes-Maritimes, 13-Bouches-

One of the signs of southern France: defendable hill-top villages.

du-Rhône, 83-Var, 84-Vaucluse

Routes   Alpilles, Camargue, Grand Canyon du Verdon, Lubéron and Roussillon, Mont Ventoux

Cols   Allos, Bonette, Cayolle, Champs, Izoard, Pré de Mme Carle, Raspaillon, Restefond, Tempêtes, Vars

This region spans a wide range of country from the high Alps to the rocky coast of the Côte d'Azur and the marshlands of the Rhône delta. The division of the Alps between this region and Rhône-Alpes may seem arbitrary, but is based largely on lines of communication, for the parts of the Alps that lie within the region look south for their influence. Five of our routes (which show a cross-section of the region) and half the Alpine cols described lie in this part of France.

Immediately south of the Alps lie ranges of high hills known as the Préalpes du Sud. These gradually give way to the high plateaux of northern Provence, from one of which, the Plateau de

Vaucluse, rises the striking Mont Ventoux, setting for one of our routes.

Provence is quintessential rural southern France: perched villages, red pantiles with broad shading eaves, whitewashed walls, olive groves and the low scrub on the limestone hills, lavender and fragrant flowers and herbs – to say nothing of the blue skies and brilliant sunshine. Do not forget the cautions we give on riding in hot weather, particularly the injunction to drink water regularly, though at times the weather can be bad in Provence – and when it is wet it can be very wet indeed. This is the country where a loaf and some cheese with fruit to finish is a roadside feast. Provence also produces a number of light wines, with the rosés the best known – take them intemperately with that loaf and cheese in the sun and you will not wake up until evening!

Provence and the Côte d'Azur were heavily settled in Roman times and there are many remains in the area, as well as notable buildings from every century since, including some striking modern work. You can reach the regional capital Marseille and Nice by rail via Paris, or fly to either direct. The European Bike Express has a drop-off point at Bollène, north of Orange, in the west of the region.

Corse *(Corsica)*

Départements   2A-Corse-du-Sud, 2B-Haute-Corse

The rugged and rocky island of Corsica lies some 170km south of the French mainland and is about 150km from north to south. The interior of the island is mountainous, rising to 2,710m in Monte Cinto – high enough for considerable snow cover to linger into late spring and early summer. While roads are sparse in some areas there are many small mountain roads. Col-seekers do not have to look far: there are over 150, with the lowest 'official' one, the Col de Guardia, only 19m above sea level! More respectably, the Col de Vergio in the north-west of the island climbs to 1,464m. The west coast is the more indented and the more spectacular with coloured cliffs and jagged headlands.

There are many forests of pine and broad-leafed trees, with olives and other Mediterranean trees in the cultivated areas. Much of the upland below the bare and craggy summits is covered in the dense low scrub known as *maquis*. The island has been settled by many invaders over the centuries, from the

Greeks – who named it 'the isle of beauty' – onwards. There is a strong Italian influence (the larger, Italian island of Sardinia lies only a short way to the south) and the Corsican dialect has many Italian words. Accommodation of all types is plentiful, apart from along the east coast where there are long gaps between settlements. A great many cycle tourists have found their personal cycling paradise in Corsica and, once under its spell, return again and again.

It is possible to reach Corsica by sea from Marseille, but by far the most convenient way to the island is to fly direct to Bastia in the north or Ajaccio in the south-west.

LANGUAGE

Although Breton is spoken in Brittany, Basque in the south-west and Catalan around Perpignan, with attempts from time to time to restore Provençal in the south, the language of France is French. You could go right across France with a smile, the right gestures and the expression *Ça va* (all right) used either as question or answer – combined with appropriate pointing or proffered money – but you will get a lot more out of it if you can use at least a little of the language. People really do appreciate it if you have a try.

If your local college or evening institute offers the use of a language laboratory, so much the better, since you make rapid progress with pronunciation, which many English speakers find particularly difficult. Do not underestimate the usefulness of phrasebooks, even if you have to use them by pointing to the word you want. A number of useful cycling words do not appear in most dictionaries, so the glossary at the end of this book includes a selection of these and other essentials such as road signs.

Many French place names have a different English spelling – such as Reims, which is spelt Rheims in English. In the route descriptions in this book the French spelling is always shown, because this is what you will find on the map and on road signs. A few very common English geographical terms (Alps, Brittany, Burgundy, Corsica, Normandy, Pyrenees) are used in place of the French equivalents (Alpes, Bretagne, Bourgogne, Corse, Normandie, Pyrénées) in the general text.

One trivial matter I originally found very

confusing, and solving which has now developed into something of a challenge, is the habit of making adjectives from the name of a place – to describe its inhabitants for example. These are always used without an initial capital letter and often crop up in French descriptions of an area. It was years before I finally cracked *mussipontain* or *mussipontaine* – which of course did not appear in any dictionary – as referring to the inhabitants, institutions or attributes of Pont-à-Mousson in north-east France. Since every drain and manhole cover in France seems to have been cast in Pont-à-Mousson, it is a name you see often. Similarly, since St Étienne means St Stephen, inhabitants of all the many St Étiennes are *stéphanoises* and *stéphanois*. You eventually get the hang of it, some are of course much easier to decipher than others, and the Michelin *Guides Verts* are a helpful reference source.

MONEY

The unit of currency is the franc (abbreviated to F, or sometimes FF to distinguish it from the Swiss or Belgian franc), subdivided into 100 centimes. Individual centimes do not count for much nowadays, and shops usually round down the odd centimes to the nearest ten. One possible source of confusion, surprisingly persistent but dying out now as those who remember it pass on, is that prices may be quoted in *anciens francs* (old francs) or sometimes as similarly large numbers of centimes. The old franc became the new centime in 1960, but some memories die hard! This should cause you no real problem: a price that appears to be a hundred times too high should be pretty obvious – a loaf just should not cost £60!

Coins are used for smaller denominations. The small change – 5, 10 and 20 centimes – is brass. Silver-coloured cupro-nickel is used for ½ (50 centime), 1, 2 and 5 franc coins. The 10 franc coin has a brass rim with a cupro-nickel centre.

Notes cover the remaining denominations, from 20F and 50F upwards. Large denomination notes – 500F and 1000F – seem to be much more generally accepted than their equivalent values would be in the UK. Even so, it is worth breaking down the 1000F notes, which banks love to supply, fairly early on in your trip. Otherwise, you are bound to end up with nothing else when you want only a loaf or a postcard – apart from the folly of having too much wealth tied up in one rather flimsy piece of paper. You will generally get a slightly better exchange rate by buying French currency from a bank before you leave. French banks will be quite happy, however, to exchange English, Irish or Scottish banknotes for you.

Major credit cards are quite widely accepted: just check on the small symbols on the back of the card, such as Visa (known as Carte Bleu in France), Eurocard or MasterCard and look for the same signs. Outside large towns and large hotels, American Express and Diner's Club charge cards are less commonly accepted. Credit card settlements for large accommodation bills or travel can be advantageous, since the values are converted at commercial rather than tourist rates with a small commission – and can take a couple of months to catch up with you. Many cash machines will also accept cash cards from foreign banks; once again just check the symbols on your card against the machine. Some machines are courteous enough to address you in English automatically; on others you have to press the button against the Union Jack symbol.

Eurocheques with their special guarantee card are becoming more widely acceptable for payment; banks have always taken them but hotels and shops have tended to be wary, often accepting them as deposits but not cashing them, leaving you to pay the whole bill in some more respectable form. Eurocheques are nowadays more convenient in France than travellers' cheques. It is desirable to take at least some cash, particularly if you are travelling at a weekend. Except for bureaux de change at airports, major stations and the like, few banks are open after noon on Saturdays. Banks also always all used to close on Mondays, but on recent trips we have noted quite a few exceptions to this. Branches in small towns and villages may open on only one or two days a week. Most close for a two-hour lunch break.

It is prudent not to carry all your money in one place or on one person. Provided every member of a group is following the same lifestyle, we have always found it easiest to make common purchases – food, meals, accommodation, travel – from a common kitty (*bourse communale* or *cagnotte* if you have to explain it), with everybody chipping in 100F each time it gets low. This avoids all manner of complex calculations.

Finally, get used to thinking in francs as quickly

as possible – do not go around translating prices all the time. In any case, apart from the few things, such as instant coffee, which are exorbitantly expensive, or those, such as bottles of wine or hotel rooms, which can be ludicrously cheap, there will not be a lot of difference between prices anyway. If you do have to work to quite a tight budget, calculate how many francs you can allow yourself per day, and work to that.

MEASUREMENTS

In France metric measurements have been universal for a couple of centuries. Just as with money, you will find it easier to begin to think right from the start in kilometres, to assess the task involved in a mountain pass by the metres to be climbed, and in the relatively few places where you have to specify quantity to think in kilograms (*kilogrammes* in French) and litres.

All French maps, guides and road signs are marked in kilometres. Rather than try to convert numbers all the time, make a once-and-for-all rule of thumb conversion of your comfortable riding speeds. If you find 10mph a suitable average at home, then 15km/h will feel much the same on similar terrain. If you prefer 8mph, then 13km/h will suit; if 12mph is your mark, then 20km/h matches, and so on. (This is quite accurate enough: if you go round trying to divide or multiply by 1.6093 all the time you will just go dotty.)

Use this translated speed to assess how you are going to progress – which is not to say you should prepare a detailed schedule. It is rather to be able to calculate whether you will make St Pierre-la-Montagne before the shops shut at noon for lunch, or reach Ste Angélique-en-Forêt at a convenient time to stop for the night. Do not forget, though, that your overall riding speed is likely to be much less when you are forever stopping to look at all manner of interesting things, and will of course be sharply reduced in the mountains.

In the routes described in this book all distances are shown in kilometres and all heights above sea level are shown in metres. These are the measurements that you will find on maps and road signs.

In shops you will recognize the size of packets or jars you want, while fruit and suchlike you will generally buy by number rather than weight, or choose and bag yourself. For any other practical purposes a kilogram is a couple of pounds – you may even hear a half kilogram (500 grams) spoken of as *une livre* (a pound). So, 250 grams serves as a half-pound, and you can take 125 or 100 grams as a quarter. In any case, the only time you will need these measures is for weighed-out items you have to ask for, such as cheese or cold meats.

Liquid volumes are measured in litres: one litre will almost fill two standard 600ml bike bottles or be just too much for one of the bigger 900ml ones. The volumes of wine and beer bottles are indicated in centilitres (hundredths of a litre). Wine bottles – if not 1 litre, as for the cheaper wines – range from 68 to 75cl, according to region although there are EU moves to standardize on 75cl. The standard litre bottles used for cheaper wines are recycled. They are distinguished by a ring of moulded stars just below the neck and you have to pay a returnable deposit. Wine in carafes in restaurants is usually specified by the *demi* (half litre) or *quart* (quarter litre).

TIME

The 24-hour clock is virtually universally used, especially for aircraft, boat and train departure times, and shop opening hours. Church and public clocks are usually marked only with the 12-hour figures.

SHOPS

The shops described here are the main ones likely to concern cycling travellers who are looking for food and one or two other staple items. Most French shops resemble their UK equivalents – but there are some differences, one of which is the prevalence of Monday closing. This affects most large shops and many small ones.

The inevitable and fundamental first food stop is the *boulangerie* – the baker's. If you wanted a symbol of France it would be the long crusty French loaf, still warm from the oven, and the basis of every cyclist's lunch-time picnic. Most boulangeries open very early in the morning – certainly by 8, often at 7 or even earlier – and stay open to around noon, reopening for the afternoon baking at perhaps 3 or 4, and then staying open to 7 or 8. French bread does not keep, partly because it does not contain added preservatives, so

You can often find your way to a boulangerie by back-tracing the tracks of a steady stream of people carrying loaves, or even by following the smell of baking bread.

If there is no boulangerie in the village where you are shopping, look for a grocer's, a café or even a private house labelled *Dépôt de pain*, where a baker's van leaves bread for the village. In remote areas you may meet a mobile bread van, and some out-of-the-way camp sites have a van that calls. Vans that are mobile shops sound their horns long and loud to signal their presence, which can be disconcerting if you are just in front.

The next basic stop is the grocer's, called an *épicerie* (literally spice-dealer's) or *alimentation générale* (general store). The épicerie usually sells not only traditional groceries but also wines, beers and soft drinks, fruit and vegetables, and a selection of toiletries and small hardware. Most are now self-service, which is helpful if you are diffident about asking for things. Just pick up a basket, fill it and pay on the way out. The quality and variety of perishables such as fruit is usually high, unless you arrive at the tail end of the day when everybody else has been rummaging. Because France extends to the Mediterranean, such products as grapes, peaches, apricots and nectarines are often cheap in season.

buy only what you are going to need before you reach the next baker's. Note that French bread also suffers from what metallurgists call hot-shortness: the warm loaves are quite brittle and liable to fall in half if you strap them too hard across your panniers. If you fancy brown bread for a change, ask for *pain complet* (wholemeal), *pain de seigle* (rye bread) or *pain au son* (bread with extra bran). *Pain de campagne* is a sort of half-way house – not brown but not as white as the usual loaf. The standard 200g *baguette* is probably the easiest to carry on a bike, though it is a bit much for one person and sometimes not quite enough for two. They will be happy to sell you either a half-size *demi-baguette* or cut one in half (ask for *la moitié d'une baguette*).

The boulangerie also sells such things as croissants and is often combined with a *pâtisserie*, selling mouth-watering fruit tarts and the like. These make a superb rounding-off for a picnic, or a delightful mid-ride snack, but are not easy to carry far even when they are packed in little cardboard boxes. Most boulangeries close for at least one day a week, often Monday. They are, however, usually open from 8 or 8.30 until noon on Sundays, while pâtisseries are often open for an hour or two on Sunday afternoons.

You don't need a sign saying 'Fruits, légumes, primeurs' to tell you that this is a greengrocers – the displays say it all. Most French fruit and vegetables are sold on the basis of taste and not regular shape, and fruit is usually exactly at the right stage of ripeness.

Many fruits and vegetables are sold on the basis of taste and not symmetrical shape (especially tomatoes!).

Market stalls are also a good source of fruit and vegetables, and in fruit-growing areas there are often roadside stalls. Even small towns may boast a moderate-sized supermarket on the outskirts; supermarkets are the same everywhere, and you may once again find self-service simpler to deal with than having to ask. Other picnic ingredients may come from a *charcuterie*, a delicatessen specializing in cold meats, pies and the like.

Some other shops have names that may be misleading. A *droguerie* has nothing to do with narcotics or even pharmacy but is a general hardware store – the place for odd cutlery items, Camping Gaz cylinders (often also sold in alimentations générales), can openers, pot scourers, corkscrews, soap and shampoo. A real honest-to-goodness ironmonger's and tool-shop is a *quincaillerie*. A *librairie* is not a library but a bookshop, which may be combined with a *papeterie* (stationer's). Many librairies sell maps and postcards. They may also sell newspapers, in which case they are likely to be emblazoned *journaux* or *maison de la presse*. In a farther overlap, the maison de la presse may also be a *café* or *tabac*. A tabac has a strange status as an outlet for officially controlled items in addition to tobacco, notably stamps – which you can also buy of course from a post office (*bureau de poste* or *PTT*). A tabac may also sell a limited range of film, but for a wider range you should go to a *photographe*, which will almost certainly have a prominent Kodak, Fuji or Agfa sign outside. Note that while film types are the same, they can be twice as expensive in France as in the UK.

The one other shop you might need, a bike shop, should be fairly obvious from the contents of the window. It may be labelled cycles or have the name of one of the large French makers such as Peugeot, Motobécane, Mercier or MBK displayed prominently. If you have to ask, you are looking for a *marchand de vélos* or a *vélociste* (the latter is really more a repairer).

TELEPHONES

Public telephone boxes are common in France and are the easiest way of keeping in touch with home. The glass-sided boxes are quite rationally labelled *téléphone*. There are two types, coin- and card-operated; in places such as airports you might find a telephone that takes both.

Coin-operated telephones are very similar to those of British Telecom, except that the older models tend to stack the coins you have put in (50 centimes, 1 and 5 francs) in little visible piles. You have to put in at least 1F before dialling. The primary dialling tone is quite high-pitched.

To telephone to the UK, you first dial 19 to get into the international network. You will then hear a second continuous dialling tone, which is a low-pitched burr. You then enter the code 44, followed by the full number without the initial 0. You may hear a series of rapid pips: this does not imply any failure to connect but means that the system is connecting you. You will then hear the familiar ringing tone – or be frustrated by the familiar engaged signal. If the engaged signal has two alternating tones, it means that the UK exchange is engaged, so it is worth re-dialling immediately. For other countries, dial 19 as before, and then the appropriate country code and subscriber's number.

When it is time to put in more money, a flickering black-and-white Maltese cross symbol appears at the top left of the dial or press-button pad on older telephones, or on the LCD display if it is a newer one. The machines return unused coins, so it is best to use a stack of small ones unless you know you are going to need 5F worth. Note that the first 30 per cent reduction cheap rate does not begin until 8pm on weekdays, and the full 50 per cent reduction not until 10.30pm. If the telephone box has a blue bell sign, you can also receive incoming calls.

If you are calling a number in rural France from rural France (anywhere outside the Paris region) you dial the two-figure département code, then the six-figure subscriber's number. Similarly, for a call wholly within the Paris area, just dial the eight-figure number. From Paris to the rest of France dial 16, wait for the low-pitched second dialling tone, then dial the appropriate eight-figure number. To call Paris from outside, dial 16, then 1, then the eight-figure number. The French ringing tone is a series of long, single beeps.

Card-operated telephones again work similarly to those of British Telecom, except that on some older ones you have to close a little cover over the card after you have put it in. Cards (*cartes de téléphone* or *télécartes*) are available from tabacs and post offices, and usually from any café near the telephone. The lowest-priced card is 40F. You may find, quite unannounced, a complete village or town taken over by cardphones; presumably the locals know and are prepared.

EMERGENCIES

For mild ailments or minor cuts and scrapes, the *pharmacie* is the place to head for. It is identified by a green cross, often an intricate pulsating fluorescent device, opulent décor (presumably to justify the prices) and frequently a location just out of the town centre. A French pharmacy does not sell films and so on but sticks pretty closely to medical items. The pharmacist is a qualified first-aider, diagnoser of ailments and prescriber of medicaments and – in autumn – distinguisher between edible and poisonous fungi. If your problem is beyond the scope of the pharmacie, the pharmacien will direct you to a doctor or hospital.

European Union nationals are entitled to reciprocal health service arrangements, which involves equipping yourself with a Form E111 before leaving home. This entitles you to eventual reimbursement of about three-quarters of any medical charges, but you will have to fork out for them first. The procedure, which is explained on the form, is quite complex and time-consuming. I would consider it essential before leaving home, therefore, to take out a travel insurance that adequately covers payment of any medical expenses. Such policies also give some cover for loss of or damage to baggage (which may or may not include your bicycle – it is important to check) and may cover costs incurred if you have to cancel or cut short your trip. Most, too, quote an emergency telephone number from which you can get assistance with such matters as interpreting between you and the French authorities.

Serious roadside emergencies are usually attended by the *sapeurs-pompiers* (fire and emergency rescue services) or the police – who may be the police (local) or gendarmerie (national). The emergency police telephone number is 17; there are instructions in the telephone boxes.

The French system for sorting out such things as accidents is largely non-adversarial. If the incident is serious enough you will probably be called on, together with any other party involved, to fill in a form giving agreed factual details – not an admission of guilt – and both parties keep a copy. This is where the emergency number of your insurance company can be essential.

2
Getting There

There are four methods of getting bicycles to France – direct by ferry from port to port, by rail by way of the Channel Tunnel, by air, or by a specialized coach service. All the travel information was correct at the time of writing, but as new services will be introduced and existing services modified or withdrawn it is important to check all details before you start your journey. Members of the Cyclists' Touring Club (CTC) may obtain information on the latest position from the Club's Touring Department (see 'Useful Organizations' in the Appendix).

Although EC citizens do not technically need a passport to travel to France, your journey will go much more smoothly if you have one. Requirements for visitors who hold passports from countries that are not members of the European Union vary and may be obtained by telephoning the premium-rate number 0898 200289. Alternatively, your travel agent will be able to advise on the position at the time you wish to travel.

PORT TO PORT

Little could be simpler than the current system. You buy the appropriate ferry ticket for yourself, usually with the status of 'foot passenger'. Cycles (including tandems) are carried at no extra charge, and usually with no extra formality. You should present yourself at the vehicle check-in point about 45 minutes before the sailing time, join the vehicle queue and follow instructions – which are usually to take the bike direct to a specified position on the car deck.

Secure it to a non-functional part of the vessel (there is usually a rail) with the rope if provided or with an elastic strap. If you do not secure it the crew may use something coarser and more damaging,

such as a heavy chain. Do not however lock it to anything, as this could cause problems if the crew have to move your bike to get at something behind it. Obey instructions given by the crew at all times, since they know which controls they will need to reach. Remove any valuables or items you may want on the crossing as there will be no access to the car deck once the ferry is under way. On arrival reclaim your bicycle – checking that such items as pumps have not been inadvertently knocked off – and ride away. You will often be waved off before the rest of the load.

Working from east to west along the Channel coast, car ferries run from:
- Ramsgate to Dunkerque
- Dover to Calais
- Newhaven to Dieppe
- Portsmouth to Ouistreham (Caen), Cherbourg, Le Havre or St Malo
- Southampton to Cherbourg
- Poole to Cherbourg
- Plymouth to Roscoff
- Cork to St Malo
- Cork to Roscoff

If you plan to travel to the western Pyrenees, the long ferry trips to Spain – from Portsmouth to Bilbao, or Plymouth (summer) and Portsmouth (winter) to Santander – offer an alternative approach. Santander and Bilbao are relatively close to the French border.

High-speed catamaran and hovercraft services run from Dover to Calais and Folkestone to Boulogne. Both are appreciably faster than the comparable ferries and, once again, cycles are carried free of charge.

There are generally more sailings in the late spring, summer and early autumn than in winter.

Fares are generally higher in the peak holiday months of July and August, though foot-passenger and cyclist fares vary less than vehicle fares. There are also reduced-price return tickets for stays of three or five days (120 hours) in France, and an additional concessionary ten-day fare on the routes from Portsmouth westwards. There are also some day or overnight-plus-day trip concessions at times.

If you are taking bicycles as part of the loading on a car roof-rack, it is usually necessary to quote the overall height of the car with load when booking, since parts of the car decks on most ferries have restricted headroom. If you are using a rear rack, its length should be included in the quoted overall length of the vehicle when booking.

It is possible to take bicycles free of charge on trains to the Channel ports of Ramsgate, Dover, Folkestone, Newhaven, Portsmouth, Southampton and Poole from elsewhere in the South East. There may be restrictions on special boat trains to Dover but there are frequent alternative services. It may not be possible to take bicycles on some peak-hour services in the direction of the main flow – into London up to 9.30am and out of London between 4.30 and 6.30pm. It depends largely on whether the trains have separate guards' vans, so it is best to enquire locally.

On most services to Plymouth a reservation is required and on all a small cycle carriage fee is payable. Similar reservation rules and charges apply if you are travelling to a Channel port from outside South East England. It is no longer possible to send bicycles by rail and sea routes in advance or as 'registered baggage' to France.

RAIL SERVICES

There are two ways of using the Channel Tunnel: by the imaginatively named Le Shuttle as a substitute for the cross-channel ferry or on one of the Eurostar services from London to Lille and Paris or Brussels.

Eurotunnel operates a minibus-plus-bike-trailer service from the Channel Tunnel Exhibition Centre to the tunnel shuttle terminal, with a comparable service to the French exhibition centre at the other end. Booking for this service is essential. Enquire on 01303 270111 for travel from Folkestone and 00 33 21 00 69 09 for travel from Calais.

The guards' vans on Eurostar trains are equipped

with cycle-carrying hooks, with a potential capacity of up to eight bikes per train. Cycle carriage is part of the registered baggage service; reservations are necessary and a charge is payable.

Bicycles on French Railways

Up-to-date information is given in the regularly revised leaflet *Guide du train et du vélo* published at intervals by the Société National des Chemins de Fer (SNCF), the French railway company. This has a section in English. For CTC members, the Club's Touring Department has explanatory booklets on taking bikes on French trains, including sample letters for enquiries.

For nearly all substantial journeys and for some others, bicycles have to be registered as passengers' baggage at the Bagages (Départ) counter up to half an hour before travelling at any station with a baggage service. Sometimes the bicycle will travel on the same train as you, usually not. You may be able to find out, by enquiring, which train it actually will be sent on so that you can take the same one. This allows you to collect it from the baggage office soon after the train arrives. Otherwise you may have to wait, particularly if the journey has involved a change of train or a journey across Paris. It follows that such changes are best avoided. SNCF state in their leaflets that you may have to wait up to five days for some journeys – and that excludes Saturdays and Sundays! If the wait is longer than the quoted time you get your money back. Once you have registered the bicycle, all handling is carried out by staff of the baggage franchise company.

On a number of local trains – many at inconvenient hours – it is possible to take a bicycle free of charge. These services are marked with a small bicycle symbol in the SNCF timetables, of which there are three types: the *Ville à ville*, covering the whole of the country but showing only services between larger stations; three regional timetables (*Indicateurs Officiels*), with separate volumes showing complete services for *Nord-Est* (north-east), *Sud-Est* (south-east) and *Atlantique* regions (the whole of western France); and pocket-size local timetable leaflets. These timetables are obtainable at bookstalls inside main French railway stations or from the addresses given in the 'Useful Organizations' section.

On these services you load the bike yourself, labelled with your name and address and where you are going, into the marked van. Some trains have room for only three bikes. The same system applies in the Paris suburban area on off-peak weekday trains (not between 6.30 and 9am or 4.30 and 7pm) or any train on Saturdays, Sundays and public holidays.

Recently the SNCF has extended accompanied cycle carriage (free of charge) to certain mainline services from Paris and two cross-country services. Most run every day. The Paris routes are to:

- Calais and Boulogne via Amiens
- Clermont-Ferrand
- Tulle, Toulouse and Nîmes via Clermont
- Nancy and Strasbourg
- Charleville via Épernay and Reims
- Culmont via Troyes, Bar-sur-Aube and Chaumont
- Limoges
- Poitiers via Blois
- Granville and Tours via Vendôme
- Rouen and Dieppe
- Alençon
- Le Mans, with connections to Angers and Nantes
- Caen

Of the cross-country routes one links Grenoble, Lyon and Nantes, and the other Toulouse and Marseille, via Perpignan, Narbonne and Montpellier, neither via Paris. The latter route involves a change at Narbonne or Montpellier. Up to ten bicycles are carried on each train, reservation is not compulsory, neither is any special packaging. French Railways Office (see the 'Useful Organizations' section), or for CTC members, from the CTC's Touring Department.

Another concession by SNCF is that a bicycle completely contained in a bag or box of maximum dimensions 90 × 120cm may be taken on any train – including the luggage stacks of TGV trains or the wide vestibules of Corail trains – provided it is loaded so as not to inconvenience other passengers.

It is possible to hire three types of bike – roadsters, ten-speed touring bikes and six-speed mountain bikes – at 47 SNCF stations, mainly in holiday areas. Some hire services operate only in the summer.

AIR SERVICES

Most airline companies will accept bicycles as passengers' accompanied luggage on scheduled flights. Make it quite clear when booking your ticket, and make sure that the travel agent and airline have noted it, that you are intending to travel with a bicycle as part of your luggage. Both the bicycle and any other checked hold luggage should be within the normal free baggage allowance – usually 20kg or about 44lb – otherwise a quite hefty excess baggage charge may be payable although this is not always applied. Since a lightweight touring bicycle weighs somewhere around 12 to 13kg on its own, this can be a limitation. Tales of cyclists walking aboard the aircraft staggering under their hand baggage, which is stuffed full of heavy items such as tools in order to keep the checked weight within the limit, are not all made up. There is a theoretical weight limit of 5kg on hand baggage, though I have never known it invoked. Expect to be asked to open up your hand baggage for search; all those tools and things look quite amazing on the X-ray screen.

Certain items are not allowed on aircraft at all: these include liquid or gas fuel (including sealed, unused canisters) for camping stoves, and mercury thermometers. Matches and lighters can only be carried on the person, while potential weapons such as the sort of sharp knife you might have for picnics or camping (but which the security people think you might use to hijack the aircraft) have to go in the checked hold baggage.

The degree to which the bicycle needs to be dismantled depends on the aircraft used (and to some degree on the whim of the handler who loads it). Most flights to major French destinations are by aircraft of the size of the Boeing 737 or larger, calling for little or no dismantling, but some flights to smaller airports use smaller aircraft with restricted loading hatches. These may be able to carry only one or two bicycles at a time. You should always remove pedals completely; do *not* refit them inside the cranks as some sources suggest, that is a sure-fire way to damage the bike if it is wheeled only a foot or two backwards by handlers. You may in addition be asked to turn handlebars sideways to make the bicycle more compact, particularly if it is a mountain bike. Sometimes you will be asked to remove the front wheel and strap it to the frame. On a touring bike it is usually necessary to remove the front mudguard as well if you have to remove the wheel. In general, dismantle only as far as you are asked.

Probably three-quarters of the recorded damage to bikes in transit by air involves the rear derailleur gear and the threaded hanger on the frame into which it is screwed. Rear gear mechanisms protrude somewhat and an impact or heavy pressure on them can damage the frame rather expensively as well as the gear itself. One suggestion is to fit for the flight one of the gear mechanism guards sometimes fitted to mountain bikes – a sort of anti-roll bar made of 6mm steel rod; another is actually to remove the gear mechanism from the gear 'hanger' that is part of the bike frame by unscrewing the 5 or 6mm Allen key fitting and then wrapping the gear mechanism separately (without separating it from the chain) in a large plastic bag and securing it out of the way. We have also found it an advantage to shield the chain and gear mechanism with a large piece of heavy card or something similar.

Some airlines supply large plastic bags into which the whole bicycle fits, probably the most satisfactory solution. British Airways, at least, no longer require

tyres to be deflated – which was always rather illogical, especially with pressurized aircraft holds – though many other airlines do. Experience suggests that bicycles are treated more gently if they are recognizable as bicycles than if they are fully dismantled in boxes, unless these are the armoured plastic crates that professional racing teams use.

Remove all loose items such as pumps, bottles, lights and bags. Since these bits are of such differing shapes we have found it worth while making up light zipped bags from ripstop nylon to keep them, the pedals and possibly such camping items as sleeping mats and tents all together as one item of checked baggage for the flight. Some airlines supply heavy-duty plastic bags for such things but you cannot depend on it.

Allow yourself ample time to carry out any dismantling by arriving at least 45 minutes before the normal check-in time. Check before you leave home that anything you may be asked to turn or remove

can be easily freed, and that you have the appropriate spanners and Allen keys with you. When air travel with a bicycle goes smoothly it is a marvellous way of reaching a touring area with the least delay; when you are asked to start taking your bicycle to pieces just as they are calling your flight it can seem less so. Things seem to be more relaxed at smaller regional airports than at large ones, and similarly more relaxed at Stansted and Gatwick than at Heathrow. The Gatwick Express rail link from London Victoria has an enormous luggage van with plenty of free bicycle space.

At the destination airport keep an eye open in the luggage hall for any spot where large 'out-of-gauge' baggage (items too big to fit on the standard baggage carousel) arrives. Depending on the airport, your bicycle may appear on a luggage trolley, or even be ceremonially wheeled in – quite a few baggage handlers at French airports appear to be members of airport cycling clubs! If there is a wide conveyor for large baggage items (as at Heathrow's Terminal 2), station yourself at the head of it; a bicycle sent up on it is not always substantial enough to activate the automatic stop mechanism. Nearly all cases of damage to bicycles when travelling by air occur during handling on the ground.

COACH SERVICES

Since 1993 a Middlesbrough firm, Bolero International Holidays, has been operating in conjunction with the CTC a seasonal coach-and-trailer service – European Bike Express – to a number of destinations, many of them in France. The specially constructed trailer can take quite large numbers of cycles with virtually no dismantling necessary. The coach is equipped with refreshment facilities. The cost is in most cases comparable with air or rail travel and CTC members enjoy a slightly reduced fare. Pick-up points along its mainly motorway route between Middlesbrough and Dover can be arranged, and there are two basic routes once across the Channel. The first goes down the Rhône valley to Orange, with a variant via Orléans and Clermont-Ferrand, then veers west to Perpignan and Carcassonne. The second goes via Orléans, then heads south-west to Tours, Poitiers Bordeaux and finally Agen and Montauban. Other routes may be introduced if demand can be shown.

Pick-up points for the return trip from France must be along the coach's route but need not be the same as the outward drop-off points. Services run approximately weekly from May to early September and homeward trips normally arrive back seventeen days after departure, although longer stays can be arranged on payment of a supplement. Details of the service are given at the end of this book under 'Useful Organizations'.

It is also possible for a large enough group wishing to travel together to hire a coach from a general coach hire company for a specific trip. The luggage compartments of most modern coaches can readily accept quite a large number of bicycles, particularly if they are compacted as for air travel and, preferably, in large plastic bags.

3

Accommodation

By UK standards – except for luxury hotels in large cities and at very fashionable resorts – most French accommodation is not expensive, although this can be undermined by falling exchange rates. Whatever its irritations for those who live there, French bureaucracy has made sure that hotels are classified and offer accommodation at a price appropriate to the classification. Since hotel rooms are reasonably priced, other forms of accommodation are relatively inexpensive too.

Information on local accommodation, and on many other things, is available from the tourist information office, the *syndicat d'initiative,* often abbreviated to *SI* or marked with the *i* symbol. Even in small villages, the *mairie* (roughly the equivalent of a town hall) may double up as a tourist information office. Some, particularly smaller, syndicats d'initiative stick strictly to office hours (including long lunch breaks) and may not be open much out of season. We have found them extremely helpful in amplifying nationally produced listings of accommodation and in making contact to determine opening times and so on. The ability to speak a little French helps, but do not let shyness put you off.

HOTELS

Hotels are classified officially by star ratings according to the facilities they offer, starting at one star. You may also see the letters 'NN' quoted; these refer to revised standards (*nouvelles normes*) introduced in the late 1970s and 1980s. In the one, two or three star range the standard of furnishing and facilities may not differ greatly, differences being mainly in the bathroom and other facilities offered with the room or elsewhere. Prices for rooms have by law to be displayed at the hotel reception desk and again in the room itself. Prices are usually quoted by the room (*chambre*), and most rooms are double-bedded (*avec un grand lit*) or twin-bedded (*à deux lits*), so that accommodation is normally cheaper if you are travelling in twos or multiples of two. There may also be family rooms with more beds, sometimes with a sliding scale according to how many people occupy them. We stayed once in a small hotel in industrial Douai in the north that offered a room with two double beds, for which prices, going up by a few francs a time, were quoted up to six occupants – followed by etc to show that the scale did not end there! You will normally be invited to inspect the room before making your decision.

At one time there were quite precise, almost class, distinctions between hotels and *auberges* (inns), *hostelleries* (also inns, but a bit up-market), *pensions* (family-run boarding-houses or small residential hotels), *logis* (lodging-houses) or *relais* (originally staging posts or coaching inns). Nowadays, whatever the title, all come within the hotel system. Motel-style hotels, often geared to business travellers, such as the Formule 1 chain, are also spreading in France. Most of these are near fair-sized towns; many are on industrial estates or are handy for main roads and motorways. They offer accommodation of quite a comfortable standard, often at quite low prices, based on at least two people occupying the room.

Breakfast is usually extra, charged per person. The normal breakfast is copious bread and jam with coffee or hot chocolate, possibly accompanied by croissants. There seem to be quite a lot of cyclists' myths that such breakfasts are inadequate for cycling on, but I have always found that the dangers with warm, crusty French bread are of eating too much rather than too little. Any inclusive prices quoted for dinner, bed and breakfast (*demi-pension*) or full board (*pension*), which includes lunch as well, are also per person. Quite a number of small hotels do not have restaurants, and have only a small breakfast room that often doubles in the day and evening as a bar. These places expect you to eat elsewhere during the evening.

Prices change with inflation and currency fluctuations, but bed and breakfast for two in a one or two star French hotel costs about the same as in a small private bed and breakfast place in the UK. In my experience, French hotels have always been obliging in finding somewhere under cover and secure to store bicycles. Ask *Est-ce qu'on peut mettre les vélos à l'abri?* (Is there somewhere under cover for the bikes?).

CHAMBRES D'HÔTE

With hotels at such reasonable prices you might think there was no scope for bed and breakfast places. However, of relatively recent years the Gîtes de France organization has been developing the idea of bed and breakfast in private homes, often farms and houses in the countryside. Some also offer an evening meal *table d'hôte* – basically meaning that you share the host's evening meal with probably no choice of menu. These chambres d'hôte are usually prominently signposted and lists are available from local *gîte* organizations and *syndicats d'initiatives*. Some are more expensive than a small hotel but generally prices are about one-half to two-thirds that of bed and breakfast accommodation in the UK.

GÎTES AND GÎTES D'ÉTAPE

The gîte or *gîte rural* (literally 'a resting-place') is the French version of the rented self-catering holiday cottage, while the *gîte d'étape* is a hostel for walkers, cyclists and horse-riders, rather on the lines of a youth hostel but requiring no membership.

Gîtes ruraux have been widely promoted, even as far as the UK, by the Gîtes de France organization. The types of property range as widely as 'cottage' does and, like them, the gîtes are usually let on a weekly or fortnightly basis. They thus make a suitable centre for exploring an area in detail. The great advantages are that you can leave your main luggage at base, travelling light by day, and that you do not have to fit in with anybody's meal times. Although letting is usually by the minimum of a week we have on occasion found, out of season, that such places may be let even by the night, sometimes as a rooms annexe to a restaurant. A limited list of properties is available through the French Travel Service in London; fuller details are available from the regional or département committees (see the 'Useful Organizations' section).

Gîtes d'étape are much simpler. They offer dormitory accommodation, with catering and washing facilities, often in converted barns or similar buildings. Dormitories are not usually segregated by gender. Some of the buildings belong to the local community, some belong to other organizations such as the climbing body, the Club Alpin Français. The degree of luxury and the costs vary: some in the more frequented mountain areas may even offer meals if there is a resident *gardien*. If there is not, you may have to collect the key from a nearby house or shop. The status of these gîtes d'étape is now semi-official and they feature on the more recent editions of the IGN 1:100,000 and larger-scale maps.

There are also two chains of youth hostels (*Auberges de jeunesse* or *AJ*) in France, run by the Fédération Unie des Auberges de Jeunesse (FUAJ) and the Ligue Française pour les Auberges de la Jeunesse (LFAJ) – for details refer to the 'Useful Organizations' section. Possibly because of the multiplicity of other types of reasonably priced accommodation on the one hand and the popularity of camping on the other, they do not seem to have achieved the degree of penetration of the hostel organizations in the UK or Germany. They appear to be polarized into large city hostels aimed at groups and very small, often rather run-down, country ones. A sheet sleeping bag is required, and can be hired at some hostels. In many the dormitory accommodation is not segregated. Visitors should hold a card from their own national hostel organization, or an International Hostel Card.

CAMPING

Camping is highly developed in France and there is an abundance of camp sites. Most campers are car-

Rural France has many attractively situated campsites, the majority very well equipped.

borne but nearly all sites have space for lightweight tents. (The once specific term for one particular type of tent – *canadienne* – has now become the generic term for all small lightweight tents.) Like hotels, camp sites are given star ratings, with luxury sites having swimming pools, restaurants and even saunas and discos. Many – and often the friendliest and best value – are owned by the local town or commune (*camping municipale*). Even quite small villages may have a well-equipped site with showers and hot water based on the village sports ground, imposingly signposted as *Stade* (stadium).

The most comprehensive overall guide is the Michelin *Camping et Caravanning*, which is issued annually and lists recommended sites. These comprise perhaps a third or quarter of the total number, and many of the very small village sites do not figure in it, but the guide is particularly useful out of season for indicating where all-year-round or extended-opening sites may be (many sites are seasonal, not opening until Easter or even later). More complete local listings are available from syndicats d'initiatives. If you are staying several nights at a site you may be asked to deposit some piece of identity at the camp office; the International Camping Carnet, obtainable from the CTC, avoids having to leave your passport, as well as conferring third-party and some equipment insurance. It can also secure slightly reduced fees at some sites.

The Gîtes organization has also developed the concept of *Camping à la ferme* – small farm camp sites. These are often quite basic with no more than a water supply and lavatory facilities, and some are geared to longer stops than overnight, but can nevertheless be worth following up.

Camping outside camp sites – *camping sauvage*

(wild camping) – by lightweight campers making a one-night stop in uncultivated country, such as in the mountains, is generally tolerated. You are supposed to be more than 500m from the road and the nearest habitation. Camping sauvage is forbidden in some départements, such as those bordering the Mediterranean where summer pressures on space are high, or where fire risk is marked. It may also be forbidden in specific spots in other areas where indicated: it is often left up to the local authority to decide. You should obviously avoid causing damage and polluting water supplies.

4

Places to Eat

There is a tradition of family eating out in France, which combines with French pre-eminence in cooking to make it probably the easiest country anywhere to find a good meal. Do not be put off if a restaurant looks crowded: if it is full of locals this probably means that it offers very good food at a reasonable price.

There are fairly clear distinctions between the functions of restaurants, cafés and bars, and brasseries. This can be quite confusing if you are familiar with the way the same words are used in the UK for often quite different establishments.

Restaurants are far more numerous than in the UK – in some areas as frequent as English pubs. They serve as a rule only full meals at accepted meal times – *déjeuner* at 12 to 12.30, and *dîner* or *repas du soir* from about 6 or 6.30 in the evening, though some may offer the option of a main course only (*plat du jour*) at lunch-time. The last service time varies between country and town. In some rural areas, particularly out of season, the latest you can begin a meal can be as early as 7.30, while in towns, cities or tourist centres it can be much later. Restaurants as such are usually closed outside meal times, although a corner may well be open all day as a bar.

All restaurants are licensed and have to provide a three-course meal at a fixed price according to the class they are allotted. These prices are well below UK levels – often half – particularly away from cities and large towns. Most also offer more elaborate and expensive meals with more courses or fancier dishes. In France the word *menu* means these set meals. Asking for *le menu à 80F* means that you wish to order a meal from the choices offered on the listing at that price. The fixed-price menu or menu conseillé may offer choices for some or all of the courses but you are likely to have to pay extra if you want to

vary it further. There is often an alternative listing labelled *à la carte* or just *carte*. You can assemble the meal of your choice from these listings but it will usually prove dearer than the fixed-price meals. The fixed menus and their prices should always be on display outside the building. The quoted price will usually include any service charge (*service compris*) and may well include a 25cl carafe or pitcher of table wine, in which case it will be labelled *boisson comprise* (drink included). Most meals include liberal quantities of bread; if you empty the basket at any stage up to the end of the savoury courses it will usually be refilled.

A French meal is a satisfying and leisurely affair – you should expect it to take about an hour and a half at the least, often much longer. On entering you will be shown to a table and offered a menu. You will be expected to order your first two courses at the same time, together with drinks; the choice of desserts, fruit or cheese to finish you make later. One aspect of French professional pride is that everybody in a party will be served with their choice for each course at the same time, so the pace of the meal is that of the dish it takes longest to prepare. If any particular item will take longer than usual you will be warned. In a diminishing number of small town and country restaurants you retain the same knife and fork for the savoury courses. Even less commonly nowadays you may find vegetables served as a separate course.

French-style cooking has been copied the world over. The main characteristics are the retention of natural flavours, largely by lighter cooking than is common in the UK, enhanced by specially prepared sauces. The light cooking is particularly effective with vegetables but can mean that some meats – in particular steaks – are very much under-cooked for many tastes. The French *bien cuit* (well cooked) is about equivalent to our 'medium rare'.

Most restaurants will list low-priced *vins de table* or *vins du pays* as well as bottles of more prestigious and more expensive wines. Often there is a wine specially selected and bottled for the restaurant, even if it is only a modest place. This *réserve maison, réserve du patron* or *cuvée du patron* is very good value; the lower-priced wines may come in a 25cl (quart) or 50cl (demi) carafe or jug; others are in *bouteilles*, bottles containing 68 to 75cl depending on the area they come from. Wine is the everyday accompaniment of a meal in France and there is no particular snobbery attached to its choice – just choose what you fancy. However, French meals are to some extent designed to be eaten with at least a little wine – Mediterranean or Provençal dishes using oils really need the astringent accompaniment of a dry wine.

For non-drinkers, water will always be provided, either ordinary water in a jug (free) or a bottled mineral water – still, such as Evian, or slightly gassy, such as Perrier. Many French diners have only a mineral water, or alternatively some red wine and a mineral water. Wine tends to dehydrate, and so does cycling, so you should be careful to ensure that your water intake is adequate.

Your bill (*l'addition* or *la note*) will not be presented to you until you have clearly finished your whole meal and not usually even then until you ask for it. Unless you are very late and the restaurant is closing around you, you are unlikely to be hurried.

Finally there are two words I used at the end of the introduction that you will hear again and again in French and whose meaning has no short translation in English (which may say something about the two cultures) – *Bon appetit*! You will hear them as you are served a meal or called out by passers-by when you are picnicking by the roadside. Such is the place of food in French culture that the greatest happiness you can be wished is that your appetite and enjoyment should match the meal. So the custom is to thank well-wishers (*Merci, Madame* or *Merci, Monsieur*) for their kind thought.

Most cycle tourists, in my experience, favour the combination of a picnic lunch – for which France offers unsurpassed components – and a relaxing evening restaurant meal. That way you get the best of both worlds. The French lunch – for most people, the main meal of the day – really does lead to a soporific afternoon.

Cafés and bars sell essentially drinks – alcoholic and otherwise, cold and hot. Some may serve simple meals – possibly a single dish (plat du jour). Almost all will serve a *casse-croûte* or French-style sandwich. This is usually half a small loaf slit lengthwise, with the filling, commonly cheese or ham, dropped in the slot. This tends to be a rather expensive way of buying bread and cheese but it is quick.

Most beers (*bières*) are of lager or pilsner types, usually from northern and eastern France where beer is a much more common drink. A draught, or rather top-pressure, beer will be advertised as *a pression*.

The choices in non-alcoholic drinks, generally better for on-the-road refreshment, are bottled mineral waters, proprietary and often very gassy sweetened drinks and colas. Of the less gassy fruit drinks the orange-based Orangina is one of the tastiest and most refreshing. Alternatives are syrups – such as mint-flavoured *sirop de menthe* – diluted with water or lemonade.

In hot drinks, a request for coffee (*café*) on its own brings a small cup of strong black coffee; *café crème* is the same with cream. The stipulation *en grande tasse* results in larger cups of the same. Tea (*thé*) will be a pot or glass of amber liquid without milk, while *thé-citron* adds lemon. Tea with milk is becoming less unknown, though in some places you might have to give a detailed specification to make it clear that you want *cold* milk. It will not be terribly strong, however, and if your deepest craving is for a real old cup of sergeant-major's then I fear you must wait until the White Cliffs are in sight again. All drinks may be appreciably more expensive if they are served to you at a table or outside terrace, particularly in cities.

The French café in a small town or village fulfils in many respects the function of the English or Welsh pub or Scottish or Irish bar – a meeting point for the community. There is no lower age limit for going into a café although there are restrictions on the types of drink that young people can buy, summarized on the large official notices in every bar. Opening hours are pragmatic: cafés tend to open when there is likely to be trade and close when there is not.

It is possible in many cases (and particularly helpful in bad weather) to eat your picnic lunch in a café, buying a drink to go with it. Some cafés even

The further south you go, the more likely you are to find outdoor café tables.

have a notice in the window saying *On reçoit avec provisions* or *On peut manger ses provisions* as an invitation to bring in your own food. After all, they reason, they are not in the food business, so you are not setting up in competition, but you *are* going to buy a drink, and possibly a coffee afterwards If there is no definite invitation you should of course ask; in my experience permission is rarely refused.

Three other sources of meals are supermarket cafeterias, crêperies and pizzerias. The supermarket cafeteria offers the components of a normal meal and is often very good value although short of the little touches of service that characterize the restaurant. Crêperies specialize in savoury and sweet pan-

cakes (many are run by exiled, even maudlin exiled, Bretons, and so specialize in cider as well), while pizzerias naturally offer baked-on-the-spot pizzas, cooked over a wood fire, often offering them as components of a full meal. Both crêperies and pizzerias allow vegetarians to escape the omelette, which is in most restaurants the only real alternative to meat or fish. (Most restaurants will be happy to supply an omelette in place of the meat or fish dish within an otherwise set menu.)

Brasseries (literally 'breweries') were originally beer houses but now occupy a spot midway between cafés and restaurants. They generally serve meals or single dishes but may have less choice and be less elaborate than most restaurants.

5
Touring Bikes

If you can, it's best to spread the load between front and rear bags: two-thirds at the back, one-third at the front, preferably low down.

It would be perfectly possible to cover the flatter routes in this book using any bicycle, but once you want to move on to the hillier routes you will enjoy it more if you have the tool for the job. To enjoy the mountain routes a properly geared bicycle will be essential. Most other factors are secondary, provided the bike is the right size and you can adjust it to give you a comfortable riding position. This is not the place to go into the detail of setting up a touring bike: fuller information can be found in the sources listed at the end of this book.

GEARING

Gearing is fundamental. The size or ratio of the gear is a measure of how far you travel along the ground for each turn of the pedals. A high gear covers quite a long distance for each pedal turn, and a low gear a short one. Life gives you nothing for nothing, of course: at a given speed you will have to push harder on the pedals, but at a slower rate, with a high gear. On the other hand a very low gear would be easier to turn but might involve pedalling uncomfortably fast. A comfortable pedalling rate or cadence for our sort of riding lies in a fairly narrow range, about 45 to 90rpm, somewhere from 80 to 90 being comfortable for normal speed riding on the flat. The point of variable gears is to enable you to choose the gear that gives a comfortable pedalling rate whatever your speed. Speed is in turn governed by your comfortable power output, the terrain and the wind. Since you will enjoy the routes if you do not hurry over them, low gears are going to be very useful. And when you cannot hurry, as on a mountain pass, they are going to be essential.

On most modern touring bikes, gears are changed by shifting the chain between different sized rear sprockets on the freewheel on the back wheel (up to eight, though six or seven are more practical for touring) and different sized chainwheels fixed to the cranks (two or three). Small chainwheels and big sprockets give low gears, large chainwheels and small sprockets give high gears. Lever-controlled gear mechanisms do the shifting, and these are nowadays 'indexed' so that they simply click into position. This improvement has largely done away with the old objections to these derailleur or chain-shifting gears. If you did not get on with them in the past because of sluggish changing and indefinite

positions, you will find modern precision set-ups a revelation.

A go-anywhere touring bike needs a wide range of gears – and the one I suggest will cover you from about 4mph (6km/h) at the natural slower pedalling rate you would use uphill at this speed to something like 20mph (35km/h), pedalling more briskly as you would when the going is easy and speed higher. But if the *range* needs to be wide, the gaps between the gear ratios should not be. Differences that are too large are uncomfortably jerky – when you change up it suddenly feels as though something has jammed, when you change down as though you are pedalling on nothing. If you are ordering a custom-built bike or setting one up yourself, I would recommend a combination of 44, 36 and 26 tooth (or 46-38-28 or 26) triple chainrings at the front and an evenly proportioned range from 15 or 16 to 26 or 28 teeth (say 15-17-19-22-25-28) on the rear freewheel, combined with an indexed gear mechanism. This is only one way of achieving the range of gears that you need, but one that I have found to work particularly well with beginners as well as experienced riders. As will be explained later, you do not go through every gear in exact sequence every time, so coping with 18 or 21 gears is not that complicated.

Proper touring bikes from big manufacturers, such as those in the Dawes and Raleigh ranges, come ready equipped with suitably low gears. However, many off-the-peg road bicycles, even some described by the manufacturers as touring models, have larger chainrings, a lot of gears that are too high and not enough low gears. The dealer ought to be able to lower the range for you, though this does seem to be something of a blind spot with those who normally deal with racing bikes. One easy way of getting a bicycle with low enough gears is to buy a mountain or all-terrain bike, though even that will still have some high gears that you will rarely if ever need. For many of the routes in this book a mountain bike would be quite suitable, though you might find you need bar end attachments to provide some variation in hand position on long rides. Most mountain bikes are not particularly light, though – perhaps a third to a half more than a conventional lightweight tourer.

You may hear gear ratios expressed in inches, following a bizarre historical system used only in the UK, Australia and the USA. It dates back to the stately old high-wheeled 'penny-farthings' and is the size of front wheel one of these would have needed to give the equivalent gear! (The distance you travel per pedal turn is pi or 3.142 times greater.) For the record, the range I suggest goes from about 75 to 77 down to 25 to 28 inches with jumps of about 12 per cent between adjacent sprockets on the freewheel.

MOUNTAIN RIDING

As already hinted, you do not go through the gear range meticulously in arithmetical sequence – and you emphatically do not work up through all the gears, ending up in top. In fact, the set-up I suggest is most easily used as a basic 'three-speed' arrangement based on the front chainrings, with the rear gear providing fine-tuning options in each range. The big, outermost, ring is for easy conditions, the middle one for general and moderately hard ones, and the inner smallest one for definite or steady climbing. You then use the rear gear to change from one freewheel sprocket to the next to get exactly the ratio that feels comfortable. To avoid pulling the chain too far out of its natural line, you use the three or four outermost sprockets with the big ring, most of them with the middle one and the three or four inner ones with the innermost, little ring. In general, start off by using fairly low gears and gradually change up to one that feels comfortable.The key is to take it steady; leisure cycling is not a race!

Everybody has their individual natural rhythm and effort of riding, which is likely to change with experience and fitness. As you gain experience, you will probably find that a rather faster pedalling rate becomes more comfortable, rhythmic and natural than a slower one in a higher gear. Your own rhythm shows most once you start going uphill, when most people find it irksome to go much slower, and uncomfortable or impossible to go faster. You have to accept this; if you are with other people, each of you should ride at your own pace. Do not try to hang back or, worse, struggle to keep up. Arrange to rendezvous at the top, or at more frequent specified points on a long climb. Sometimes you can even speeds out by arranging for stronger riders to carry more or heavier parts of the luggage.

All this means that it is not possible – although people continue to try – to specify a 'correct' gear for a particular climb. The best gear for you depends on your natural attributes, the wind and weather, how you feel on a given day and at that particular time –

as well as the gradient. Everyone has a natural length of time for which their comfortable effort can be sustained. If you are new to cycling this may be no more than an hour or two, followed by a fairly long rest. At least to begin with, be prepared to underestimate your abilities – you can always explore an interesting detour at the end of the day if you are still full of beans. You may well surprise yourself at the distance you can cover. After all, four hours' riding, spread over a day, at a quite modest 11–13km/h will take you some 50km.

All your normal calculations about average speeds are turned on their heads once you reach the mountains. With suitably low gears you can potter relatively comfortably up the passes (where gradients are usually much gentler than short, steep British hills) but you will not be going very fast, possibly only 6–10km/h. You have to learn to pace your efforts, not to rush at what seems to be a relatively gentle slope. You have to cultivate a sort of fatalistic patience: you know you will eventually get to the top – and it does not much matter how long it takes.

Interestingly, the brain seems to have an illusion about the apparent steepness of hills: gradients look less when you are going up than when you are going down. (As more than one person has observed, if you are going to have an illusion, better that way round than the other!) This tends to induce a natural caution going down, which is no bad thing. When going up a pass with hairpin bends do not be put off by the violent-looking difference between the zig going up to the bend and the zag going away. What you are seeing is the gradient doubled.

Not only does everybody have a different natural tempo, they also differ in such preferences as keeping going once they have settled into a rhythm or stopping to rest at relatively frequent intervals. In any case, there will be things to stop and see, so average as opposed to actual speeds will be very modest. This may mean that, say, a 25km climb rising by perhaps 1,500m may take a total of five or more hours. You certainly should not be dispirited if it takes most of the day.

Although it is impossible to recoup entirely the time taken up by climbing, at least you know it will not take very long to go down a pass; even if it is five in the afternoon when you reach the top, you can be down in the next valley and in the hotel bar before six. And you know that it will not take much effort, either. Nevertheless, there are certain precautions

An avenue in the valley of the Durance.

On long downhill runs you need brake only for bends if you sit up on the straight stretches and let the wind slow you down.

about going down passes.

The first need is to be adequately dressed; that is dealt with in Chapter 7. The second is to remain in control. This does not mean keeping the brakes on – or at least very rarely. The slopes of most passes are such that if you sit up with your hands on the tops of the bars – using what is in effect air braking – then your speed will naturally be held to an exhilarating but quite safe 40 to 55km/h, depending on the gradient. You will then find that you need to use your bike's brakes only for slowing for bends or tricky sections. Thus you avoid problems that can arise from overheating the rims, which can happen if you keep your brakes on all the time. I have found this method to work well even when quite heavily laden with camping kit.

If you do find yourself going into a bend too fast, however, the first thing is to slow drastically in as nearly a straight line as possible: do not worry about negotiating the bend, just concentrate on stopping. Remember that it is the front brake that does most of this; the rear one is much less effective when you are decelerating – its real role is to supplement the front one and spread the braking at relatively steady speeds. It is actually quite difficult to apply the front

brake so hard on a loaded touring bike that you lift the rear wheel but quite easy to put on the back one hard enough for it to skid.

Be wary of loose gravel on corners and avoid as far as possible having either brake on if you have to cross a patch of it. And, naturally, take extra care on wet roads. The other obvious hazard on long downhills is traffic coming up. Some long vehicles such as coaches have to use the whole width of the road to negotiate a hairpin bend, or may even have to take two bites at it – so be prepared.

Carrying It All

All the clothing, and anything else you want to take with you, has to be carried. In general all loads should be carried on the bicycle, in suitable saddlebags or panniers securely fixed to appropriate carriers, not on your back. Some mountain bike users prefer a small securely held back-pack for day trips, but for on-road use bicycle-mounted loads are much more comfortable. If you are carrying a particularly bulky load – if you are camping, say – then spread your bags between the front and back of the bicycle. There is more detail in some of the titles listed in the 'Useful Books' section.

Let the bike carry the load while you travel light.

6
Roads and Maps

RIDING ON THE RIGHT

The first obvious difference for a British (or Irish, Australian, New Zealand or Japanese) rider is that you ride on the right-hand side of the road. If you have never done it before you might think it would be difficult, but in practice even beginners are into the swing of it within minutes. Many people even claim to find it more natural. Generally speaking, ordinary roads present no problem, particularly if there is other traffic to remind you, and the same goes for right-hand junctions, where you stay on the nearside of the road (the right). Left-hand junctions call for the same precautions as right-hand junctions in Britain; and having turned left, remember to cross to the far side of the road. This – and when setting off after a lengthy stop, particularly if it is on the opposite side of the road to the one you should be on – is where you are most likely to make the mistake of trying to ride on the left. Roundabouts look a little daunting at first, but you merely go round them anticlockwise instead of clockwise, giving way to traffic already on the roundabout.

NATIONAL ROADS

The *routes nationales*, N-roads, are the close equivalent of British A-roads or Irish T-roads. The classification is based on a rough pattern of cardinal routes numbered from N1 to N15 radiating from Paris. Other N-roads complete the spider's web. In general the one- and two-figure N-roads carry the heaviest traffic, and are not very pleasant to cycle on, but you may have to use them for short stretches to link more agreeable roads or to get into a town. It

is best to avoid them as far as you can, though in mountain areas you may not have much choice. Traffic is less dense than on comparable roads in the UK (no French N-road carries the sustained traffic of England's A1 or A3, for example) and except for holiday and cross-frontier routes, they are quieter the farther you are from big cities.

Some smaller N-roads can be very quiet indeed. Many of these smaller roads are being reclassified as local roads and quite a bit of general renumbering is taking place, so do not be surprised if road signs and your map disagree about the number of your road while agreeing on its destination. N-roads are marked in red on maps and on road signs, while kilometre stones are also topped in red.

As a result of historical factors – among them the Napoleonic need for military links, the relative absence at the time of powerful local landowners, and the altogether sparser population – there are very many more dead straight roads than in the UK. This is particularly so in the flatter or gently rolling parts of the countryside and also more obvious when the road is a main one. Long straight roads can be very dispiriting to cycle along, especially in heat or a nagging headwind. Sometimes there are the characteristic (but disappearing) long avenues of plane trees or poplars, which give some shade but not a great deal of shelter.

LOCAL ROADS

Most other roads, including some very minor ones indeed, are classified as *chemins départementales*, D or sometimes CD for short. These roads, as you might guess, come under the control of the local département, which leads to one slightly confusing feature.

Each département numbers its own D-roads, so the numbers usually change when you cross a county boundary. One minute you can be bowling along the D76, which has been happily following its own intricate but well signposted route, only to find when you get to the next complex village that the D76 has vanished, while the D2 now leads to your destination. But the newly defrocked N-roads, which now have three-figure D-numbers, do not change in this way.

Major D-roads are marked in yellow on maps, road signs and kilometre stones. Others are uncoloured on maps but still have yellow sign-toppings or kilometre stones (where these exist). D-roads are the key to pleasurable traffic-free cycling in France – they are the roads you are likely to use most.

OTHER ROADS AND TRACKS

Slightly down the scale from the smallest D-roads come some local roads, which may be signed *chemins vicinales* (CV) or sometimes *chemin vicinale ordinaire* (Vo). The distinction between some of these and the smaller D-roads seems quite arbitrary, since both are narrow lanes. Many CV roads are, however, dead-ends leading to isolated communities.

In forest areas, particularly the national forests (*forêts domaniales*, roughly equivalent to Forestry Commission lands), minor roads may be classified as *routes forestières*, abbreviated to RF. These range from very good metalled roads – just like any other minor road – to quite rough tracks. In sandy or hilly areas, the firm-based unmetalled tracks often offer a very reasonable riding surface and in the mountains may yield spectacular views as a bonus. Some lowland ones, though, can be very muddy – and all forest tracks are liable to be churned up by timber operations. Forest roads are meant to enable forestry work to be carried out and may well be closed to motor traffic, or closed altogether for timber extraction. Some may be marked *route privée* (private road) – which can be off-putting at first sight – but you can use them if they carry the qualification *circulation publique tolerée*, a legal device to allow the forest authority to retain ownership and control of the road.

Some other roads and tracks, often in border areas, are *routes stratégiques*, abbreviated to RS. These roads were originally of military origin but some are now open. Check any notices carefully.

There are also in a few places paths designed or adapted specially for cycling. These are marked as *pistes cyclables* (cyclable tracks). The longest of these that I know of wanders through the forests and sand dunes of the coastal Landes south of Bordeaux. Another fairly long one runs the length of Lac d'Annecy at the foot of the Alps, following the bed of a former railway. In addition, quite a number of French towns and cities, notably Strasbourg, have initiated extensive schemes of special cycle routes.

France has a network of numbered long-distance paths, the *sentiers de grande randonnée*, marked GR on signs and maps. While primarily a walking chain – and a pretty tough one in the high mountains – parts of them are reasonably ridable and may even be marked as cycle routes. Many winter ski resorts, particularly cross-country ones (*ski de fond*), are now opening up their ski runs in summer as mountain bike routes, marked with VTT signs, and frequently associated with a mountain bike hire facility (*location de VTT*).

Finally, there are numerous rough mountain passes, some merely mule tracks, others at least partly ridable. A few have become challenges for adventurous French cycle tourists – the best known of these is the Col de Parpaillon, 2645m, paralleling the Col de Vars near Barcelonette.

You may take it that there is no objection to cycling on any road or track unless there is any specific indication that it is private (*chemin privé* or *route privée*) or forbidden (*interdit* or *interdite*), or if the standard 'no cycling' sign is shown. Some small roads carry a standard 'no entry' sign with the qualification *sauf riverains*, which means that they are open only to traffic belonging to or having business with inhabitants of properties along the road. I have never encountered any objection to cyclists using such roads; the signs are intended to prevent motor traffic using them as short cuts.

SPECIAL RULES FOR CYCLISTS

Bicycles are generally considered as vehicles and are subject to restrictions lying between those of the pedestrian and the car. The ultimate authority is the *Code de la route*, the equivalent of the *Highway Code*, but having the force of law. The relevant sections regarding cycling (Articles 189 to 199) may be summarized as:

Some canal towpaths are open to cyclists, making very easy off-road routes. This is a stretch of the Canal du Midi.

ing fairly common on main roads leaving towns. These comprise about the inner metre and a half of the carriageway, separated from the other traffic by a bold white line and marked by white cycle symbols.

- If the road is cobbled or is being dug up for repair, cyclists may ride on the footpath – carefully and giving way to pedestrians – outside built-up areas.
- All cycles must have two effective brakes.
- From sunset to sunrise, and during conditions of poor visibility, bicycles should have a front lamp and a red rear lamp and reflector. (However, French urban cyclists seem to flout the lighting laws in ways that make even the most anarchic of UK students or cycle couriers look positively conformist!) You may wheel a bicycle without lights along the edge of the road. Pedal reflectors and reflectors visible from the side are also required.
- All cycles should have a bell or horn (and no other similar device) audible for at least 50 metres.
- Cycles should have a metal plate showing the owner's name and address.

It is obviously common sense to use lights if you are riding after dark, but it is unlikely that a bicycle temporarily imported by a visitor will attract official attention by having no pedal reflectors, side reflectors, bell or nameplate. I have certainly never known these rules invoked for foreigners, nor their absence remarked on after an accident.

ROAD SIGNS

Most French road signs are similar to those used in other European countries, but there are some important exceptions:

- The 'give way' sign is a plain inverted red triangle, often without wording.
- A round blue sign with a white bicycle symbol indicates a compulsory cycle path; it may also bear

- Cyclists must not ride more than two abreast, and must ride in single file where traffic conditions demand it and at all times after dark.
- Bicycles with sidecars or trailers, and tricycles, must always proceed in single file. Bicycles may not be towed by another vehicle. Passengers may only be carried in special seats (such as child seats) or in trailers specially adapted for their carriage.
- Cyclists must use marked cycle paths or lanes alongside roads where they exist. They are marked with the appropriate blue circular sign. These paths are usually beside roads leaving or entering large or fairly large towns. If there are cycle paths on both sides of the road you should use the one on the right. Special cycle lanes (*bandes cyclables* or *couloirs cyclables*) are also becom-

the words *piste cyclable* (cycle path), perhaps with the additional word *obligatoire* (compulsory).

- The same sign crossed out in red indicates the end of the cycle path.
- A sandy-yellow diamond with a white surround indicates that you are on a major road with priority: all joining roads will have 'give way' or stop signs. These signs appear at intervals on trunk and major roads, often approaching junctions.
- The same sign crossed out means that you no longer have priority.
- A point-upwards triangular sign showing a thin horizontal black line crossing a thick vertical one means that you are approaching a junction at which you have priority.
- The general hazard sign, which in the UK is an exclamation mark, is in France a vertical black bar, often with wording beneath giving the nature of the hazard.

Less important, but worth noting are:

- Nearly all other road junctions are marked with a triangular sign with a diagonal black cross, a generalized crossroads sign. This is usedwhether the junction is a crossroads or a T-junction to either side; in other words, the sign is not a diagrammatic representation of the junction as it is in the UK. One other useful indicator of an often unsigned junction is two

The borne de kilometrage at its best, with everything you need to know: road classification (yellow = D), which road, how high up, how far to the top.

white posts, about 1.5m high, with a red reflective band near the top, either side of the turning. Lines of similar posts (usually hollow plastic) are often used, with white reflectors, to mark the path of the road at a bend.

- Sequence-of-bends signs are the schematic double zigzag and do not indicate which way the road actually bends. Single bend signs, however, do.
- Hill gradients are expressed in percentages.
- All speed limit signs are in kilometres per hour.

Quite unimportant:

- The humps on the two-humped bumpy road sign are much shallower than on UK signs. The bumps on the bumpy road, however, emphatically are not, although many French traffic-calming humps, which are often cobbled or textured, have a little smooth tarmac section at the side for cyclists.
- The character shovelling on the road-works sign has a quite different pose.

There are in addition quite a lot of word signs, official and unofficial, often used with the vertical bar hazard sign, sometimes with others. For convenience they are listed in a glossary at the end of the book.

ROAD SIGNALS AND PRIORITIES

Most road junctions in France used to be governed by the *priorité à droite* rule – you always gave way to a vehicle joining your road from the right, irrespective of the relative importance of the two roads. Nowadays, most junctions, at least down to most D-road ones, are marked by give way and stop signs, while the major roads have either the sandy-yellow diamond with a white surround or major/minor crossroads signs noted above.

There are now only three situations where you are likely to encounter the priorité à droite rule. These are:

- In built-up areas – that is, between the sign indicating the town or village name and the crossed-out version showing that you are leaving it. Even here many side-roads now have give way or stop signs.
- Occasionally after you have passed a crossed-out diamond priority sign, perhaps if a main road of comparable importance is joining yours. This will almost certainly be confirmed by a priorité à

droite sign.

- At junctions with a flashing orange light or at traffic lights that have been set with the orange light flashing.

Roundabouts (*ronds-points*) used also to be covered by the priorité à droite rule. This, combined with driving on the right, is a recipe for gridlock, so now roundabouts (which were much less common than in the UK but are rapidly multiplying) usually accord priority to traffic on the roundabout – a 'priority to the left' rule. There is always a warning roundabout sign, marked *Vous n'avez pas la priorité*.

Many junctions are governed by traffic lights (*feux de signalisation* or just *feux*). The phases go in sequence: red (stop), green (go), orange or amber (prepare to stop), red again. Note that there is no red-plus-amber 'get-ready-to-go' phase; the sudden appearance of the green does wonders for speeding up your reactions. When traffic is light the amber or orange light alone may be set to a flashing sequence as a warning to take care and to treat it as an ordinary junction with priority from the right. If a flashing amber light comes on where the green normally is, it means 'proceed with caution'. At some sets of lights a right filter arrow flashing in orange may come on during the red phase. This means that you can filter right if there is no traffic crossing and it is safe to do so. A green filter arrow means that you have right of way.

Bus lanes (*couloirs d'autobus*) are marked in some towns and – unless marked for bikes as well – are restricted to buses and taxis.

SIGNPOSTS AND KILOMETRE STONES

French signposting is excellent – but different from UK signposting – in the country, and often indifferent or dreadful in towns. The standard country route signpost is a blue-edged white plaque mounted on a stubby concrete pillar relatively near to the ground. There is usually another small square plaque at the top of the sign giving the road number, white on red for N-roads, black on yellow for D-roads. Distances to villages and towns (and sometimes to major road junctions) are given in kilometres. Below five kilometres they may be given to 100m, marked, for example, as $3_{,7}$. Although the signposts are pointed at one end to show the direction indicated, the placing can often take a bit of getting used to. An apparently left-pointing sign often turns out to be intended to indicate straight ahead.

In towns, signposts to individual destinations can be quite obscure – perhaps fairly high up a wall and rather unofficial-looking, with no road number. It is quite common to find a single through route marked *Toutes directions* (to all destinations), with the individual place names not cropping up until you actually have to turn off left or right.

You are bound to notice very soon one other feature of the signposting system – *the bornes de kilométrage*, the kilometre equivalent of the milestone. The bornes are uniformly shaped with rounded tops. The main body of the stone (now often plastic or metal instead) is white and the top red on N-roads, with the road number in white, and yellow on D-roads, with the road number in black. Some carry only this information plus a number that shows how far you are from the nominal start of that particular road. The best, however, are a mine of information, stating how far it is to the next village or the top of the pass, and in mountain areas giving altitude above sea level in metres – very useful on a long climb. Unfortunately, this useful information is not always renewed when the stone is repainted. On many roads there are also 100m stones – small square stones numbered from 1 to 9 – between kilometre markers, but they are often quite obscure.

Villages and towns – built-up areas subject to a speed limit of 60km/h – are indicated by a simple sign with the village name (plus the ever-useful road number) as you enter, and a similar sign crossed out in red as you leave. All villages of commune status or higher have name boards in black capital letters on a cream background. *Hameaux* and *lieux-dits* (hamlets) of lower status have their names in white upper and lower case italic letters on a navy blue ground. These slightly theoretical distinctions can help you judge the size of marking you may be looking for on the map. Another useful locating feature is that most bridges of reasonable size have a sign giving the name of the river, stream or canal that they cross.

MAPS

France is well served for maps at cyclist-friendly scales. There are two main map makers: the pub-lishing subsidiary of the giant tyre firm Michelin, and the Institut Géographique National, IGN. For the latest availability you should contact one of the suppliers listed at the end of this book.

All French maps are much cheaper to buy in France than elsewhere: Michelin sheets, for example, are about one-third of the UK price in France. In addition, since they are updated quite frequently, you are more likely to find the latest edition locally where there is a rapid turnover. But part of the fun of any bike tour is spending winter evenings planning with a map – so get the Michelin atlas and the 1:1,000,000 map in advance at least.

Michelin Maps

Maps at two scales produced by Michelin are particularly useful. The first is a small-scale sheet, No. 989, which covers the whole country at a scale of 1:1,000,000. At this scale, 1cm on the map represents 10km on the ground (about 16 miles to the inch) – so 6in or 15cm is about 100 miles or 150km. This is a useful map for route planning since – because of the size of France – it is often difficult to get an idea of the relative positions of places from a succession of larger-scale maps. However, it shows only major roads and a few selected minor ones, while railways are not shown at all. Mountainous areas are indicated by hill-shadowing, and forests by green shading. Major mountain passes are marked and there are useful marginal maps showing when during the spring and early summer they may be expected to be clear of snow. Distances between towns and major junctions are marked, so that you can easily form a rough idea of what length of stages you can manage between stops. Département boundaries, names and numbers are marked, which is useful for checking such things as accommodation lists.

The other Michelin map is the most practical on-the-road reference, at a scale of 1:200,000 (1cm to 2km, or just over 3 miles to the inch). This is produced in two series, using the same map as a basis, both highly visible in shops by their tall, thin shape and bright yellow covers. The most useful series for on-the-road use is what Michelin call the *Cartes détaillées* (detailed maps). Thirty-six sheets, numbered 51 to 86, cover mainland France, while there are an additional three sheets, 87 to 89, giving duplicated cover of three areas (Alsace-Lorraine, northern Alps, and the area round Lyon) that fall

Not a 'no-cycling' notice in sight! This is actually a road in a southern village.

The Michelin 1:200,000 mapping shows most of the things cyclists want to know. Major roads (either N-roads or principal D-roads) are shown in red, important D-roads in yellow, and the remainder, irrespective of classification, uncoloured. There is some indication of importance and quality of surface, shown by width (on the map) and solid or dashed road edges (note that these do not indicate unfenced roads as they do on Ordnance Survey maps). Some very minor roads, particularly in towns and villages, are not marked but in general coverage is excellent. Most major topographical features and man-made landmarks are indicated.

It is only in the representation of relief that these maps become a bit sketchy. The general bumpiness of hilly areas is indicated by hill shadowing but there are no contours and relatively few spot height markings. There is no hill shadowing in areas judged to be insufficiently hilly, with the result that a whole sheet (such as that covering upper Normandy and Picardy) might have no indication of

awkwardly on the sheet lines of the main series. The final sheet, 90, covers the whole of Corsica. Each sheet portrays an area about 214km west-to-east by 94km north-to-south, with a simple concertina fold that opens up without awkward unravelling to show an almost square 45 × 47km area. This makes it possible to follow a route in any direction with a minimum of refolding. There is a single fold horizontally across the middle, giving a total of 20 numbered panels. Michelin and other guides often refer to the map panel number to help you locate a place or feature on the map, for example *Michelin 76, pli 9* (Michelin map 76, fold or panel 9). The much less handily folded version, called by Michelin *Cartes régionales* (regional maps), covers mainland France in sixteen double-sized sheets, numbered 230 to 245, with an extra sheet, 246, covering the lower Rhône valley. Corsica does not feature. These maps share with the IGN maps the same awkward and wear-and-tear-prone fold of UK Ordnance Survey maps.

the quite steep sides of some of the river valleys. However, road gradients are marked by a system of chevrons or arrows that point uphill – the opposite of the convention adopted by the Ordnance Survey, but a good deal more logical to a toiling cyclist. One chevron indicates gradients between 5 and 9 per cent (1-in-20 to 1-in-11), two chevrons slopes from 9 to 13 per cent (1-in-11 to 1-in-7½), while three mark steep hills, those over 13 per cent, usually with the percentage marked alongside. Only the three-chevron hills would qualify for a gradient marking on an Ordnance Survey map. On many very minor roads, however, the chevrons do not appear, even on quite steep slopes. Nevertheless the system does give a pretty good idea of how up and down a region is or how tough a particular climb will be. Distances between towns, villages and even quite minor junctions are marked to the nearest 0.5km in discreet red figures.

The maps also show features of tourist interest –

châteaux, caves, churches, monuments and so on (with those that Michelin judge interesting differentiated by a solid infilling of the symbol from those presumably considered dull) as well as spots with a view. Recent sheets incorporate an alphabetical gazetteer of places of interest, referenced to the quarter (north-west, north-east, and so on) of the fold of the map on which they appear. Roads of all classes may be marked with a green edging if Michelin judge them picturesque. The criterion appears in places arbitrary and to rest on a permutation of any two from trees, water, mountains or vineyards; maybe the jibe of philosopher Roland Barthes – 'the picturesque begins as soon as the ground becomes uneven' – is not too far out.

Hamlyn have recently joined forces with Michelin to produce the 1:200,000 series of maps in atlas form as the *Michelin Motoring Atlas France*. As a thick A3-format paperback this is hardly the thing to carry on a bike but is an excellent reference to have at home in conjunction with the 1:1,000,000 map. The atlas is revised at frequent intervals.

Michelin also produce a number of sheets with the same style of mapping at double and four times the scale – 1:100,000 and 1:50,000. These mostly cover areas around large towns and cities: Paris, Toulouse, Bordeaux, Nantes, Clermont-Ferrand and the Lille conurbation. There is also useful coverage of the hinterland of Nice as far north as the Grand Canyon de Verdon. Michelin appear to be withdrawing superseded sheets and introducing new ones rather rapidly at these scales.

IGN Maps

IGN produce maps at a range of scales, denoted by the colour of their covers. Red covers (*Serie rouge*) are at a scale of 1:250,000, green covers (*Serie verte*) at 1:100,000 and blue covers (*Serie bleue*) at 1:25,000. There used also to be a useful orange set at 1:50,000 but this scale is being abandoned by IGN. Local overprinted versions are also on sale, with specialized information such as ski runs, lifts and trails or waymarked footpaths. There is also a special series at several scales covering National and Regional Parks.

The 1:250,000 map (the same scale as the Ordnance Survey Travelmaster series) has roughly the same scope as the Michelin 1:200,000 but, while perhaps prettier to look at, is neither so handily folded nor quite so detailed, while the dramatic hill shading tends to obscure practical detail.

The 1:100,000 scale of the Serie verte is close to the cycle tourist's ideal, giving scope for considerable detail while at the same time covering a respectable area. This series shows appreciably more detail than Michelin and, as well as hill shadowing, there are contours, whose interval varies according to the terrain. Road gradients are not indicated. The 74 sheets are, however, folded in the same cumbersome way as Ordnance Survey maps, so that they soon wear holes at the topologically impossible double fold of the corners, while at the same time being less simple to unfold on the road, particularly in anything above the lightest breeze. My general experience is that they are very good to consult for the tricky bits, but noticeably less easy and convenient than the more diagrammatic Michelin maps for following a route on the road.

The larger-scale 1:25,000 is, as in the UK, a very useful if not essential tool for riding off-road. Topographical features, including scree and crag, are clearly marked, as well as the detailed courses of paths and tracks. Gîtes d'étape, mountain refuges and emergency telephones are also indicated.

7

Cycling the French Way

WATCHING

Cycle road racing is France's summer – or spring, summer and early autumn – sport. European professional bike racing is a highly commercial and slickly run operation, but behind it all there is a tough, demanding, colourful, highly tactical and highly athletic sport.

The big races take two forms: 'classic' single-day place-to-place races and stage races. The latter last several days or even weeks, and performances on each daily stage add up to the final result. Supporting these, and where most riders make their money, are a host of local races (*critériums*), often on short round-the-the town circuits. Part of the appeal of all these is that they bring the sport to the public. Having the Tour de France pass through your village is as though a few minutes of the Cup Final – which might well turn out to be the crucial ones – were played on the village green before the show moved on. At some stage in its history, the Tour de France has visited all the areas described in this book, and been over most of the passes.

The classic single-day races are concentrated in late March and April, with a few in early autumn, and are shared between France, Italy, Belgium and the Netherlands. The great French spring classic is Paris–Roubaix, which nowadays usually starts at Compiègne outside Paris on the Sunday nearest 10 April unless it clashes with Easter. It is notorious for taking in sadistically treacherous cobbled roads in the north as it approaches Roubaix near the Belgian border. Lesser French classics are Paris–Camembert on the Tuesday after Easter, Paris–Brussels in April and Paris–Tours in October. Others near to the French border are Milan–San Remo in Italy (San Remo is not far east of Nice on the Riviera), held on

the Saturday nearest St Joseph's Day (19 March), and the two April races in the Belgian Ardennes near Liège, the Flèche Wallonne and Liège–Bastogne–Liège, the longest established of them all. The dates of the April races vary according to the date of Easter.

The three-week Tour de France in July is the stage race that everybody knows. The Tour (*tour* means 'circuit' and has nothing to do with touring) follows a different route each year, sometimes clockwise, sometimes anticlockwise, often going beyond the borders of France, but always finishing in Paris. The route takes in many different types of terrain, with the great dramatic battles being fought out in the mountains of the Alps and the Pyrenees. Most stages are straightforward races, where the first over the line wins, but others may be individual or team time trials, where riders or teams ride separately against the clock. Although the holder of the famed yellow jersey (*maillot jaune*), which the current leader wears each day, is the rider whose times for each of the daily stages add up to the lowest total, there are other awards for the most consistently placed rider on all the stages (*maillot vert*, green jersey) and the best mountain-climber, officially the *meilleur grimpeur* but always unofficially *le roi de la montagne* (the king of the mountains), who is entitled to wear a natty jersey with red spots. The abilities to sprint to win bunched flat finishes and to climb mountains are, largely, born gifts and for once life is fair in that both are not usually vested in the same people.

For the spectators at least part of the spectacle is the gaudy cavalcade of advertising vehicles that precedes the riders – a noisy, brash, vulgar, speeded-up carnival procession that is immensely amusing and enjoyable. The roads are closed to other traffic for some hours ahead of the event, so you may have to set out early to get your viewpoint, although the gendarmerie are usually much more tolerant of cyclists than of car drivers. Once you have found your spot you may have to stay there for some time, so stock up with food, drink and sun-screen cream.

To see the drama of the race, pick a spot in the mountains, where things happen and where the race is unlikely to come past in seconds in a great swishing bunch; to study riders' style and technique watch an individual time trial stage; but to see the sport come to the people, see it in a village or small town in the French countryside. Do all three if you can.

There are other, shorter stage races, including a spite of minor, almost training races, in the south in February and March, culminating in the week-long Paris–Nice race that directly precedes Milan–San Remo. This is billed as 'The race to the sun' and almost always meets appalling weather on its way. The emphasis in April and May switches to Spain and Italy (occasionally the Giro d'Italia or the autumn Vuelta a España venture into France) but in the weeks leading up to the Tour de France there are several events about a week long. These include the Grand Prix du Midi-Libre in the Cévennes and Provence, and the Critérium du Dauphiné-Libéré in the Dauphiné Alps – both traditional warm-up rides and indicators for the Tour de France. Both are named after the promoting newspapers, which naturally give them a great deal of coverage. Others are the Tour de l'Aude in the eastern Pyrenees, the Route du Sud in the central Pyrenees and, in the north, the Quatre Jours de Dunkerque (which lasts five or six days, not four).

Throughout the season, but concentrated in the weeks after the Tour de France, come the local critériums up and down the country, where the newly crowned heroes of the Tour race in front of their public, perhaps riding so many races in a week that they might just as well be riding another stage race – but with a great deal more travelling in between. These races often form part of some local celebration and the whole town or village is in festive mode. Most spectacular and atmospheric are the late evening lamp-lit *nocturnes*.

So, how do you find out about these events? First, UK cycling magazines (particularly *Cycling Weekly*) publish, usually in the autumn of the preceding year, a calendar of the main European events. The route of the Tour de France is usually released in the preceding November, whereupon nearly all the possible contenders claim that the particular combination of flat and mountainous stages and time trials has been tailor-made for one of the others. Once you are in France, local papers or the daily sports paper *L'Équipe* give start and passage times, and exact route details of imminent events, particularly those they are engaged in sponsoring or organizing. While the events are actually taking place, each daily paper will give full details of the next day's route and timings. (Note that France has few national papers but instead a series of regional dailies, which provide a mix of local, national and international news.)

Underpinning this professional side of the sport there is a vast array of local and national races for amateurs, from whose ranks the future stars come. To these have been more recently added events for mountain bikes (VTT or *vélo tout terrain*). It has been a rare summer trip when we have not come across one or more of these races completely by chance. Local bike shops often have posters and information on what is on.

TAKING PART

A world away from the battles of the racing cyclist, it is quite possible to join in with a French cycle touring club on one of its organized trips. Each weekend, up and down France, clubs organize rides over local routes and invite outside cycle tourists to take part. The promotions range from lavish affairs sponsored by local commerce with astronomic numbers of entrants (one we took part in, the Randonnée de la Montagne de Reims in the Champagne area, had about 3500 riders!) to quite intimate rides with perhaps a score of participants. A typical event will have a choice of routes, from perhaps as short as 25 miles (40km) up to 100 miles (160km) or more, often with a common rendezvous point for a picnic lunch or snack. Routes are usually arrowed, and progress is checked every so often at control points (contrôles). There may or may not be an overall time limit.

Most of these events start quite early (or even horribly early) in the morning. Many of them close with a little reception (*vin d'honneur*) with interminable speeches by local dignitaries and awards for the youngest and oldest participant, the farthest-travelled and so on. We have had one or two occasions on which our little group of Britons on a cycle

French participants ride gently up the 1068m Col de Macuègne in the 95km Randonnée des Monts du Buc et d'Albion.

number of French cyclists is lunch, you will often see determined groups of not-so-young and frequently corpulent males hammering round the route so that they can rejoin their families at the noontime table.

As with races, local newspapers will often give details of forthcoming rides, under the rubric Cyclotourisme, usually on a Wednesday or Thursday for the approaching weekend. Bike shops may also have a noticeboard or poster for the local club and its activities. Most cycle touring clubs are affiliated to the Fédération Française de Cyclotourisme or FFCT (see the 'Useful Organizations' section) – roughly the equivalent of the CTC. The organization is in the hands of the local club and under the aegis of the regional committee. The FFCT publishes for its members an annual listing of events; for an outsider it is probably easier to obtain from the FFCT the address of the appropriate regional committee (there are fourteen, covering regions that do not quite coincide with the administrative ones) who will then supply a leaflet listing rides in their area, with contact addresses, dates, distances and entry fees.

In addition to specific promotions, the regional committees have available, or can direct you to, lists of *randonnées permanentes* – detailed routes for rides taking in the best of their countryside, which you can do at any time for your own satisfaction. There is usually a small charge for the route card and information.

camping holiday has ended up with an embarrassing and quite uncarryable trophy for the 'foreign club from the greatest distance' or some such. Sometimes they seem to arrange the categories so that everybody gets something!

While the French view of cycle touring is often quite a sporting one, and many ride out-and-out racing bikes but with an extended gear range, the routes are usually quite cleverly devised to show off the local countryside at its best, often taking in very minor roads that you would never find for yourself. Since the other Sunday preoccupation of quite a

CLOTHING, COLD AND HEAT

Cycling is an athletic exercise, even at gentle speeds. In addition, the range of latitude and especially altitude in France means that you may well meet very hot or quite cold conditions, possibly within hours or even minutes. You need clothing that will allow you freedom of movement, protect you from heat and cold and not chafe where you sit on it.

You can wear virtually what you choose for the flatter routes, but clothes should still follow the same precepts as special cycling clothing. Shirts, sweaters and jackets need to be quite long at the back because of the leaning-forward riding position – even with flat handlebars or on a mountain bike – and shorts or trousers must be soft enough to allow full movement. Jeans usually do not. Proper cycling shorts, made from stretchy elastomer-nylon mixtures with a smooth seat lining, and otherwise known as skin-shorts, may look strange or excessively revealing but they are much the most comfortable to wear. They have no hard seams across the saddle area, which conventional trousers and underwear often have, leading to discomfort for which the saddle gets the blame. (Saddles are very personal; you may have to try several before you find a really comfortable one. The softest and springiest are not necessarily the most comfortable after a few miles. There is much fuller guidance in my *Cycle Tourer's Handbook* and *Pedal Power!* – see the 'Useful Books' section.)

Cold

Because of the effort you put in uphill going slowly and the cooling effect of the air going down when you are putting in no effort at all, cycling has the effect of exaggerating climatic temperature differences. Sweating is the way the body naturally cools itself, so uphill clothing has to be porous enough for sweat to evaporate and do its job. Modern fabrics such as woven polypropylene, which 'wick' moisture, can be effective in keeping you dry but also entail a risk of overheating in warm weather. Going downhill, clothing has to be windproof enough to prevent chilling; with road speeds downhill on a long open pass often over 30 mph (50km/h). If there is a slight headwind, as there usually is going down a valley, you can be facing a full gale's worth of wind-chill while still possibly being damp from sweating on the climb to the top. Add to that the lower temperatures at the summit – the 'lapse rate' or decrease is about 1°C per 100m, so the top may be 10 to 15°C or more cooler than the valley bottom – as well as the probability that it will be windier, and you will soon appreciate the need for gloves, an extra sweater, some sort of windproof top and long trousers for at least the first

part of the descent. The slip-over style of cyclist's track suit bottom – closely cut with zipped ankle fixing – is convenient and effective. If you know that you tend to sweat heavily and will consequently reach the top quite damp, it can be worth having a change of dry shirt or cycling top to put on before setting off downhill.

If you are travelling in the colder seasons you will certainly find gloves necessary. I find two or three pairs of woollen gloves or nylon fleece, rather than heavier gloves or gauntlets, offer the best compromise between wind-proofing and steaming up. You can then adjust by using the layers you need. The same applies to upper-body garments. It is far better to have two or three discardable layers than a single heavy jacket.

Heat

South of the River Loire, and sometimes surprisingly far north of it, you are likely to find yourself

You can't rely on good weather in the mountains – so have enough clothes. This is 1,600m up on Mont Ventoux at Easter!

riding in hot conditions. It is one of the pleasant features of leisurely cycling that on a hot day it is often more comfortable just riding gently along, making your own light breeze, than sitting still. While you are riding, the passing air cools you by evaporating any sweat as soon as it forms – you realize this as soon as you stop and it pours off you for a few minutes. This moisture has to be replaced. Much the best replacement is plain water, either from the tap or one of the bottled mineral waters. A great deal of hot-weather discomfort, including some digestive disorders, derives from mild or even more marked dehydration, so you should take good care to replenish body water. Drink frequently and before you are really thirsty. If your urine becomes darker and decreases in volume it indicates that dehydration is already under way and you urgently need topping up. Bike bottles, best fitted to special bottle cages on the bicycle frame tubes, are essential. Most touring bikes have provision for two, and sometimes you can fit three. The standard bottles hold about 600ml but you can increase capacity by using the larger 900ml version, often sold as 'triathlon' bottles. Tap water in France, despite travellers' tales from the past, is as good as anywhere in the world, while most continuously-flowing public fountains – one of the attractive features of many southern villages – supply drinkable water. If it is *not* suitable, it will be marked *Eau non potable* (not drinking water). It is also worth remembering that there is a tap in many village churchyards.

Avoid too much beer, wine or coffee while you are on the road; as diuretics they do virtually nothing to replace your moisture content. Following some youthful excesses, we have even gone so far as to agree not to drink alcohol at lunch time to avoid excessively lethargic afternoons. Except in extreme effort in very hot conditions there should not be much need to replace salt since the body fairly quickly reaches equilibrium, but if you do experience persistent cramp, a little salt, or better still an isotonic salt mix in one of the proprietary athletic drinks, may help. Individual needs vary enormously.

The other hazard of hot weather riding is from the sunlight. Because you tend to ride in one direction for a fairly long spell at a time – particularly on a place-to-place trip where this might be for several consecutive days and because your arms, face, neck and to a lesser extent your legs, are held in much the same position all day – it is easy to become quite

badly sunburnt. This is often true of places on the body that you might not expect, such as behind knees and elbows, on your ankles and on the top of your head. The early stages of burning can be masked by the subjective coolness of riding through the air, particularly in the mountains. At altitudes above 1000m, and even more above 2000m, the burning ultra-violet component of the sun's radiation is appreciably greater, although the air may be cool or even cold. You should have some idea of your own susceptibility to sunburn; high-factor screening creams, light but long-sleeved shirts, a sun hat or headscarf, even tights, can all help.

Beware of heavy exposure of parts of the body unused to it; these are often unsuspected, such as narrow bands of the leg, arm, shoulder or back exposed by briefer shorts or tops than usual. In the extreme south the only answer may be to take a siesta after lunch during the hottest part of the day – 2 to 4 pm. After all, the locals do. We have found it necessary to take particular care when camping, since you tend to be out in the sun for most of the day. The backs of your knees and upper arms are particularly vulnerable to low-angle sunlight.

CYCLE SPARES IN FRANCE

France is at least as well supplied with small bike shops as Britain, although a higher proportion of them deal also with mopeds and small motorcycles. In addition many of them sell the products of only one firm or group. Nevertheless most basic spares are available from most shops.

Such items as brake or gear cables (*cable de frein* or *dérailleur*), inner tubes (*chambre à air*), brake blocks or shoes (*patins de frein*), chains (*chaîne*) and the ever-useful toe-straps (*courroies pour les cale-pieds*) are universal and standard. Most nuts (*écrous*) and bolts (*boulons*) on bicycles are now metric; Allen-key fitting bottle cage bolts and mudguard bolts (*écrous a six pans creux*) are 5mm, and their corresponding Allen keys also in millimetre sizes. In addition many more elaborate components, such as bottom-bracket axles, chainrings and seat pillars, are international – and those available in Britain are imported from France, Italy or Japan. The golden rule if you want to replace anything is to take along the damaged or worn-out component for matching.

There are, however, a few items that are subtly or widely incompatible, though failures of most of these should not happen to you. Before travelling (and this applies as much to Britain or anywhere else as France) check that:

- Tyres have adequate life left in them
- Rims are not excessively worn or scored and that wheels are true (not wobbling from side to side) with a full complement of properly tensioned spokes
- Brake and gear cables are in good condition and not frayed (pay particular attention to the lever end of the cables)
- The chain and freewheel are not excessively worn
- Mudguard, carrier and brake fixing bolts are all present and secure; brake-blocks or pads are not excessively worn
- All bearings and cables are correctly adjusted and lubricated (if you are travelling by air it may be better to avoid lubricating the chain, as a courtesy to handlers and fellow-travellers' baggage, until you reach France)

Possibly incompatible items are:

- **Tyres** These seem to cause the most confusion. If you fit new tyres before you go, they should last at least for your trip. Even so, mishaps can occur and you may have to buy a replacement (*pneu de rechange*). There are many confusing size designations marked on the tyre, but international standards are now established. All tyres of European origin now have, in addition to any other marking, a standard designation of the form '32–622' on the side of the tyre. Here '32' is the nominal cross-section in millimetres, '622' the diameter in millimetres of the rim on which the tyre fits. If your touring bicycle was made after 1985, it will almost certainly have the 622mm size (also known as 700C). This is the most common size in France, too, so replacement is easy. Other sizes that are fairly easily obtainable in France are: 28-, 32- or 35-590 (known in Britain as 26 × 1⅜ and in France as 650A); 32- or 37-584 (known in France as 650B but rare in Britain); and from 32-559 upwards to much fatter widths in the universal mountain bike size (often referred to vaguely as '26-inch' (*vingt-six pouces*), although there are four other '26-inch' sizes in use!) . The British 27 × 1¼ (32-630, sometimes in other widths such as 28-630 or 35-630) is only very rarely found in French shops and the exclu-

sively British 26 × 1¼ (32-597) never. Inner tubes are much less critical: 700 (also fitting 27in) or 650 (also fitting 26in) are readily obtainable. The standard valve is the narrow-diameter Presta type; if you want a mountain bike spare you may have to ask for a tube with a Schraeder valve.

- **Cranks and pedals** Although the square taper by which cranks (*manivelles*) fit to the bottom bracket axle (*axe du pédalier*) is universal, the thread (*filetage*) at the other end of the crank for the pedal differs in Britain and France. If you break either you will probably have to replace both pedal (*pédale*) and crank. The French size is slightly smaller (14mm diameter, 1.25mm thread pitch), so a British dealer should be able to re-tap a French crank to a British thread (14.28mm diameter, 1.27mm pitch) when you get home.

- **Freewheels and hubs** The now-common free-hub design in which 'splined' or notched sprockets slide onto the freewheel section of the hub is made only in two patterns, Shimano or Sachs/Campagnolo compatible, each accepting the appropriate sprockets. The threading of the French hub (*moyeu*) and the screw-on type of freewheel (*roue-libre*) differ slightly from the English. It is possible to force a British freewheel (34.92mm diameter, 1.058mm pitch) onto a French-threaded hub (35mm diameter, 1.00mm pitch) but you may damage the softer aluminium alloy thread on the hub. A French-threaded freewheel will be a sloppy fit on a British-threaded hub – it may hold; it may not. Sprockets will be interchangeable, though, so that if an individual sprocket is damaged, or too worn for use, it may be possible to replace the sprocket (*couronne*) on the existing freewheel body. Sprockets may not be readily available (in Britain or in France) for older models of freewheel. Quick-release hub axles for adjustable hubs are universal; solid axles differ slightly, 10mm rather than ⅜in, although we have succeeded in forcing British cones onto a French replacement axle. This is not advised, though. At one time, all British front wheels had 32 spokes and rear wheels 40, whereas Continental countries used 36 in both. Now 36/36 is common in Britain, while 32-spoke hubs and rims, and to a lesser extent 40, are available in France. Do not necessarily expect them to be in stock. The term for the drilling of the rim is *perçage*, so *perçage trente-six* indicates a 36-hole rim.

• **Bottom bracket fittings** Many new touring bicycles and virtually all mountain bikes are now fitted with 'sealed' unit bottom brackets, with Shimano again dominating the market. However, while the bearing unit itself may be identical from country to country, the actual fitting of both unit types and the traditional cup-and-cone adjustable type depends on the threading of the frame. Not only is the threading of the cup bearings slightly different between Britain and France (although you might be able to get away with using a left-hand French bearing cup at some risk to the frame threading) but the French right-hand side cup has a right-hand thread, as opposed to the British, which has a left-hand thread. These are completely incompatible. The British-style threadings have now been adopted by the International Standards Organization and ISO-dimensioned components are beginning to find their way onto new bikes sold in France, in particular mountain bikes. Check carefully.

Taking part: riders at a contrôle in the Randonnée de la Montagne de Reims.

Routes

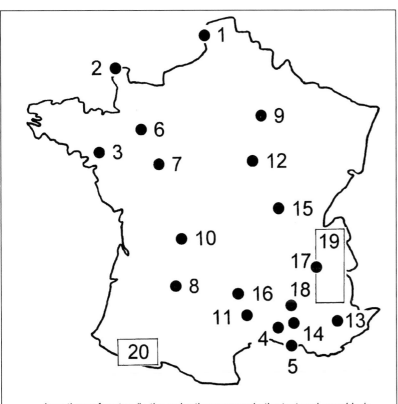

Locations of routes (in the order they appear in the text and, roughly, in order of hilliness). 1–Boulogne; 2–Cherbourg; 3–Grand Brière; 4–Alpilles; 5–Camargue; 6–Alpes Mancelles; 7–Loire valley; 8–Quercy Blanc; 9–Montagne de Reims; 10–Haut Limousin; 11–Gorges of the Dourbie and Mt Aigoual; 12–Morvan; 13–Grand Canyon du Verdon; 14–Lubéron; 15–Beaujolais; 16–Tarn and Jonte gorges; 17–Vercors; 18–Mt Ventoux; 19–Alpine cols; 20–Pyrenean cols.

rather unevenly across the country and avoiding cities and large towns. The map shows where they are. If you are a novice or infrequent cyclist it is obviously better to measure yourself against some of the easier itineraries first. If you are moderately experienced but have not cycled abroad before, then I would suggest warming up on some of the easier or moderately hilly regions before attempting the high mountains. Even experienced cyclists find that spending a day or two in the foothills to get used to the different rhythm of life before tackling the high cols is no bad thing. It is often difficult to put across to newcomers to cycling that it is the mountain areas that will eventually attract you – and that there actually is pleasure to be found in spending a large part of your holiday in riding uphill! The special techniques involved were covered in Chapter 5 and a couple of necessary cautions are given at the beginning of Chapter 12.

The less strenuous routes show you representative parts of rural France, most of them not the parts that the average tourist sees. Although for many years now I have made at least one annual trip to the mountains of France or elsewhere, it has been an enlightening pleasure to turn my wheels away from the mountains for once towards some more delicate and intimate landscapes.

THE ROUTES

The routes described in this book have been chosen to introduce you to a fair cross-section of rural France, from fairly flat to mountainous, spread

At the end of each route there is a short series of entries of practical information in the following order:

Approximate total distance   gives the approximate total distance of the ride.

Maps   gives the sheet numbers and panels of the relevant Michelin and IGN 1:100,000 sheets. The large Michelin regional map sheet numbers are not given.

Region   gives the name of the administrative region in which the route is situated. This may be useful if you wish to obtain general tourist information or listings of gîtes, which are often prepared on a regional basis.

Départements   gives the numbers and names of the départements through which the route passes. This is to enable you to find information locally on items such as accommodation, restaurants and things to see that tend to be classified by département.

Accommodation   lists the names of towns or villages in which there is some sort of accommodation, including gîtes d'étape and camp sites. This section is intended to give some idea of places to look up in accommodation lists and is unlikely to be complete; not all places named have all types of accommodation.

Access   quotes main road routes from the nearest large town, the nearest railway stations and, where appropriate, airports or sea routes. The railway service may in some cases be infrequent.

Restrictions   gives (for the more upland routes) available information on the probability that the route, or some of it, may be snowbound for part of the year.

The following additional information is given for the cols and detours described towards the end of the book:

Approximate total climb   shows the approximate height climbed in metres, in the direction described.

Linking   gives the names of towns or villages that the col links, with distances to the summit.

Closed period   gives the time of year when the col is likely to be closed or blocked by snow.

8

Cross-Channel Weekends

THE HAUT PAYS D'ARTOIS – THE HINTERLAND OF BOULOGNE

Geologically, there is not a great deal to distinguish the rolling country behind the French Channel port of Boulogne from the very English counties of Kent and Sussex that face it across the Channel. There are the same chalk hills and little valleys, and much the same crops in the fields. Small wonder, then, that this is the route most like England – or, rather, southern England. (I recall the observation of a cycling friend originally from Blackburn in Lancashire. For him, the boundary between northern and southern Europe lies somewhere around the River Trent, with the Channel a mere hiccup between two sets of soft, southern landscapes.)

But look closer and the differences appear. The way of life is quintessentially French. The villages are distinctively French, although there is a touch of East Anglia with whitewashed cob walls and warm red pantiles. There is an almost Mediterranean sun-blanched look to the houses and the squares in the little towns, even though they are farther north than the Isle of Wight. The big houses hidden behind their screens of dark mature trees have that utter symmetry that so marks the French manor or château. The chalk that forms the hills is less steeply folded than in the North and South Downs – more like south-west Hampshire, with the clear streams in the tree-lined valleys strongly reminiscent of the Test, Itchen and Meon.

For a cyclist living in southern England this route is quite a feasible proposition for a weekend trip. The high-speed catamaran from Folkestone to Boulogne takes just under an hour, while there is a sharp discount on fares if your stay in France is to

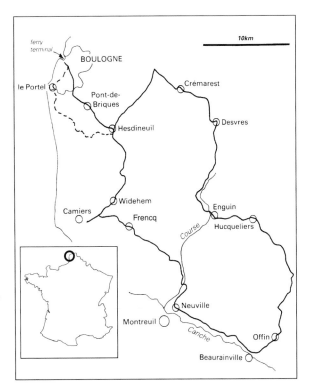

be no more than three days.

Boulogne, like most ports, takes a little escaping to the east and south. There are basically three choices: two hilly and one flat. The catamaran terminal is quite close to the historic centre of the town, and one hilly way out would be to follow the town centre signs and then the St Omer (N42) road, from which you can fork right onto the slightly quieter Desvres and Arras road (D341). This really makes a better way in than out, although there is still some climbing involved; Mont Lambert, a village on the outskirts of the town, was not awarded its 'Mont' for nothing.

The other hilly way out, and again one probably better on the return, is to follow the signs to Le Portel, the more residential part of the town perched some 50m above the beaches below. This road, the D119, follows a very up-and-down course to rejoin the D940 at Neufchâtel-Hardelot.

The flat route, which we took, begins a little drearily with 4 or 5km of industrial development, beside the (at this point) rather uninviting waters of the Liane. The road is signposted to Paris, Montreuil and Le Touquet. At a quite complex junction at St Léonard the road to Le Touquet (D940) breaks away to the right. This road seems to carry just as much traffic as the main N1 Montreuil and Paris road, and it is quite a relief to leave it after only a few hundred metres for the D52 to Hesdineuil-lès-Boulogne. Hesdineuil is the start of the route.

Shortly after the church, a road, signed Condette (D240), bears off to the right, under two railway bridges. A left turn leads beneath a third bridge and then climbs steadily through the eastern fringes of

the Forêt d'Hardelot. Once in the open again, the climbing becomes a little more earnest, with quite a steep pitch through another wood just after crossing the D215.

The open country is now beginning to be typical of the Haut Pays d'Artois: wide rolling wolds, golden with vast fields of ripening wheat and barley on the hot July weekend that we chose. The next few villages – Haut Pichot, Halinghen and Widehem – and many more that follow are really no more than hamlets. Clusters of a few dozen whitewashed pantiled cottages are grouped round a little slate-roofed flint-built church. These place name endings -hem or -hen and -thun are reminders that only a little way north is the beginning of Flanders; we would recognize them as the closely related English -ham and -ton.

We climbed out of Widehem up a long rising shelf of a road that gradually lifted to give immense views over the great cornfields and the clefts of the dry valleys picking their way into the scarp. The heads of these little valleys are too steep to plough, and the close-cropped green turf glowed in contrast to the universal gold. We were to stop overnight in the next, and much more substantial, village of Camiers, but the route itself bears left at the top of the hill to run along the very edge of a ridge and then down a long dry valley to Frencq.

Even if you do not need to drop to Camiers, it is worth making the detour to the top of the hill above the village, with its all-embracing view over the dunes to the Channel. To the left are the resort towers of Le Touquet, while the broad beaches sweep away to the north, with the faint white band of the cliffs above Folkestone just showing across the water on the horizon.

From Frencq you could be forgiven for thinking there was not a flat spot on the route. The villages lie in the valleys of the little streams, nameless on the map, that run south

Open cornfields near Frencq.

to join the Canche. Each stream is marked by a green line of willows, while as you drop to them the black line of the road climbing away again on the far side lies etched against the wold. This is definitely not country to hurry through! Shortly after the climb from Longvillers, though, there is a change as the road twists suddenly through delightful open woodlands before crossing the main N1 in a right-and-left dogleg to drop through more woods to Recques in the much larger valley of the Course.

There is rather more of a feeling of opulence in this valley; there are quite a few obvious second homes hereabouts (increasingly English owned) and a suburban feel to the trim lawns and varnished shutters. The road down the valley is, for a change, easy, with a twisting crossing of the clear stream at Estrée, to follow the left bank to Neuville-sous-Montreuil. The green lines of the willows and poplars along the stream and the neat copses and rectangular fields make a sharp contrast with the openness of the uplands.

A cottage doorway near Beaurainville.

If you have time, Montreuil itself is well worth a visit, perched above what is now the valley of the Canche. The walled town with its citadel has a maze of cobbled streets flanked by seventeenth- and eighteenth-century houses. There are fine views of the valley of the Canche from the town ramparts. Montreuil has suffered the fate of Rye and Winchelsea across the Channel, mediaeval ports that have watched the sea recede as their valleys silted up. Montreuil was still marked on maps until a few years ago as Montreuil-sur-Mer; it is now a good 13km from the sea.

The route bears left at Neuville to follow the Canche upstream. The road stays some way above the river, climbing and falling a little but always giving fine views down across the maize fields to the alignments of willows and poplars among the greenness of the wetlands in the valley bottom. Here and there are little ponds, some artificial, some apparently natural, with dots of anglers motionless

around them. (There is a fish-breeding centre a little farther up the Course valley.) The route is punctuated by a series of flower-bedecked villages: Marles-sur-Canche, Marenla and Beaurainville; the plainer squat whitewashed houses suggest that these are the flowers that those who have lived here a long time feel it is natural to mark the summer with, rather than the more formal and pretentious arrangements of the villas of Recques-sur-Course.

From Beaurainville it is possible to make a detour to the equally delightful and rather more intimate valley of the Authie, which runs parallel to the Canche some 10km to the south. We, however, bore north-east up the tributary valley of the Créquoise, through more whitewashed villages, bearing left after the unexpectedly sharp little climb through Offin to follow the even smaller stream of the Embrienne to Embry.

In Embry the almost-straight-on D149 through Rimboval would have been an easier route through to the junction at Hénoville than the more main and obvious D108 with its steep pull away from the village. From Hénoville, the D343 runs along the ridge that here seems to mark a divide in the scenery. To the left lie the familiar open cornfields, while to the right the landscape is one of bocage country: small enclosed mixed-cultivation and grazing fields. On a hot parching afternoon our lives were saved at Maninghem by a man watering his garden who willingly filled our empty bottles before we swept down to Hucqueliers, quite the largest village we had been in for some time, with its broad and café-lined square.

From here the little valley of the Baillons leads west through the hamlet of Preures (where it is better to take the fork by the left bank of the stream) to Enquin-sur-Baillons, perched above the junction of the stream and the Course. From here a right turn, after the bridge over the Course, takes you up the final part of this delectable little valley, past the village of Course, which gives it its name, and on to the small town of Desvres.

From Desvres the straight D127 leads down and then up into the Forêt de Desvres. Just after the top of the climb a forest road, marked RF (route forestière) on the map, bears left along a broad ride in the forest down to the small village of Crémarest. Here the Liane, so uninspiring as it oozed slowly and greyly past Boulogne's industry, is a clear bright stream. A steady climb on the D254, signed for La Capelle – through towering banks of maize when we passed – leads up into the Forêt de Boulogne. About 1km into the forest, another route forestière bears sharp left. After some 400m motor vehicles are banned and you enter a *zone de silence* – an area where passers-by are expected to respect the quietness of the forest. The forest road continues across the D341 to plunge down to the village of Hesdin-l'Abbé, from which a crossing of the N1 and about 1km of descent to the Liane brings you back to the starting point, Hesdineuil-lès-Boulogne.

From here it is possible to follow the flat route back into Boulogne (although the multiple junction at Pont de Briques is rather trickier in this direction, tending to send you along the N1) or to head out to the coast road. This involves setting out from Hesdineuil in the direction in which the route started, but turning right instead of left after the second railway bridge, up to Condette and Le Choquel to join the undulating D119 coast road.

Once back in Boulogne, ignore the signposted road layout to the catamaran terminal, which is geared, as you might expect, to car traffic, resulting in a horrific long-way-round one-way system to stream vehicles into the right place. Aim instead for the landmark of the pedestrian walkway to the terminal – a prominent tower. Close by here is a level crossing over the railway that serves the Gare Maritime. Cross the railway here, or by the pedestrian railway crossing a few metres farther to seaward. Once across the railway, or at the end of the path from the pedestrian crossing, turn sharp right to follow the car and motorcycle symbols to the terminal check-in points.

Approximate total distance   119km
Maps   Michelin 51, panels 1, 2, 11 and 12; IGN 1
Region   Nord-Pas-de-Calais
Département   62-Pas de Calais
Accommodation   Boulogne, Hardelot, Camiers, Montreuil, Beaurainville, Hucqueliers, Desvres, Pont-de-Briques
Access   High-speed catamaran from Folkestone

NORTH COTENTIN

The Boulogne route may be the most southern English of the routes, but the coastline of this northern tip of the Cotentin peninsula, that finger of Normandy that sticks north into the Channel, is surprisingly reminiscent of shores much farther away. More than once the narrow walled fields running down to the shore and the deserted sandy bays hemmed in by low cliffs recalled the west coast of Ireland or parts of Skye or Argyll. Yet this coastline is only about 150 miles from the centre of London.

As will probably seem a recurrent theme in this book, geology is at the root of much of the resemblance. The northern fringe of the Cotentin peninsula is formed of a hard reddish granite, related to Brittany, Dartmoor and Land's End. The coasts, even the cliffs, of southern England are for the most part soft chalk limestones, clays and sands, so the ruggedness of the shore around Cherbourg is in sharp contrast.

The coastline is not all there is to Cotentin, of course. The other parts of the peninsula are excellent for gentle cycling. The inland countryside is largely bocage, and has many of the characteristics of much of rural England, particularly such counties as Shropshire and Herefordshire. It consists of an

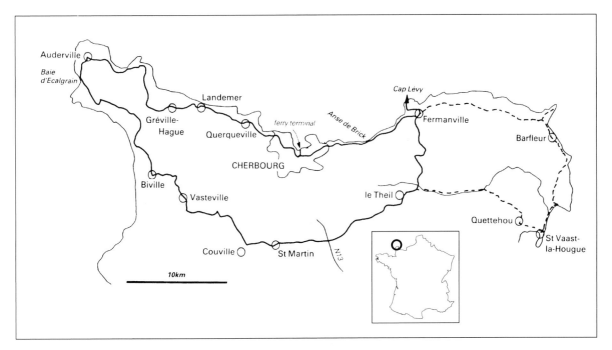

intricate pattern of small, hedged fields, some grazed, some cultivated, with occasional small copses. Quite often the hedges, which frequently contain many mature trees, are on raised banks or even turf-covered and overgrown walls – a feature that had a marked influence on the fierce mechanized fighting throughout Normandy in 1944. Add to this green and varied countryside the sun-washed sturdy little stone villages and the relative lack of traffic, and you have a sumptuous cycling recipe.

Exploring this route was a very pleasant revelation. I had crossed to Cherbourg many times before – my very first steps on French soil were on the tarmac of Cherbourg's intimate little airport at Maupertus. But Cherbourg had always been on the way to somewhere else. Cherbourg was just a starting point; our wheels were always to take us away south, to Easter weekends with the cycle touring club at St Lô at the base of the peninsula, or much farther afield. So, the moral is: do not always rush on to the next place until you have looked around.

For those with reasonable access to Portsmouth, Southampton or Poole, weekend trips to Cherbourg are quite feasible. There are concessionary three-day return fares on all services. Overnight sailings land you possibly bright and certainly early in Cherbourg, ready for the road.

Cherbourg is a much easier port to leave than Boulogne – and many others. From the ferry terminal, you follow the signs west to the town centre (*Centre ville*), over the lifting bridge and then right along the Quai de Caligny, skirting the fishing-boat harbour. The centre of the town, to your left, is worth a visit with its maze of narrow streets and old houses. There is also a wealth of places to eat – useful when you are waiting for the night boat back.

The route out follows the D901, signed to begin with to Equieudreville, then to Hameau-de-la-Mer. After about 2km the D901 is fringed by a cycle lane and then a separate cycle path curves away on the seaward side of the main road. The D901 was rather busy when we passed that way on our September exploration, since the overnight ferry and our wait for the autumn dawn to break had landed us in the rush-hour traffic to the naval dockyards. These are prominently signposted l'Arsenal and the road tries to take you to them from time to time; do not let it. At other times the road seems relatively quiet.

From the relief of the cycle path there are good views back across the harbour of Cherbourg. This is an entirely artificial haven; two lines of breakwaters shelter the outer harbour (Grande Rade) and the inner harbour (Petite Rade). The first works to link the Île Pelée to the east and the Pointe de

Inner harbour, Cherbourg.

and shops, and modern desirable residences. A signposted left turn up a short steeper pitch brings you to the church, which has been a prominent landmark on the left for several kilometres. Beside the large and fairly new parish church there is the small and solid tenth-century chapel of St Germain, claimed to be the oldest in western France. From its steps there is a fine view along the coast in both directions.

To rejoin the D45 you drop back down the hill and turn left. The road winds for a while between fields running down to the sea and a low wooded ridge to the left. The fields are long, narrow and stony, divided here by turf-covered stone walls, with sporadic patches of heath. It was the pattern of walls that first suggested the west coast of Ireland to us, with the low stone slate-roofed houses dispersed among the fields much like those distant crofts.

Just before Landemer, a strangely ornate grouping of fairytale castle towers and turrets to the left of the road proves to be the manor of Dur-Ecu. In Landemer itself, bear right off the D45 into the very narrow Rue des Douanes, which leads to the start of the coast path, the GR223. A short, stiff climb through a pine wood brings you up to an overgrown wartime pillbox, the roof of which serves as a belvedere, commanding extensive views along the coast. This part of the coastline is higher and wilder, patched when we were there with the purple of heather and the lush green of bracken against the pale red granite of the low cliffs and rocks. Unfortunately the coast path is for pedestrians only from this point and you have to rejoin the pleasant D45.

The road climbs gently away from the viewpoint, back into an agricultural landscape. One of the things to strike us, bearing in mind the ruggedness of parts of the coast, was the gentleness of the gradients on most of the road. The next hamlet of Gréville-Hague was the early haunt of the painter Jean François Millet, of whom a bust adorns the little traffic island in front of the bakery.

After about four more rolling kilometres, partly

Querqueville to the west began in 1776 but the sea destroyed the defences almost as soon as they were put up. Nevertheless, seaborne accretions slowly built up and some 70 years after the work began there were solid enough foundations for the breakwaters; by 1853 the work was complete. For about a century the port was frequented by transatlantic and cruise liners – and a few still call today – but the rise of air travel has left the port a little quiet and faded, though it is now the centre of a thriving cross-channel trade.

The cycle path ends just before Hameau-de-la-Mer, where the route leaves the D901 to turn right on the D45. After about 1km take a left turn into the road signposted to the centre of Querqueville. The road climbs steadily into the middle of the village – now a slightly amorphous mixture of tall old houses

through sparse bocage, partly through heathland, the road dips seawards again, to the little port of Le Hâble, where we basked in the rapidly warming morning sun for a while. As in all the small ports along this coast there is a pleasing leaven of real working boats among the pleasure craft. After the slight climb over the headland the road drops once more, this time to the first of several fine, curving sandy bays, the Anse St Martin, bounded by red ribs of granite thrusting seawards. At the west end of the bay lies the minuscule jetty of Port Racine, which proudly proclaims itself France's smallest port.

From here the road strikes inland again, through the straggling village of St Germain-des-Vaux (which, we were to discover, has the last food shop for quite some distance). The next village, Auderville, although prominent on the kilometre stones almost since Cherbourg, turns out to be no more than a few houses and a small restaurant.

At the D901 turn left and then shortly right to the viewpoint above La Roche, which looks out over the Cap de la Hague and the stark lighthouse of Gros du Raz. The tidal race, the Raz Blanchard, is one of the fastest and most treacherous in Europe. Out to sea, the bulk of Alderney seems quite close, while Sark and Guernsey loom on the south-western horizon. In La Roche itself, turn left to climb again up to the D401, where you turn right.

Suddenly the road comes over the brow of the hill to reveal tremendous views over the broad, rocky and sandy Baie d'Écalgrain. This magnificent and quite unheralded bay, its soft sands deserted on this warm early September day, curves south to the rocky cape of the Nez de Voidries and, when we were there, looked out over a sea of a blueness that would have done the Mediterranean cred-it. Behind the sands, the rounded hills are carpeted with bracken and heather. For us, this unexpected bay was perhaps the highlight of the whole route and we lunched lazily above it, a few metres along the coast path.

The road drops steeply to the shore and then climbs away again up a steady but not too difficult slope through the heathlands towards Jobourg. There is a possible detour seawards again here, to the twin promontories of the Nez de Voidries and the Nez de Jobourg. From here there is unfortunately no alternative, except for some rough paths, but to join the main D901 for a few kilometres – along this stretch the southern boundary of a nuclear fuel reprocessing plant.

Extensive views soon open up to the right over the 12km beach of the Anse de Vauville, stretching away south. It is possible to make a rather hilly detour to Vauville and Biville; the direct turn is now bridged, so you have to turn into the bypassed village of Beaumont and then pass under the D901 on the D318. From Vauville there is a steady climb up to Biville, with views over the almost desert landscape of the Anse de Vauville with its hinterland of dunes and out to sea. After Biville the D318 turns east to

On the coast path near Auderville.

rejoin the direct route, the D37 at La Croix-Frimot.

There is quite a sharp down-and-up before the road reaches the compact village of Vasteville, and a steady climb away from the village until you reach the left turn of the D122 to Teurthéville. This is a delightful little road, winding between straggling hedges through the bocage, eventually joining the D22 after Teurthéville.

Continue on this road, which climbs gently but quite perceptibly to join the D56 to St Martin-le-Gréard. Once over the bridged crossing of the main N13 the landscape changes. There is much more woodland, mostly beech and oak – indeed the road is mostly wooded with patches of bocage and orchard until it drops to the valley of the Saire just after Renievast.

Here there are several alternatives. The Val de Saire road, the D120, follows the stream east along its pleasantly green and lush pastoral valley, giving a chance of visiting the small fishing ports of St Vaast-la-Hougue and Barfleur, on the eastern coast of the peninsula. It was at Barfleur that the boats that brought William the Conqueror's successful invaders to England in 1066 were fashioned, while some centuries later Richard the Lionheart left from the port.

Alternatively, as we did on our short September trip, you can head north to the coast. On reaching the main D901 turn right for about 1km, and then left, skirting the airfield, on the D612 to Fermanville. There is quite a maze of walled lanes in the little village, but the lighthouse (*phare*) is quite clearly signed.

A short ride by walled fields and patches of heath where horses graze soon brings you to the lighthouse (which can be visited) and the rocky promontory of Cap Lévy. As we watched, the receding tide revealed a chaos of rocks ranging from pale cream to deep reddish-brown, with dozens of little rock pools with mysterious weedy depths. To the west there is a long view along the coast to the towers of Cherbourg and beyond. By now the September afternoon had turned softly grey and nearer at hand the narrow walled fields and low houses even more recalled Scotland's and Ireland's Atlantic shores. Then, as if to complete the illusion, the faint hint of what could have been a peat fire drifted across to us as we sat on the rocks. Maybe it was no more than the tail end of a bonfire – who can tell? – but for a few moments we were far away.

The return route to Cherbourg follows the D116, which hugs the coast for the first 8 or 9km, before coming to the outer suburbs of the town. There are a couple of points along the route that give particularly fine broad views out over the sea: the first is by a track that leaves the road to seaward just at the beginning of a road cutting about 2km west of Fermanville, the other at the sharp inlet of the Anse du Brick, about another 2km farther on.

Just after Bourbourg, at a set of traffic lights, do not follow the 'Car ferry' sign that directs you to the right: this just leads you through a rather desolate industrial stretch. The route straight ahead, although built up, is a good deal more pleasant and brings you to a crossroads only some 400m from the entrance to the ferry terminal.

Approximate total distance 111km
Maps Michelin 54, panels 1 and 2; IGN 6
Region Basse-Normandie
Département 50-Manche
Accommodation Cherbourg, Port Racine, St Germain-des-Vaux, Bricquebec, Valognes, St Vaast-la-Hougue, Barfleur, Cosqueville, Anse de Brick
Access Car ferry from Portsmouth, Poole (summer only), Rosslare

9

Fairly Gentle France

THE MARSHLAND OF LA GRANDE BRIÈRE

It is a common belief of non-cyclists that flat places are ideal for cycling. It seems quite perverse to them that anybody should deliberately seek out hills or mountains to cycle up, no matter how splendid the views. As far as using bicycles as everyday transport goes, there may be something in this. After all, three of the towns and cities in England with the highest proportion of cycle journeys are three of the flattest: Cambridge, Peterborough and York. And is Holland not the country where everybody cycles everywhere? However, it is not long before a fledgling cycle tourist discovers that the broad horizons of a flat countryside can take a long time to change, and heads for somewhere with more variety.

But there is, in short spells at least, a fascination in utterly flat country – like the Fens, Somerset Levels or Romney Marsh. The scene is totally dominated by the sky and on the right day the immensity of the space can be awe-inspiring. There is a fascination, too, in water, so we found this relatively short route round the wetlands of the Grande Brière was full of interest.

Rises and falls in sea level and silting at the mouth of the Loire over tens of thousands of years led to the formation of this unique marshy area. Prized for the richness of its fish and game, it has certainly been inhabited for something like 10,000 years, for neolithic remains have been found here. Parts were drained in the Middle Ages and in 1461 special rights over the Brière were conferred by the Duke of Brittany on the inhabitants of the 21 villages surrounding the marsh, privileges they still hold to a degree. Briérons of the 21 villages have regulated rights to hunt, fish, cut reeds, graze animals and extract peat from the marshland. Up to the beginning of the twentieth century, the extraction of peat took place in a ten-day late summer festival with revelries comparable with those of harvest or haymaking in other places.

Keeping a wetland in a stable state calls for skilled maintenance, and following the neglect of the war years and the consequent choking and silting-up of some of the vital channels, the Brière Regional Park was set up in 1970 to restore and manage the marshland. The result is an intriguing oasis of greenness surrounded by its villages, many on their 'islands'. There is an intricate network of waterways

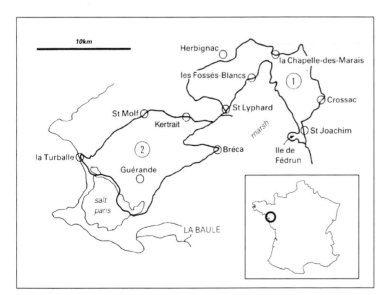

and channels, on which Briérons – even if they work during the day in St Nazaire – still pole their flat-bottomed boats and plunge their square nets.

The route takes the form of two separate but combinable loops. The first visits the Brière proper; the second visits the salt-marsh and salt-pans to the south-west. We chose as our base the marshland village of St Lyphard, about 15km north-east of the seaside resort of La Baule and a similar distance north-west of St Nazaire. The neat little village has enough small shops to provide all the necessities and an attractive camp site set beside a small lake. There is a viewpoint in the bell-tower of the church, which gives an extensive view across the marsh. Our visit was early in June.

The Grande Brière

St Lyphard is now bypassed by the main D47 so the exit north-east through the hamlet of Marlais is very quiet. At the junction with the bypass, a left-and-right dogleg leads to the D51, which skirts the northern edge of the marsh.

The countryside just outside the wetland is green grazing: small, hedged fields with prominent willows and poplars. It was along this stretch that we passed stacks of reeds destined for thatching. Once cut, the reeds are dried in bundles, like giant wheat-sheaves, then stacked horizontally in neat ricks, each with a conical thatch of sheaves to keep it dry.

The marsh is crossed by several main channels and at Les Fossés-Blancs, about 3km farther on, the road crosses the long, straight Canal du Nord. Here there were several of the characteristic flat-bottomed boats drawn up. Unlike punts, although poled along in much the same way, they have a sharp bow. Several were out of the water being tarred for the autumn season. At Les Fossés-Blancs there are several small canals as well as the main one and we watched for a few minutes as a couple of water rats plied purposefully to and fro, noses just clear of the water and their fur seeming, miraculously, to stay dry. At this time of year the yellow iris – with water-lilies, one of the characteristic plants of the marsh – was just beginning to come into flower.

After Les Fossés-Blancs, the road leaves the marsh proper to join the D33, where the route goes right and then shortly right again at some unexpected traffic lights on the D50 to follow the eastern side of the Brière.

After just over 1km it is possible to detour to the right through the pleasant twin hamlets of Camer and Camerun, with some reed-thatched cottages. Back on the D50 there are glimpses of open water to the right, but here the marsh is mostly sedge and reed. It was here that we saw the first of the large iridescent blue dragonflies for which the Brière is noted.

The showpiece village is the Île de Fédrun, one of the original islands. Its highest point is some five metres above

Traditional net fishing at St Malo-de-Guersac.

Briéron boats at les Fossés Blancs.

It was on the canal here that we saw Brièron fishing in progress. A central mast on one of the flat-bottomed boats supports a second pole that can be winched up and down. From the end of this, by four hooped supports, hangs a square net, and this is lowered into the water and lifted out with its catch, then tilted to decant the fish into the waiting keep.

The stretch of partially drained marsh south of here is known as the Petite Brière and is noted for wildfowl and other birds. From here the route retraces on the D50 for about 4km to St Joachim, one of the 21 Briéron villages and one of several whose prominent spire is a landmark from many points on the Brière. In case of need, St Joachim has a bike shop. In St Joachim turn right on the D16 to Crossac, across lush grazing on the drained marsh; here there are more trees, largely willows.

In Crossac go left on the D4 to cross the main D33 at the compact large village of Ste Reine-de-Bretagne. About 3km beyond Ste Reine, turn left at a crossroads near the straggle of houses of Le Gravelais – the road appears to be unnumbered, but is named Rue

the level of the marsh. An oval of road goes round the island – known as the Circuit des chaumières – lined by thatched white-rendered cottages. Many of these originally had a small adjoining outbuilding used for housing stock and the tools of the marsh-dweller's trade. One of the cottages has been restored to display a typical Briéron interior, which with its dim light and earth floor recalls the black houses of Scotland's west coast and outer isles.

Several small creeks lead down from the gardens of the houses to the open water that separates the island from the marsh. From the Île de Fédrun a fine avenue of poplars leads to the next 'island', the Île d'Aiugnac. At Rozé, just south of here, is a bridge over the River Brivet canal and one of the sluice gates used to control the water entering and leaving the marsh. The former sluice keeper's cottage is now a museum of Briéron waterways and water traffic.

Restored Briéron cottages at Kerhinet.

du Dolmen. A couple of hundred metres down the road a hard-surfaced but untarred track is signposted to the dolmen, which is quite an impressive stone slab on three pillars in a field to the right. You need the permission of the field's owner to visit it.

The track curves round to rejoin the road, which you follow through La Chapelle-des-Marais – another of the 21 villages – to join the D2. It was on this road that we were halted momentarily by a partridge unconcernedly shepherding her eight minute and unsteady chicks across the road. Just after a sharp little dip and climb there is another dolmen on the right, similar in design – according to the information plaque nearby – to the West Kennet barrow near Avebury in Wiltshire.

A left turn about 1km farther on takes you across the D33 past the ruins of the Château de Ranrouet, an impressive moated fortress in process of restoration. Follow the road round to cross the main D774 at a rather complex junction south of Herbignac to join the D33 towards Asserac.

Unexpectedly, the road climbs here through woodland (do not worry – the highest point is only 28m!) and after about 4km you turn left on a road signposted to Trément. After a sharp left-hand bend in the road, turn right on a hard-surfaced but untarred track, turning left when you regain the metalled road. This is the rolling D83, which takes you straight back into St Lyphard.

There are two other little 'ports' like Les Fossés-Blancs near St Lyphard. The first is La Pierre Fendue, reached by a track at the southern end of the St Lyphard bypass, the other Bréca, which is visited on the second loop of the route. Both have boats for hire and trails into the marsh.

Just north-east of St Lyphard there is another track leading to the marsh, to the end of the channel of Les Gros Fossés. Here we spent a pleasant couple of hours, just watching the towering evening cumulus clouds march across the great dome of the sky, with their shadows darkening and then spotlighting the white steeple of St Joachim, 10km away across the marsh. The breeze dropped as the sun set, the sighing of the reeds fading into the faint plashing of water against the soft banks.

The Coast and the Saltings

Leave St Lyphard south-west on the Guérande road (D51) and then fork right after about 2km on to the D52 to St Molf. There are several attractive rows of thatched cottages in the hamlets along this part of the route.

In St Molf you can continue, forking right, on to the D52 out to the rocky coast at Quimiac, following the coast road (D452) round through Piriac-sur-Mer down to La Turballe. Your other option is to bear left on the D33 direct to La Turballe. All these roads are gently rolling and, although rarely above 30m, there are frequent ups and downs. It was along the D33 that we saw red squirrels scampering away into the hedgerow trees.

In La Turballe go straight ahead to the sea front and then left on the D92. This little road winds its lonely way between farmland on the left and the salt-marshes and salt-pans on the right. The salt is first collected in square shallow pools. These are flooded with sea water, which is then allowed to evaporate, and the resulting crude salt crust is cleaned up and recrystallized. The large black sheds where the salt is recrystallized are a prominent landmark on the first part of the road.

Interspersed with the salt-pans are coarse salt-marsh and small lagoons, with a varied bird life. The last part of the road through the salt-pans is quite wild, almost a dyke between the brown salty squares, with the church of Batz-sur-Mer dominating the horizon beyond the lagoon.

The route continues through the narrow streets of the village of Saillé, turning left at a T-junction about 1km east of the village into the Rue de Guaine to join, briefly, the D92. Turn left and then at the top of the slope fork right on an unnumbered road past the Camping de l'Etang to reach the D47 just on the outskirts of the village of Sandun.

Go straight across on the narrow road. After about 2km this reaches the attractive little 'port' of Bréca. There are some very fine and well cared-for thatched cottages in the Briéron style in this picturesque little hamlet, as well as a small wharf and nature trail. A wartime defensive blockhouse has been skilfully converted to make a useful picnic shelter.

The road curves sharply left after the waterfront to cross the D47 again; go straight across and follow the signs for Kerhinet. This village has an extensive open-air museum of Brière cottages – not quite typical in that they are grey stone rather than rendered and whitewashed, but well restored, neatly thatched and mostly inhabited. When the project is completed there will be exhibitions of Brière life and crafts.

After Kerhinet the road passes a couple of dolmens reached by a grassy track – and the tower of an old windmill. The next village, Kerbourg, just on the other side of the D51, is worth a visit too, after which a right turn along a fine little road, bordered with hedges of foxgloves when we passed, leads back to the D51 and St Lyphard.

Approximate total distance Grande Brière circuit 68km; Coast and Saltings 60km
Maps Michelin 63, panels 14 and 15; IGN 24; also IGN Regional Natural Park sheet 308
Region Pays de la Loire
Département 44-Loire Atlantique
Accommodation St Lyphard, Hoscas, St Joachim, Herbignac, La Turballe, Guérande
Access By road, N165 from Vannes or Nantes, then D774; by rail to St Nazaire, La Baule; by air to St Nazaire, Nantes

THE ALPILLES

The Alpilles are the last fading out of the limestone ridges of Provence, the westward extension of the Lubéron. But whereas we found the slopes of the Lubéron tough enough to class the route there as 'moderately mountainous', the Alpilles are gentle. The highest point on the route is only 280m above sea level – hardly higher than England's Chilterns or Berkshire Downs.

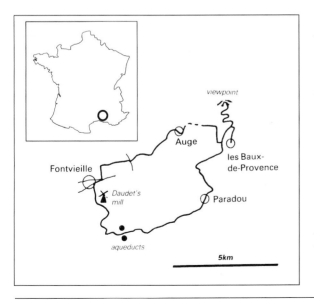

The miniature mountains of the Alpilles display all the characteristics of limestone areas – through which many of the other routes pass – but on a smaller scale. There are little gorges and diminutive crags, all looking much bigger than they are because the Alpilles rise from the flat valley of the Rhône. The mountain illusion is enhanced by the jagged rocky crest of the ridge and the glaring whiteness of the limestone bones that protrude through the thin red earth.

This little range of hills was my first introduction to Provence as I rode south many years ago from the train at Avignon, so they have perhaps a disproportionate place in my affections. The route is much the shortest in the whole book but I was determined that the Alpilles and their intriguing village of Les Baux-de-Provence should have their place.

For this trip we were based at Fontvieille, a fair-sized village about 10km north-east of the town of Arles. Fontvieille is best known for Alphonse Daudet's windmill, from which his *Lettres de mon moulin* were said to have been written (although in fact they were composed in Paris). Nevertheless, the windmill is preserved and the route passes nearby. There is a range of hotels, shops, restaurants and a pleasant camp site in the village. Fontvieille has two nearly parallel main streets, which are incorpo🌸ed into a one-way system, confusing at first but quite logical once you become familiar with it.

The route leaves Fontvieille north by the D82^C, a small lane at the east end of the village, just where the two limbs of the one-way system join up again. In a short distance – soon after the village cemetery – the road bears right. The route continues straight on when, about 200m later, the D82^C turns left. This is a narrow road, beside market-garden fields, all carefully shielded from the powerful winds by bamboo and cypress windbreaks. The smallholdings and market gardens of the fertile valley of the Rhône are the source of most of France's early-season vegetables and fruit.

Cross the main D33^A by a right-and-left dogleg, which leads into a another small road. This winds through olive groves, almond orchards and patches of woodland, climbing gently towards the Alpilles. At the hamlet of Auge, the road becomes an unsurfaced track. There are two or three tracks here; provided you keep basically to the right they converge after the hamlet, skirting more olive groves. The landscape becomes a good deal more craggy, with low white limestone cliffs rising behind the grey-green olive groves, laid out in neat lines against the red soil.

After rather less than 1km of unsurfaced track the road becomes metalled again and begins to climb, not too steeply, eventually reaching a T-junction near some new, and patently second-home, houses. This does not appear on the map. Turn right, disconcertingly downhill for a spell, to the junction with the wide D27. Turn left on this road to climb the well-graded slope up towards Les Baux-de-Provence, with the cliffs of Les Baux rising to the right and views of little hamlets in the valley to the left.

Where the road bears right for Les Baux itself, it is worth continuing for a bit on the left-hand road, still the D27 although it becomes much narrower. It climbs a little and passes into a miniature gorge, bordered with grotesquely weathered limestone shapes that the imagination readily turns into mythical beasts. Then, after perhaps a kilometre, at the top of a twisting climb, there is a superb viewpoint towards Les Baux. From this point the village, dominated by the ruins of its stronghold right on the top of the crag, looks almost carved out of the living rock. A short freewheel leads back to the turn up to the village.

There is no denying that Les Baux is a very popular tourist destination, and equally no doubt that the Easter Saturday when we came to it is not the best time to call. Fortunately, cars are kept out and the steep cobbled streets and alleyways leading up to the ruins of the castle and the old deserted village are traffic-free. Entry to the castle is normally by ticket, bought from the Lapidiary Museum at the top of the main street, but in the evening and early morning – probably in any case the best times for views from the top – you can go in free.

The old stronghold of Les Baux, with its castle perched on a rocky ridge no more than 200m wide and protected by sheer cliffs each side, was a natural fortress and had its years of glory between the eleventh and fourteenth centuries. Over the centuries it and the small town it governed harboured many whom the establishment saw as troublemakers and the castle and town were eventually destroyed by Louis XIII in the seventeenth century. The site remains spectacular, with the new village clambering up the slope towards the old. There are magnificent views to east, south and west from the castle, and to the west down into the little gorge of the Val d'Enfer from the walls of the village.

From Les Baux, return to the D27 and turn downhill to the left, bearing right when you get to the D78^F (which is the continuation of the major

Rock shapes of the Val d'Enfer, Les Baux in background.

road). This is a glorious free-wheel for about 3km, to the junction with the D78^D, where you turn left, to the village of Paradou.

In Paradou go straight across the main D17 by the church, and then right at the next crossroads. After a few hundred metres you come to another crossroads; ahead there is a fine avenue of plane trees leading out of the village, but our route goes left. This road runs along the foot of the low limestone ridge. To the right are the low shrubs and pines of the open heathland, while to the left lie olive groves, lines of cypresses and small fields with their windbreaks, incredibly green when we passed.

This is one of those roads that we found an utter delight to ride along, yet if we were forced to say what it was we found delightful we should find it hard to be specific. It is one of those mysteries of cycle touring: sometimes a trick of the light, the warmth of the evening sun,

Les Baux-de-Provence.

the herby resinous scent of Provence, the chatter of the crickets, a compatible companion, all combine to make the everyday memorable. Trivial happenings stick in the mind – in this case, a family of mice scampering across the road one by one, freezing as we stopped to look.

Just before you reach the crossroads leading back to Fontvieille, there are the remarkable ruins of two Roman aqueducts, the Aqueducs de Barbegal. It is worth leaving the bikes where the ruins are closest to the road and walking up to the cleft in the rock to the left where the two channels pass. One channel supplied Arles with water, the other served to power a water-mill.

Once back at the road, and about 500m beyond the ruins, turn right on the D33 to climb gently over

the shrub-covered hill and through pines to pass Daudet's windmill, which is on a rocky bluff on the right. The mill is now a museum to the nineteenth-century writer. The last few hundred metres back down into Fontvieille are a pleasant freewheel through an imposing avenue of umbrella pines.

Approximate total distance 24km
Maps Michelin 83, panel 10; IGN 66
Region Provence-Alpes-Côte d'Azur
Département 13-Bouches du Rhône
Accommodation Fontvieille, Les Baux-de-Provence, Maussane-les-Alpilles
Access By road, D17 from Arles, D5 from Istres, then D17; by rail to Avignon, Tarascon, Arles; by air to Marseille-Marignane

THE CAMARGUE

The Camargue, like the Grande Brière, is an utterly flat area of marshland – but there the similarity ends. Whereas the Brière is a freshwater marsh, the Camargue is salty; the Brière consists of low-lying saturated wetlands criss-crossed by channels – the Camargue has lagoons and islands; and whereas much Briéron activity is concentrated on its waterways, that of the Camargue is centred on the salt-marsh surrounding the lagoons.

Just north of the historic town of Arles the great river Rhône splits in two: the Grand Rhône continues the main course and accounts for some 90 per cent of the flow; the Petit Rhône heads west before turning south. Between the two lies the Plaine de la Camargue, the delta of the Rhône. The land of the delta has been naturally reclaimed from the sea over the centuries by the accumulation of silt carried down by the river. The process is still going on – the mouth of the Grand Rhône extends by perhaps ten metres a year into the near tideless Mediterranean – but a complex interplay of storms and currents has ensured that at other points on the delta the sea is actually encroaching.

The northern part of the Camargue is cultivated.

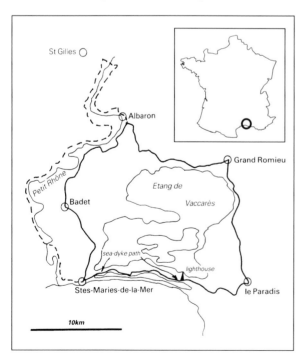

In some parts, rice is grown in paddy fields, flooded through the spring and summer. The flooding and draining help to remove the salt from the reclaimed marsh and prepare the way for other crops, so that as they take over the area used for rice declines. The peak was reached in the 1960s, when France had lost its colonies in South East Asia and needed to be self-sufficient in rice.

The main interest of the Camargue, though, is the wildlife of the lagoons and marshland. A large part of the area – including the biggest lagoon, the Étang de Vaccarès – has been a nature reserve since 1928 and is a noted haunt of migratory birds. Semi-wild black cattle and white horses roam the marshes and there is an almost Western-movie-style cowboy tradition of rounding up and breaking by gardiens. For the cyclist there is a bonus: a chance to experience some of the wild remoteness by leaving the road to follow the dyke path along the low bank that separates the Camargue from the outermost lagoon.

The one drawback of this part of the world is the mistral, the strong and chilly northerly wind that pours down the Rhône valley from time to time, turning placid citizens irritable and crotchety – and making cycling quite hard if you are riding into it. Make allowances for the hard north-facing stretches if the wind is blowing. Onshore breezes can become quite strong, too. You soon appreciate why the rice paddies and small market-gardening fields have their windbreaks of cypress trees and bamboo.

I was first introduced to the Camargue in the early 1970s when I took part in a ride – the Randonnée de la Camargue – organized by the cycle touring club in nearby Martigues. That brisk ride was on a baking July day; this time we made our rather cooler trip at Easter. The route described here – a continuous loop – starts and finishes at the hamlet of Grand Romeu, about 12km due south of Arles but on the opposite bank of the Grand Rhône.

Arles, we felt, was not a terribly cycle-friendly town (we were staying about 10km north-east, at Fontvieille), but it is possible for cyclists to avoid the horrific near-motorway bridge that direct traffic uses to cross the Rhône. This involves turning north from the town centre road, the Boulevard de Lices, up the Rue Gambetta and crossing the river by the old Pont de Trinquetaille. From here there is a marked cycle path that passes under the two new major east–west and north–south roads and out into the country.

The route leaves Grand Romeu south on the

D36[B], down a pleasant tree-lined lane (trees are surprisingly numerous, if patchily distributed, on the Camargue – at least by comparison with our own Fens). Quite soon you come out onto the first of several open stretches offering views over the Étang de Vaccarès to the right, and over drying salt-marsh to the left. It was from this road that we spotted dignified grey herons standing alone and aloof, or wheeling slowly over the brackish pools, and small flocks of white egrets. There are also one or two of the traditional stone huts formerly used by the gardiens.

The plants of the Camargue are all salt-loving – grey-green and remarkably prickly sea thistle and tall feathered reeds predominate, with some low scrub and juniper. Like much of Provence, many of the plants are green in the spring and grey in the summer, but they turn quite red during the winter months, with the reeds becoming a soft, shimmering pale yellow.

After about 5km the road turns away from the Étang de Vaccarès, onto what we felt was a rather featureless stretch, bordered for the most part by low scrub and in places by coarse grazing. At the hamlet of Le Paradis the road bends sharply right and, some 500m farther on, the route forks right again. This road has a tarred surface for about 6km and then becomes a hard, compacted gravel track.

Just after the bridge and sluice across the head of the Étang du Fangassier, there is another junction. Turn sharp right here towards the rather stumpy Gacholle lighthouse, clearly visible ahead with its small clump of trees. After about 2.5km, at the bridge and sluice between the Étang de la Dame and the Étang de Galabert, the road ends and you embark on the sea-dyke path proper – the Digue de la Mer. The path is open only to cyclists, horse-riders and walkers. It is hard surfaced and fairly easily ridable, although a little loose in places, favouring fatter rather than narrower tyres.

From here you begin to get more of the true flavour of the Camargue. As the dyke threads its way between islands and beside the sea lagoon, the landscape assumes an almost desolate, melancholy beauty, apparently suspended between sea and sky. I have never had the luck to be there at such a time, but it must be truly impressive under a sky of tall clouds. On our day it was a soft pearly grey, and this and the neglected wooden piles embedded in the waste of pebbles only served to emphasise the isolation and openness.

From time to time small flocks of flamingos passed overhead, their airborne shape bizarre with their long necks in front and their long legs tucked behind – only the direction they are flying reveals which end is the head. There are several points along the dyke where – at that time of year – flocks of these pink flamingos are easily spotted, one-legged and upright in the overwhelmingly horizontal landscape. There are a couple of official hides from which you can watch these and other birds.

The total length of the path, from the car park just before the Phare de la Gacholle to the surfaced road at the western end, is about 14km. Allow plenty of time, since the going is rather slow. The church of Stes Maries-de-la-Mer seems to take a long time to come near over the last stretches.

According to legend, Stes Maries is where the boat containing Mary Magdalene, Martha, Lazarus, Mary mother of James, Mary mother of John, Suedonius and Sarah landed safely after being cast adrift and abandoned following the Crucifixion. The legend has it that Mary Magdalene and the other disciples dispersed to found other churches, while the other two Marys and Sarah remained nearby, eventually being buried here. Subsequently their tomb became a place of pilgrimage, venerated in particular by gypsies from all over Europe. It is now best known for its annual gypsy gathering at the end of May. Maybe due to the gypsy influence, this is very much horse country, with riding establishments at nearly every *mas* (farm).

There is a choice of routes back from Stes Maries. It is quite reasonable to follow the main D570, which carries a fair amount of traffic at holiday times but is otherwise quiet. An alternative to the first 9 or 10km of it is offered by the D85[A], which rejoins the D570 at Pioch Badet. It may also be possible to follow the path that turns right off this road after 4km and skirts the Étang de Vaccarès, rejoining the main route at Méjanes. We were not able to research this path and have not been able to find any information on it.

A third possibility is to follow the D38 along the left bank of the Petit Rhône, then turn right on the D38[C] to rejoin the D570. Finally, a rather longer alternative is to leave Stes Maries by the D58, cross the Petit Rhône by the ferry after 6km, and then follow the D85 to Sylvéréal. Here turn right on the main D58 to the far end of the village, then go left on the D202, which passes through rice paddies along the right bank of the Petit Rhône. This road joins the D179 at La Fosse, where you go right to the main N572 just short of St Gilles. Go right again for 2km, then very sharply right on a small road by Figarès and along the left bank of the river, through more rice paddies. At the junction with the D37, go right through Albaron to the D570.

All the routes turn south-east on the D37 to return to Grand Romeu. Although this road passes through a generally unexciting cultivated or grazing landscape, there are several spots on or near the road that give extensive views to the south over the Étang de Vaccarès and its wildlife.

Approximate total distance   68km
Maps   Michelin 83, panels 9, 10, 19 and 20; IGN 66; also IGN Regional Natural Park sheet 303
Regions   Languedoc-Roussillon, Provence-Alpes-Côte d'Azur
Départements   13-Bouches-du-Rhône, 30-Gard
Accommodation   Arles, Stes-Maries-de-la-Mer
Access   By road, D570 from Arles, then D36 and D36[B]; by rail to Arles; by air to Marseille-Marignane, Nîmes, Montpellier

THE ALPES MANCELLES

Whoever coined the name Alpes Mancelles (the Alps of le Mans) for this southernmost tip of Normandy was either a bit of a joker, someone with an ear for a good promotional slogan, or romantic beyond belief. For, although the route takes in one of the two highest points in western France – the 417m Mont des Avaloirs – the Alpes Mancelles themselves owe their name to a short rocky section of the infant River Sarthe near St Léonard-des-Bois. So do not expect Alpine splendour, nor many Alpine gradients – but the route does take in one col named on the map: you will be able to boast to your friends of your exploits on the Col de St Sulpice. You need not tell them that it is only 246m at the top!

The route takes you through two distinct types of landscape: the forests and the largely bocage country between them. From one or two vantage points on the road the pattern of small, hedged fields – some grazed, some cultivated –

The River Sarthe and the church of St Céneri-le-Gérei.

with occasional small copses, showed up in the mid June in which we passed as a vast chequered patchwork of greens, yellows and gold, much like Shropshire and Herefordshire seen from Clee Hill. Like the Welsh border counties, too, the rounded hills, where they are not fully forested, are crowned with small woods that emphasize their distinctness from the rolling bocage only a few metres below them. Farming the bocage is quite labour-intensive, so the area has a generally hardworking look without the easy affluence of some of the other places.

Most of the route lies within the Regional Natural Park of Normandie-Maine. We made our base near the small compact town of Sillé-le-Guillaume, some 30km north-west of Le Mans, which sits facing the sun on the southern slopes of a low ridge of hills. Earlier in its history it had been one of a string of fortified strongholds separating Maine from Normandy. Among the incidents in its past was the complete sacking of its fortifications by the English at the end of the Hundred Years War.

The ridge of hills, the Coëvrons, is covered by the Forêt de Sillé, and among the hollows in the forest are several ponds and small lakes. We camped in the forest on the southern side of the largest, the Étang du Defais, some 3km from the centre of Sillé. The opposite (north) side of the lake has been developed into a small resort with restaurants, extensive lake beaches and space for water sports.

This forest and the others on the route are mostly open woodland, with small oaks and chestnuts, and here and there plantations of conifers. The openness gives almost the impression of a succession of small sunny glades – a long way from the dense ranks of conifers of the high mountains. Several of the small reed-fringed lakes – which you come on quite unexpectedly – are nature reserves, others the haunt of anglers.

In the Forêt de Sillé.

Our route begins, then, at the Etang du Defais, and follows the forest road east until it meets the D105. Do not be put off that the occasional forest road is marked Route privée (private road); lower down, the notice explains that traffic is permitted. The Eaux et Forêts are merely pointing out that they own the road and may need to restrict its use if forestry work is in progress. The D105 falls away with quite an exhilarating twisting downhill stretch through the forest, sweeping past an angling lake on the right, to emerge into the open fields before Mont St Jean. A steady but not too hard climb leads up to the village, with the chance of a detour to the left to the viewpoint of the Butte Voyère, reached by a track from a signposted road.

A word of caution here on the Michelin map: one of the characteristics of bocage country is the number of small dispersed hamlets, perhaps only a farm and half a dozen cottages, hidden away down minute dead-end roads. Very few of these roads and hamlets

closes in, with steep tree-fringed cliffs beyond the river (the very cliffs of the Alpes Mancelles) as you approach St Léonard. This is a rather touristy if pleasant little village, busy with trippers on the Sunday morning that we came through, and with several cafés and hotels. A short walk up from the church gives some rocky views of the little gorge of the fancifully named Vallée de Misère.

There is quite a little climb out of St Léonard, through orchards and little enclosed fields. Just over the brow you get a good view of the huddle of stone-built houses and the church of the next village, St Cénéri-le-Gérei. A fine swoop down and a swing to the left bring you to the picturesque hump-backed bridge over the Sarthe, with the angular church perched high above the stream. 'This village,' says the Michelin guide, 'has inspired many a painter'. The process has left it somewhat self-conscious, seeing itself rather as the Castle Combe of the Alpes Mancelles, with several up-market restaurants and their attendant coach parties. Perhaps a Sunday lunch-time in mid June is not the best time for a visit.

The next two villages, St Pierre-des-Nids and Champfrémont, in the heart of the bocage, are much more workaday places and have rather more varied shops. From here the road climbs steadily but not too steeply up into the next forest, the Forêt de Multonne, passing on the way a pleasant open space round the little chapel of Ste Anne, where there is a useful bottle-replenishing tap.

The road route continues over the hill towards Lalacelle, turning very sharp left about 1km before the village to climb back up to the Mont des Avaloirs. In dry weather it is quite feasible to cut off the corner – and avoid losing height – by taking the bridleway of the GR22^C to the left. Like all sentiers de grande randonnée (marked GR on the map) this is signed by white and red bands on trees and the like, and is very easy to follow. It climbs at first, then levels out just before rejoining the road. The path makes a very agreeable change, plunging right into the quiet heart of the forest, but looks as though it might be sticky after wet weather.

are marked on the map, so quite often what you expect to be a bend turns out to be a junction. Even the IGN 1:100,000 map does not mark them all, so you have to use some common sense in navigating. The principal junctions are well signed, and many of the small ones have a diagram naming the farms they serve.

From Mont St Jean the road, still the D105, rolls down and up across several small valleys, through St Georges-le-Gaultier to St Paul-le-Gaultier. A right turn on the D15 takes you through the village – like most of the villages on the route it usefully has a shop or two. At the eastern end, a left fork on the D146 brings you onto a delightful little road that emerges from a small wood to drop to the Sarthe at Pont de la Folie. The river is actually quite substantial here, bordered by short lines of poplars, and unexpectedly rocky. Turn left directly after the bridge. The valley

The climbing is not all over, however, when you reach the road and turn left, for there is quite a stiff pull up through the forest to the top, the 417m Mont des Avaloirs. At the top a short dead-end road leads to the viewing platform marking the summit. Unfortunately, the trees have obviously grown since the tower was installed and in summer there is virtually no view from the top of any of the places the table d'orientation tantalizingly lists. There is another hill near here of identical height – the Signal d'Ecouves, some 15km to the north-east. These hills share the distinction of being the highest points in western France; they are higher than anywhere in much more rugged Brittany.

If the views from the top were disappointing, then there is ample recompense on the way down, with fine panoramas south over the bocage to the ridge of the Forêt de Sillé. It is a fine freewheel, too, with only a couple of crossroads to interrupt the rhythm. A gentle rise brings you to the junction with the D20, where you turn left.

This road is known as the Corniche du Pail, and as it climbs steadily broad views of the bocage chequerboard open up, with the blue hills above the little spa town of Bagnoles de l'Orne on the horizon. On our June visit, the bracken- and fern-covered slopes of the Corniche were speckled with the pink of tall foxgloves and the white of marguerites, with attractive groups of small birches. The open Corniche gives way at the top to more forest, rather denser this time, but mixed with beeches and birches, then a pleasantly fast if slightly nondescript road leads into the small town of Villaines-la-Juhel. Here you turn left on the D119, an open road through cornfields, to the next rather English-sounding village of Averton, where the route turns left on the D149 Gesvres road. The inconspicuous turning between two walls is easy to miss but you have a second chance when you reach the church, with a penalty of only a short distance.

This is a delightful road, starting beside a stream with a bluff rising behind it covered with heather and bracken. The road then climbs quite gently through the south-eastern end of the Forêt de Pail to emerge at the Col de St Sulpice. There is no summit marker, just a crossroads with the turning up to the chapel of St Sulpice itself to the left. The route, however goes right (D268), on a long and quite exhilarating descent through the forest.

It is possible to shorten the route considerably, although it means missing the Corniche du Pail, by turning left on the D204 at the second crossroads after the Mont des Avaloirs. This gentle foxglove-fringed road follows the valley direct to Gesvres, from which the D149 climbs directly up to the Col de St Sulpice.

On the main route, a short climb from the Merdereau stream at the foot of the forest descent brings you up to a point with broad views all round of the hills, before a left-and-right over the D119 leads, still on the D268, to the village of St Aubin-du-Désert. The route bears left at the church in the square, onto the D222, a rolling road that after some 5km reaches St Germain-de-Coulamer, a village that seems at first glance to have a maze of little streets. Here there is a slight error on the Michelin map: the minor road you need goes to the right (west) of the village cemetery, just beyond the church, not to the left as the map suggests. This narrow road twists through hamlets and between open fields and is as fine as any on the route, with tantalizing views before it plunges to join the D203 in the valley bottom. Another brief downhill after turning right is followed by the steady tree-lined climb back up to Sillé Plage and the lake.

Just at the top, though, there is another small lake on the right, this one a reed- and iris-fringed nature reserve with water-lilies floating gently in great rafts. On our warm June evening we sat there quiet for a few minutes as the frogs called from the far shore and a few ducks paddled quietly across the smooth mirror of the surface. It was as good a way to end the day's riding as any we could have imagined.

Approximate total distance   105km
Maps   Michelin 60, panels 2 and 12; IGN 17
Region   Pays de la Loire
Départements   53-Mayenne, 72-Sarthe
Accommodation   Sillé-le-Guillaume, St Léonard-des-Bois, St Pierre-des-Nids, Villaines-la-Juhel
Access   By road, D304 from Le Mans or Mayenne, D30 (becomes D21), then D15 and D310 from Alençon; by rail to Le Mans, Alençon

THE LOIRE VALLEY

The Loire is one of the great rivers of France, and the longest at over 1000km. It rises beneath a rocky outcrop, the Gerbier du Jonc, in the southern Massif

The Loire valley from the north.

quite a short compass – open rolling wheatlands of the type that stretch across hundreds of kilometres of central France, forests and lazy river scenery. The area is often known as the 'Garden of France'. By way of contrast, to show that not everybody lived in manorial splendour, the route visits several cave dwellings, complete villages dug out of the soft chalky tuffeau rock.

The valley is criss-crossed by a maze of tiny roads that offer gentle cycling, for this is one of the easiest of the routes, with only two fairly long climbs. Because of the intricacy of the roads, the directions for following the route – which takes the form of an elongated near figure-of-eight loop – are quite detailed in some parts.

We chose Azay-le-Rideau as our base, because it was convenient and we liked the place. The route description begins and ends there, but it is rather toward the eastern end of the route. It would be equally easy to start at any point, while a base in Chinon, Candes, Montsoreau or nearby would allow it to be split into two smaller and nearly equal loops with little modification.

Central, flows north for 400km, and then – almost within sight of Paris – turns abruptly west at Orléans to flow into the Atlantic. Earth movements many millions of years ago opened up an easier route west for north-flowing rivers, including the Loire, which was until then a tributary of what is now the Seine. Although it is well north of half-way, the Loire is a natural divide between northern and southern France, not least in the minds of French weather forecasters.

The Loire valley is synonymous with châteaux and wines. The fifteenth and sixteenth centuries particularly saw the construction of an unparalleled variety of great houses along the hospitable banks of the Loire. The route gives the chance of visiting the great châteaux of Azay-le-Rideau, Villandry and Ussé, quite a variety of smaller houses, and the stronghold of Chinon. It also passes through the appellation contrôlée wine-growing regions of the Côteaux de Layon, Saumur, Saumur-Champigny, Chinon and Touraine-Azay-le-Rideau, with ample opportunities for tasting.

But the area also has a variety of features within

One of the attractions of Azay-le-Rideau is its château. Beautifully set in what is an ornamental lake rather than a moat, the present building dates from the sixteenth century, with a surprisingly modern appearance, while its relatively modest size gives it a unity that escapes more elaborate and excessive structures, such as Chenonceaux. The interior is furnished with a relatively simple and highly evocative elegance. There is a son et lumière display of the château's history during the summer months.

The route leaves Azay-le-Rideau by the D84, the road that goes past the entrance to the château and then follows the green valley of the River Indre, with plantations of poplars sloping down to the hidden river. After about 6km you leave the valley, turning left up a small road signposted to Druye, just after the turning on the right to Saché. This starts with a sharp climb, then levels out through the forest to

(right) *The château of Azay-le-Rideau.*

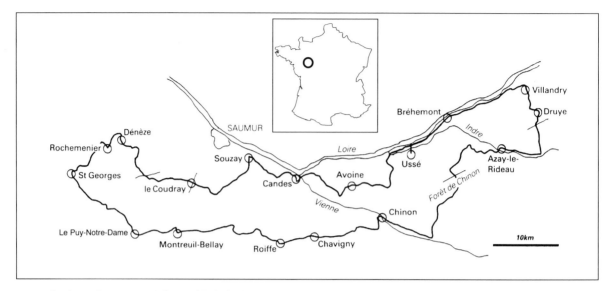

cross the busy D751 in a right-and-left dogleg. At the time we passed by, early in June, the roadside verge down to Druye was dotted with purple orchids among the grasses.

Druye looks from a distance remarkably like a demonstration collection of agricultural buildings, dominated by large silos. Turn left by the church to follow the D121 down to the outskirts of Villandry. Here the wall surrounding the garden of the château begins and you fork right down a narrow road that skirts this wall, giving views of the château and its formal garden on the way down. The best view is from a bend about 150m from the top.

The present gardens – the pride of Villandry – are a patient reconstruction of the sixteenth-century design, with geometrically shaped beds emphasized by yew trees and square-trimmed box borders. The château itself is an imposing square building dominating the flat river terrace below.

On reaching the main D7 go straight over, along a very pleasant avenue of dwarf sycamores and limes. The lane emerges from this avenue to climb to the bank (*levée*) of the River Cher. It was here that we saw rows of herons standing stately in the placid waters. Shortly after, as the road bears right along the river bank, it drops away to a section of large cobblestones (*pavé*). There is enough space at the edge to avoid the worst of the bumps, and in any case this cobbled stretch lasts no more than 500m or so, but for that distance you can appreciate what the riders in the Paris–Roubaix race suffer.

The Cher soon joins the River Loire. Just beyond the little quay at the next village, La Chapelle-aux-Naux, is a set of markings on a flight of steps leading down to the water showing the levels the river has reached during floods over the years. The highest mark, only about a metre below the road, dates from 25 October 1872. Imagining the terrifying scene of the great river flooded from bank to bank only served to show how different was the lazy summer stream before us, with its broad sandbanks and narrow channel.

The road now follows the river downstream for some 18km, mostly along the top of the high levée, skirting several small villages. To the right is the river and to the left the fertile vegetable and fruit market gardens on the flat plain. Quietly and unobtrusively the River Indre comes in from the left and for the last 5 or 6km the road follows the narrowing spit of land between the two rivers.

At the turning signposted to Rigny-Ussé, continue along the river bank; the turning towards the château of Ussé is the next one. This fifteenth-century château with its complex pattern of roofs, turrets and chimneys sits starkly white against the dark green of the wooded cliff behind, seen at its most impressive from the road as you approach. It is said to have been the inspiration for the castle of the Sleeping Beauty – and presumably a great many fairytale castles since.

To avoid the D7 – which is busy in the tourist season – it is best to retrace to the riverbank road and follow this round through Île-Martin. This little lane winds its way past poplar plantations, crossing the Indre and then the D7 and reaching Huismes. After Huismes, turn right at the crossroads with the D118 to Avoine, once more through alignments of poplars, with – at the time we passed – fields of early sunflower plants.

In Avoine, aim for the church, then turn left on the D118 for Savigny and Candes. At the crossed-out name sign at the end of the village, turn left down an unsigned road into a stretch of woodland that goes through to a hamlet called Montour. Here turn right to Savigny, where you follow signs to Roguine and Candes. As you cross the Vienne, at the Pont St Martin, close to its confluence with the Loire, there is a fine view of Candes ahead.

In the next village, Montsoreau, which is pretty well continuous with Candes, turn left up the road signposted to Loudun (D947), then after about 400m turn right up a small road signposted to the Moulin de la Herpinière. This windmill (there is another about 1.5km away on the other side of the Loudun road) is now rather over-restored and used as an art studio and gallery.

By now you are well into the Saumur and Saumur-Champigny vineyards – the road is signed as a Route du vin – and the slopes of the hillside and laid out in neat rows of vines. The route follows the vineyards (*vignobles*) as far as the outskirts of Souzay. Here you turn left uphill on the D205, and after Champigny at the top of the hill, follow the D405, signed to St Cyr-en-Bourg, not the more prominent turn to Chacé, which bears round to the right. Here we seem to have regained the Route du vin that we left at Souzay. Soon there appears to be a patch of a different style of viticulture, with vines trained along wires, showing perhaps a metre of clear stem above the ground, rather in the manner of standard fruit trees.

Continue straight on at the broad D93, and straight on again to the left of the cemetery and over the level crossing, always on the D405, to St Cyr, a village of very high walls. It also boasts the largest wine-growers' co-operative in the region, which has a very high reputation. Do not take the obvious turning signposted Samoussay but bear left to St Just-sur-Dive where, just after the canal bridge and the plantation of poplars, turn right on the D162, signposted Le Coudray-Macouard, where continue on the D162 across the N147 following the Doué road.

This is a picturesque green landscape with plantations of small trees and honey-coloured villages. Beyond Courchamps, the next village, the road opens out again; it is higher up and there are extensive views over to the left of a gently rolling landscape with woodland and large open cornfields. In Montfort turn momentarily left on the D174, then right at the church with its little open square, on the D163, to cross the main D960 to Forges. Here turn right at the church, then fork left, following the signposts for La Fosse, where there is the first of the underground farm villages on the route.

La Fosse underground village consists of three farms dating from the seventeenth century. Do not be put off visiting because the site looks rather featureless from the outside; all the action is underground, excavated below the level, chalky plain.

The next village, Dénezé-sous-Doué, has another cave, this one noted for its carved sculptures. The cave was discovered as recently as 1956 and the figures are dated to the sixteenth century. Authorities differ as to their origin and significance: some consider the cave to have been the hidden meeting-place of a secret guild of stone-carvers, others believe the figures to be the work of persecuted sects, meeting literally underground around the time of the religious wars of the late sixteenth century, and expressing in the caricature figures their opinion of establishment personalities of the time.

In Dénezé, after a pleasant avenue of trees, take a small turning on the right, which leads round past the church, then right on the D69 for about 1km, turning left at the road signposted to Villeneuve. Turn left again just before the hamlet of Villeneuve itself, down an unsigned road to Rochemenier.

Rochemenier has an extensive underground farm settlement, inhabited until the 1930s, which has been restored as a village initiative and is open to the public. These farms were excavated in flat ground, unlike the still-occupied dwellings in other parts of the Loire valley that are cut back into vertical cliffs. There are some very fine examples of the latter in the village of Villaine-les-Rochers, on the D57 about 6km south-east of Azay-le-Rideau.

The first excavation took the form of a deep pit in the soft tuffeau chalk (misleadingly, sometimes known locally or translated as tufa, which is properly the name of a soft volcanic rock). This pit now became a courtyard, with the various dwelling rooms and farm 'buildings' cut back into the artificial cliffs of the

The church at Rochemenier.

side of the pit. The chalk from the digging could be sold for liming more acid fields in the valley – often yielding enough to cover the cost of constructing the farm.

The settlement on view consists of two seventeenth- or eighteenth-century farms: at its height the complete underground village had some forty similar farms, the oldest dating from the Middle Ages, the latest from the nineteenth century. As far as possible the appropriate tools and contents have been restored to their original rooms: barns, winepress and cellar, cow sheds, bedrooms, dining-room and kitchen, oven, stable, even an underground chapel and village hall. The modulating effect of the rock kept the temperature even, making the caves quite snug in winter and relatively cool in summer. The entry to the farms is close by the church in the centre of the village, and the whole makes a fascinating visit.

From Rochemenier turn west on the D177, sign-

posted to Louresse, and in Louresse turn left just past the church, on the D159, to St Georges-sur-Layon, then on D178 to Concourson-sur-Layon. Here you are back in vineyards and have once more regained the Route du vin (this time the Côteaux de Layon), following the winding stream of the Layon to Les Verchers-sur-Layon. Here you turn briefly right on the D69 and then left on a small road signed Les Fontaines, then right on an unsigned road immediately after Bussy-Fontaine.

From here it is effectively straight on to the prominent water-tower and the impressive church of Le-Puy-Notre-Dame. Turn left just before and immediately under the walls of the church and follow the green little valley through to Montreuil-Bellay. There are some imposing glimpses of the château of Montreuil-Bellay, perched high above the river, from this road.

In Montreuil, turn right over the river Thouet and up into the town. Take the left turning signed to Méron and Epieds. The village of Méron is perched on a small hill, dominating the surroundings, one of those sights that seems typical of rural France. In Epieds turn right, then left to join the D19 to Saix. After the village, turn right on the D50 to Roiffé and then follow the signs for Lerné. This road runs gently down a broad open valley to the golden stone village of Lerné, where the château of Chavigny is prominent below the trees on the hillside to the left. A little farther on, the château of La Roche-Clermault dominates the horizon ahead.

Once more this is gently rolling country, part wooded with occasional vineyards. After La Devinière (the birthplace of the satirist François Rabelais) it is impossible to avoid turning left to cover a short stretch of the main road to the roundabout that marks the start of the Chinon bypass. Here turn right, following the sign to Chinon St Jacques, turning left just before the level crossings. You enter Chinon by a fine avenue of plane trees that frame a view of the castle ahead.

Still-inhabited cave-dwellings at Villaine-les-Rochers.

The preserved 'troglodyte' farm at Rochemenier.

Follow the road system round its little right-hand loop and across the bridge over the river Vienne. The direct route out is a sharp right just after the bridge, but to visit the historic old town and the castle turn left. Chinon castle is largely a twelfth-century fortress, perhaps best known as the site of Joan of Arc's identification of the Dauphin Charles and her prophecy that he would be crowned Charles VII of France. The setting is one of the most impressive along the Loire.

The road out of Chinon, the D8, bears right in parkland to the east of the bridge and on the north side of the Vienne: it is named here the Rue Déscartes. This road follows the valley of the Vienne, past maize fields and vineyards through two hamlets whose names appear to have been borrowed from distant places: Briançon and Le Puy. There appears to be a dolmen built into the wall of a house at Briançon.

In Le Puy, turn left on the D44 to Cravant-les-Côteaux, where after a left-and-right the road begins to climb through the old village (*Vieux Bourg*) coming to a pleasant poplar-lined valley, like a miniature mountain road. It is quite a steady gradient – only the second major climb on the whole route – up first into the heathland area of the Landes du Ruchard, then into the attractive Forêt de Chinon.

Continue to the main D751, where you have to go right for about 1km, then left onto a forest road, Route Forestière de la Pucelle, marked with a 50km/h speed limit. At the next eight-way crossroads, turn right down the firm-surfaced, untarred road, Route du Henri II, to the village of Cheillé, through fields of fruit trees and cornfields.

In Cheillé you can either drop directly to the D17 in the valley for Azay, or take the right-hand turn at the bottom of the street below the church, to follow a rolling up-and-down road, past orchards once more, as well as a small château, which brings you back to the outskirts of Azay-le-Rideau.

Approximate total distance 204km
Maps Michelin 64, panels 11 to 14; IGN 25, 26
Regions Pays de la Loire, Centre and Poitou-Charentes
Départements 37-Indre-et-Loire, 49-Maine-et-Loire, 86-Vienne
Accommodation Azay-le-Rideau, Villandry, Montsoreau, Doué-la-Fontaine, Montreuil-Bellay
Access By road, N138 to Saumur, D751 from Tours to Azay-le-Rideau and Chinon; by rail to Tours or Saumur; by air to Tours

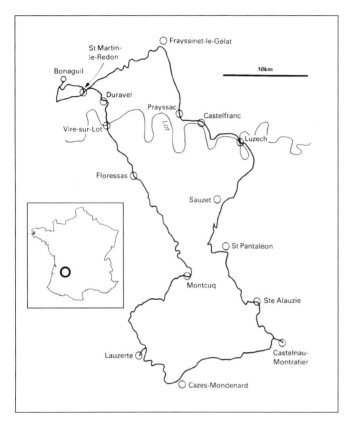

THE QUERCY BLANC

The Quercy is one of the historic divisions of France, covering the region between the volcanic mountains of the Massif Central and the plains of Aquitaine. The area we picked for our route covers only a small part of the southern half of the old province: Bas-Quercy, the area to the south and west of Cahors. We do, however, make an excursion across the River Lot to visit the magnificent castle of Bonaguil.

The southern part of the route lies in the Quercy Blanc, an area of chalk ridges (*serres*) and valleys, running roughly south-west to north-east. It is rolling but not particularly tough cycling country. Farther north the chalk gives way to a harder golden to reddish-brown limestone, not unlike Cotswold stone in its range of colours. The fertile valleys are heavily cultivated with a wide range of crops. The uplands· are often barer with cereal fields and clumps of cypress, or woods of characteristic dwarf oak trees – the sort that in parts of the Quercy harbour truffles among their roots. Towards the Lot valley the woods become denser and more mixed with ash and other trees.

The whole area is much what England's Lincolnshire and Northamptonshire Wolds, or Cotswolds and Chilterns, might be if they were transported 600 miles south and had been fought over for 300 years. It was the continual Anglo-French quarrelling between the twelfth and fifteenth centuries that gave rise to so many of the striking fortified hill-top towns and villages.

We came to this area directly from prospecting routes in the Tarn gorges and the Cévennes – which meant travelling a little north as well as west. We were immediately struck by how southern the countryside appeared by comparison. There is a general sun-blanched feel, abetted by the hard white chalk showing through in the fields, and by the pinkish pantiles of the jumbled roofs. The crops in the valleys, too, are southern: tobacco, maize, vines and sunflowers. Officially this is part of the Midi-Pyrénées region.

We chose as our base the compact hill-top town of Castelnau-Montratier, perched on a spur of one of the serres. It owes its imposing position to the destruction in 1214 of an earlier settlement, Castelnau-de-Vaux, which lay at the foot of the hill. The towers of three windmills – one of them still with sails – are a feature of the town's skyline, and it was on a shaded grassy terrace below these that we camped while exploring the route.

Since Castelnau-Montratier is on a 250m ridge, it seemed to make good sense to stay on it for a while, so we headed west along the easy D19. As in my native Chilterns, it is easy to get the impression that the country is flat as you bowl along the top of one of these broad-backed ridges, but every so often there was a little wrinkle in the swell of the hill, or the road went nearer to one edge to give an open view across the cornfields to the woods on the top of the next ridge, slightly blue in the summer haze.

After some 6km or so you reach the boundary between the Lot and Tarn-et-Garonne départements and the road number changes to D16. A farther 3km brings you to a five-way crossroads, and it is time to leave the ridge. Turn right on the D31, only to be faced with another choice after a few hundred metres. Going straight on, on the D31, soon brings the first surprise view over the deep and broad valley of the Barguelonne, while the left turn, unnumbered, is a delightful little road leading into an almost hidden valley.

Both roads meet again after about 4km, and the now combined route (D57) continues to the crossroads below Cazes-Mondenard. Here you bear right past a small industrial estate, followed by a right-and-left dogleg, still on the D57 and still tracing the little Barguelonne. After a little over 1km, the D81 turns off to the right, crosses the stream and heads over the hill to Lauzerte between the twin chapels of St Cernin and St Jean. This is a fine miniature mountain pass, reasonably graded with twists and turns, first through fields of hay, then up to thin woodland.

It was on this climb that we noticed for the first time in the Quercy the abundance of butterflies once so characteristic of chalk country in England – small blues and darting brown fritillaries – among the thin grass and chalk-loving herbs. At the top, at Le Chartron, the road emerges into a brief patch of heathland dotted with dwarf oaks, before dropping in a broad fast descent to the valley. Rounding a bend near the bottom – in a sea of young sunflower plants when we passed – the view quite suddenly opens out to give a striking first impression of Lauzerte, perched four-square on its hill.

Lauzerte was one of the true *bastide* (fortified) towns, built on its limestone bluff by a French count in 1241, only to fall to the English a little later. These towns were all built on a more or less rectangular grid pattern within stout walls, often round a further stronghold such as a castle or fortified church to which the inhabitants could repair if necessary. Quite a bit of the old town remains in Lauzerte, with a mixture of styles especially evident in the central square with its covered arcades. There is a very fine view over the Barguelonne valley from the town walls.

From the town the route drops back to the valley road, giving a choice of routes. The straight alternative, the D953, continues past the varied fields of the valley towards Montcuq. However, we were intrigued by the sails of a windmill on the hill to the north and climbed out of the valley on the D2, turning right at the top of the slope to Bouloc. In the village follow the *vers D953* (towards D953) signs. The

windmill, another tower mill with rotating cap like those at Castelnau-Montratier, is one of the few remaining of what was once a common feature round here. To reach it you have to make a detour of about 1km east. Despite its superb position, we found that it was impossible to get close to, since it has been converted to a private dwelling.

There was a bonus, though. Shortly after regaining the route there is an unsigned fork, where you have to go against natural inclination by going slightly uphill on the left-hand road (the other one goes down). This road proved to be an extremely pleasant winding byway, past a couple of small woods and attractive hamlets. It was on this road that we began to appreciate how much we were in a land of spires, much like Leicestershire or north Hertfordshire in England. The fertility of the valleys led early to intense mixed cultivation, with a multitude of small hamlets dotting the valley bottom and the lower slopes of the hills, each with its little spired church or chapel. The effect is intensified by the square-spired dovecote towers on so many of the farmhouses. Apparently the pigeons were cherished for their droppings, much prized as a fertilizer.

The next village up the valley, Montcuq, was also once fortified but all that remains is the surprisingly tall and straight castle keep perched on its rock. There are very wide views from the foot of the tower, which you can reach on a just ridable steep path. After Montcuq the route leaves the valley north by the D28, climbing through woods to reach more open country, with a mixture of hedgeless fields and small vineyards. There are one or two up-and-downs and then, shortly after you cross the D656, the view suddenly becomes more dramatic as the road emerges onto a narrow ridge between two steep-sided chalk valleys, followed by a brisk descent through dwarf oaks.

Shortly after the next village, Boulvé, the route bears left on the D58, signposted to Floressas. The soil and the woodland change quite abruptly: gone is the white chalk and in its place a vivid reddish marl, while the woodland is much more mixed with ash and plantations of white poplar. There is quite a little climb up to Floressas, and at the same time the view opens up behind of range after range of wooded hills. It was here that we saw the first of several bee-eaters, with their characteristic long curved beaks.

After Floressas the road begins to drop gently, mostly through woodland to Vire-sur-Lot and its

The valley of the Barguelonne at Cazillac.

near the towers.

From Bonaguil it is possible to follow an easier route, by way of the D158 back to the D673 at Boussac. It is possible to take any of several routes over to the Lot valley but we followed this road up the very pastoral and green valley of the Thèze. This flat-bottomed valley with its low limestone cliffs and plantations of poplars and willows is quite different from the valleys of the Quercy Blanc farther south. In places the limestone has been quarried and used for building; like Cotswold stone it is golden or even reddish when fresh, and weathers to a soft grey.

Just before Frayssinat-le-Gélat, turn right on the D44 to Pomarède, keeping straight on (on the D67, signposted Prayssac, where the D44 bears right). From Prayssac there is no real alternative to about 2.5km of the D911 to Castelfranc. There are, however, as compensation fine views over the River Lot.

In Castelfranc bear right on the D9, just before the church, to continue to follow the right bank of the Lot. There are two choices here. For the adventurous, a stretch of disused railway line has been preserved as a pedestrian, horse and cycle path. It is quite firmly surfaced, and you can follow it upstream for about 6km to the little chapel at Camy. The D9 itself is attractive, too, though rather farther away from the river than the old railway. In Luzech – a village of some antiquity and history, having been a dominating point since Roman times – turn left across the narrow isthmus between the two arms of the Lot, over the bridge and then right on the D23.

This road, through St Vincent-Rive-d'Olt, follows the valley of a small tumbling stream through lush green mixed woodland, climbing gently all the time, to emerge into more open country near Sauzet. Cross straight over the D656 by the cemetery on the outskirts of the village, to follow what is now the D185. Near Bagat-en-Quercy there is an abrupt and dramatic change of landscape. You have been climbing steadily all the way and suddenly the greenness of the valley gives way to a miniature mountain climb (with hairpin bends) to an open chalky upland, followed by a stretch of open scrub with dwarf oaks and

bridge over the river. The route crosses the main D911 at Duravel and climbs quite sharply to begin with up a steeply banked lane through woodlands. Follow the signs to St Martin-le-Redon. In St Martin, an attractive and floral little village, follow signs for Bonaguil. There is a hairpin bend as the road climbs away from the village, followed by more woodland.

Then, suddenly, as the road begins to go downhill, a tremendous view of the castle of Bonaguil opens up to the right. This impressive fortress, in its present form dating from around 1500, marks the boundary between Quercy and Perigord, and stands on a commanding pinnacle of rock, high above its little village. The suddenness of the view and the way in which the golden stone of the towers stands against the dark trees behind are quite breathtaking, enhanced by the buzzards that hover and wheel

The castle of Bonaguil.

through Blayon. Blayon is an exquisite hamlet of no more than four or five golden stone houses. When we passed, it was set in fields of young sunflower plants that were lit vividly green by the low sun. This delightful road then winds past the next hamlet, Ste Alauzie with its stark white church tower, to climb up through more golden corn to rejoin the direct road. By now the three windmill towers of Castelnau-Montratier are prominent on the horizon, though you still have one last climb past the vineyard to reach them.

Approximate total distance   141km
Maps   Michelin 79, panels 6, 7 and 17; IGN 57
Region   Midi-Pyrénées
Départements   46-Lot, 82-Tarn et Garonne
Accommodation   Castelnau-Montratier, Cazes-Mondenard, Lauzette, Montcuq, Puy-l'Éveque, Luzech
Access   By road, N20 from Cahors or Montauban, then D19; by rail to Cahors, Montauban, Fumel

chalk flora. At the same time a broad view of the way ahead opens up: you are back in the Quercy Blanc.

The road drops once more to the valley of the Barguelonnette, but the obvious continuation marked on the Michelin map as going straight on turns out to be no more than a chalky track. It is better to turn left on the D653 for a couple of kilometres and then right on the D37, signposted Castelnau-Montratier. This is a determined little climb, followed by a superbly scenic winding descent past the hamlet of Escayrac and between fields of the most golden corn I have ever seen.

It is possible to continue on the D4 direct to Castelnau, but we followed the detour to the left

In the bastide town of Lauzerte.

10

A Bit Hillier

THE MONTAGNE DE REIMS

I first heard of the Montagne de Reims when an invitation came through the post. The invitation was to take part in the Randonnée de la Montagne de Reims, an organized cycle ride being put on by the local cycle touring club in Reims. We had passed that way a year or two before and had no recollection of any mountain. I was intrigued; the date was convenient and I sent off my entry. This is how, in the company of 3452 other cyclists, I made my first acquaintance of this delightful area.

The Montagne de Reims is in fact one of a series of escarpments facing outwards from the Paris basin, rather in the way that in England the Chilterns and North Downs face outwards from London. It is formed of a chalky rock – the basis of the slopes on which the Champagne-producing vines grow – capped with a flinty clay. Like the Chilterns and the North Downs, the region is quite hilly, although the highest part is only 283m above sea level – no more than 20m higher than the Chilterns.

The hills are topped with some very mixed woodland and lie between the valleys of the Vesle (the river that flows through Reims) to the north and the Marne, one of the great gentle rivers of France, to the south. With vineyards occupying much of the space between, there is a good variety of landscape in quite a small area.

Champagne is the great preoccupation of the region, and the route passes the premises of many large and small producers of the bubbly beverage, giving ample opportunity for tasting and buying. There is a practical limit to the number of bottles one can take back as souvenirs on a bicycle, so it might be better to make the circuit an occasion for enjoying on the spot the lesser-known still wines that rarely make it abroad – the Côteaux champenois appellation includes reds and rosés as well as the expected whites.

The whole of the route lies within the Natural Regional Park of the Montagne de Reims. We began our circuit near Épernay, where we were staying, although it would be equally easy to start from Reims, or indeed from any of the villages on the route. Our first detour was to the village of Mareuil-sur-Ay, about 8km east of Épernay, to look at the River Marne and its canal, and we begin our route from there.

We left Mareuil by a little road almost opposite the church, and within 100m we were among vines, dominated on the right by the statue of a gilded angel on a knoll. Just over the brow of this first small hill you cross the Mareuil bypass by a tiny chalky road that leads up to the little village of Mutigny, past vines proudly proclaiming their Mercier allegiance. From the church here there is a superb panorama south over vineyards down to the valley of the Marne, with the neat squares of the vines draped like a giant patchwork quilt over the curves and folds of the escarpment.

From Mutigny we dropped swiftly to Avenay-Val-d'Or with the scent of fermenting grape juice hanging heavy in the air. This was the end of September, and a fine summer and early autumn had allowed an early harvest (recolte). The scent was to waft up to us again and again, either as we passed through villages or where the debris of crushed skins and stalks was piled ready to fertilise the soil.

In Avenay the route keeps left, parallel to the railway, and at the north end of the village turns left again on the D71 for Germaine under a low railway bridge. The road climbs steadily, first through fields of maize and then through forest, to the almost-

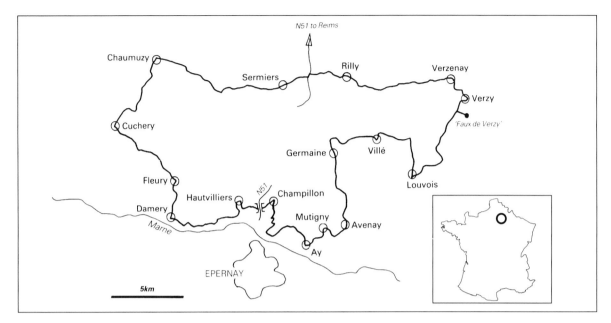

perched village of Germaine. Here there is a forestry museum (*Maison du bûcheron*). The road drops to cross the railway again and embarks on a sweeping climb past the beautifully situated and compact hamlet of Vauremont, with its neat pantiled roofs and ornate church tower. The woodland here is very open, with beech and hornbeam mixed in with some pines and larches.

The next village, Ville-en-Selve, is followed by a steep drop below the church, still on the D71, out onto a wide open cultivated area. At the more major D9, turn right for about 2km to the long straggling village of Louvois, where there is a rather complicated junction. The route, now on the D34, doubles back rather to climb through open woodland once more; it is a long but steady climb, rather straight in places.

Just over the brow of the hill, there is a right turn to a very unusual feature, the Faux de Verzy. The road is closed to motor vehicles after about 300m but is still cyclable, and leads down a woodland ride from which many of the *faux* can be seen. These are beech trees with a genetic oddity that causes them to grow with gnarled and twisted limbs to form dense domed canopies of intertwined twigs and leaves, mostly 3 to 5m high. They grow very slowly, are very long lived, and propagate by re-rooting rather than seeding. They also tend to come into leaf at widely differing times. At the last detailed survey in 1977

there were nearly 700 examples of beech and 13 oaks similarly affected.

The forest is remarkably quiet: at one point we stopped and the silence was broken by a loud crashing – which turned out to be no more than the noise of an acorn tumbling branch by branch from the top of an oak. One or two forest areas on the route are marked zone de silence; one of these is between Vauremont and Ville-en-Selve.

After leaving the forest road from the faux, the route turns right down a brisk hill through beech-woods to the compact and busy village of Verzy. From here the road begins its twisting and decidedly up-and-down progress through the vineyards of the north-facing side of the Montagne. These lie part-way up the face of the scarp, so that there are from time to time extensive views over Reims, and the plains and hills beyond.

In Verzy, take the Verzenay road, D26, north-west. Verzenay is a very intricate village with many fascinating back streets: as we passed it was a hive of activity, with everyone busy with some aspect of the grape harvest. Nearly every other building seems to harbour a champagne house, with name and emblem proudly displayed, many of them very small enterprises. The street layout is quite complex: take care that you do not deviate down the hill towards the main road.

The route, still the D26, is signposted to Mailly-

Champagne and Ludes, as well as the windmill. This landmark dominates the vineyards just beyond Verzenay and achieved fame as a lookout post during the 1914–18 war. From here there is a succession of champagne-producing villages, just a kilometre or two apart: Mailly-Champagne, Ludes, Chigny-les-Roses, obviously well-to-do Rilly-la-Montagne (where we had lunch in the little square on that first Randonnée de la Montagne de Reims) and Villers-Allerand.

The character of the countryside changes as you cross the N51 (left

The Marne valley vineyards from Mutigny.

ously also not believed that there could be a mountain hereabouts, and struggled to climb the little hill in their enormous flat-country gears. Turn left at a fountain labelled Eau non potable (not drinking water) on the D24 for La Neuville-au-Larris. The road climbs up through an attractive green avenue of sycamores on a long sweeping curve, with a very English-wold view backwards over the cultivated valley. La Neuville, on a small plateau, has a pleasing layout with an attractive church facing a minute open square.

and right) at Montchenot, just beyond Villers-Allerand; indeed the area west of the road is known as the Petite Montagne to distinguish it from the Grande Montagne to the east. West of the N51 is much more a mixed farming area, with fields and pockets of woodland beginning to supplant the vines.

In the next village, Sermiers, the route bears left by the church to follow the D22 up a steady slope, which yields fine views over the last patch of vines towards Chamery and Ecueil. The drop from the summit in the forest is brisk and it is only too easy to sweep past the next turning. This is at a crossroads rather before the bottom of the hill; turn right on the D22^E (signposted Ferme de la Presle and Pourcy).

In Pourcy, with its prominent church spire, the route joins the D386. Just before the next hamlet, Marfaux, there are two immaculately kept military cemeteries side-by-side, one British, one German, which serve to remind that this part of France has been fought over many times and to show the ultimate futility of it.

Chaumuzy, 2km later, is a another compact village set in wide open maize fields. These bring back memories of a large Dutch contingent at that first Randonnée de la Montagne de Reims, who had obvi-

The countryside changes to vineyards once more as the road bears quite sharply right and drops steeply to Cuchery, where we had another strong waft of fermenting grapes. There are several turnings in Cuchery; the route takes a small one just before the mairie, signposted to Orcourt. There is a sharp little uphill pitch out of the village, after which you bear left through the vines just before the hamlet of Orcourt, to follow the road signed to Épernay and Fleury-la-Rivière.

The fields at the top are surprisingly featureless but must have hidden treasure, since they were dotted with the bent figures of mushroom gatherers. There is an abrupt drop into the narrow streets of Fleury-la-Rivière, with more champagne producers, and then the route turns right, on the D22 once more, for a gentler descent to Damery, the largest village since Verzy and Verzenay.

In Damery, turn left along the valley road (D1), which runs between vineyards to the left and the tall stands of poplars beside the river to the right. In Cumières, 4km farther on, the route turns left at the eastern end of the village on a steep little road signposted to Hautvillers, which climbs between rows of Moët et Chandon vines, with views of the Marne valley and Épernay opening up behind.

Hautvillers is a rather self-conscious village, where Dom Perignon, the seventeenth-century buyer and cellarer for the abbey here, is said to have studied the phenomenon of secondary fermentation and so initiated the méthode champenoise for making sparkling wines. The village has kept and restored many of its old houses and made a feature of its wrought-iron signs showing the trades of the artisans and shopkeepers who formerly lived in each one.

From the eastern end of the village begin by taking the Épernay road and then take the first left on a very narrow lane, which branches off by a small tree-lined square. This drops steeply through the vineyards, under the new N51, and then climbs even more steeply to Champillon, which from below looks almost to be a perched village. Here you bear right at the church, which brings you out on the old main road, now very quiet.

There are two very good viewpoints on the way down this road, the first at a calvary on the right, which gives a fine view across to Hautvillers, and farther down a more official one. This downhill swoop to Dizy is very fast on the broad, smooth and largely deserted road.

In Dizy, you turn left at the traffic lights and then left on a very insignificant-looking road just after the church, the Rue des Gouttes d'Or (the street of drops of gold). This is a tough climb, which levels out at last to be a superb winding narrow road among the vines, with views to right and left in turn. There are one or two patches of slightly rough surface: watch out for potholes.

After the drop to the outskirts of Ay, take the first left turn on another small road, signposted Champagne Bollinger. This goes over the brow of a little hill, then, at a crossroads at the bottom of the hill, the route goes left. A right fork in the bottom of the valley leads to the steep climb past vines with Moët and Chandon markers once more to regain Mutigny and complete the circuit.

Approximate total distance 86km
Maps Michelin 56, panels 16 and 17; IGN 9 and 10
Region Champagne-Ardenne

Département 51-Marne
Accommodation Épernay, Verzy, Rilly-la-Montagne, Montchenot, Damery, Ay
Access By road, N3 to Épernay, N44 to Reims; by rail to Reims, Rilly-la-Montagne, Avenay Val d'Or, Ay, Épernay

HAUT LIMOUSIN

The first thing to strike us as we came into the Limousin was the luxuriant greenness of everything. Trees, hedgerows and fields were rampantly verdant. There is an obvious explanation: the rainfall on this plateau is quite heavy, particularly in winter. Since the underlying rocks are crystalline igneous types, covered in places by clay, the water does not soak away and there are numerous small lakes and streams. The village and plateau of Millevaches, just on the edge of our area, takes its name not from a thousand cows but from a thousand springs (*batz* in the original Celtic of the region,

Lac de Vassiviére from Auphelle.

mutated to *vatz*). Part of the greenness stems from the prevalence of chestnut trees, whose leaves are the most vivid of greens, although familiar oak and beech are common, too.

Not all the lakes are natural, and the focus – or at least starting point – of the routes is the artificial Lac de Vassivière, a stretch of water some 6km by 4km, give or take a few islands and promontories. It lies about 50km east of Limoges.

This is not a prosperous nor particularly populous region, and you will not find for the most part great houses or architecturally distinguished towns. Apart from the little resorts on the Lac de Vassivière itself (which even boasts a cruising restaurant), it is not particularly developed for tourism. What it does have is a rolling upland countryside, much of it some 650 to 750m above sea level, part cultivated, part moorland but mostly wooded – and some excellent cycling.

For our base while exploring the region we chose a pleasant camp site on the shores of the Lac de Vassivière, at Auphelle. The lake, formed in the 1960s by damming the little stream of the Maulde, lies in a natural hollow; the dam is quite narrow considering the volume of water it keeps back. There is a road round the lake that keeps as close to the shore as the numerous promontories allow. Our routes, however, venture farther afield. There are two loops, one heading south towards the valley of the Vézère, the other remaining on the plateau to make an enlarged circuit of the Lac de Vassivière.

South to the Vézère

The bowl of low hills within which the Lac de Vassivière lies is perched some 650m up, so the route starts off downhill. After a short climb from the lake shore – through small fields and the woodland where we had spotted the almost feline shape of a pine marten the evening before – there is an exhilarating and gently curving drop down the D13 to Peyrat-le-Château, the nearest large village. Peyrat nestles against a small and picturesque blue lake that laps against the walls of a grim square tower, all that now remains of a former stronghold, the château of the title. The lake is a favourite of anglers, of whom quite a number were sitting motionless in the sun on the shallow wall beside the water when we passed. Peyrat has quite a selection of everyday shops, hotels and restaurants and a comprehensive little market. The village lies in the

valley of the Mauldre – the stream dammed about 200m higher up to form the Lac de Vassivière – and the road south, the D940, climbs gently away from the valley, none of it steep enough to warrant even a single Michelin arrow.

Much of the route is through woodland, interspersed with small bocage-style fields, fields of hay or grazed by tan-coloured cows. The woodland is here mostly chestnut with a fair sprinkling of hazel: once again we were overwhelmed by the greenness of it all. Along this road we seemed to see an enormous number of jays, swooping across our path or calling raucously as they disappeared into the low trees.

Shortly before Eymoutiers the road crosses the river Vienne, which we had last seen as a broad placid river flowing beneath the battlements of Chinon castle, just before joining the Loire. Here, however, it was a boisterous youthful stream, tumbling noisily over boulders in a little green ravine. Just after the Vienne the route goes left, still on the D940 into Eymoutiers, a busy small market town with its church (all that remains of an eleventh-century monastery) prominent on a granite bluff above the streets.

In Eymoutiers the route bears right on the D30, which climbs away from the town in a much more determined fashion, through beech and birch woods, reaching soon an open heath area with heather, bracken and broom, liberally dotted with foxgloves. This is obviously timber country and we passed numerous neat piles beside the road, including one continuous wall of logs that towered above us.

Once over the top of the climb, the road follows for a while the valley of a small stream flanked by grassy meadows full of such familiar flowers as the buttercup. Once again we were reminded how the indiscriminate spraying of roadside verges and meadowland in the UK in recent years has killed off the variety of our grassland; fortunately, with enlightenment, it is now slowly returning.

Riding past these meadows, we began to hear the chattering of crickets and grasshoppers, a sound that was to be with us for the rest of the day. Crickets are often silent until they hear the gentle call as you freewheel past, which unleashes the response of dozens of answering freewheels. High above the valley were many birds of prey, including kites, readily identifiable by their prominent and slightly forked, square tails. Just before the village

woods and small fields, with the tar melting in patches beneath our wheels in the hot afternoon sun. Disappointingly, the view at the top promised by Michelin did not materialize: not for the first time we were to find that the rapid growth of young trees had obscured it. There were, however, glimpses south down towards Treignac and the blue hills beyond.

From the top there was a beautiful, gentle run down to the main D940, with an incredibly blue reed-edged lake on our left. Once on the main road – quieter than many southern English lanes – there was a fairly gentle but unrelenting climb past St Hilaire-les-Courbes, mostly through woodland, followed by a quite thrilling descent into Lacelle. For a stretch after the village the road is lined by a fine avenue of tall beeches, beside a minute tributary of the Vienne.

About 2km beyond Lacelle, the route turns sharply right under a railway bridge on the D132, which soon becomes the D69 when it crosses the département boundary back into Haute-Vienne. There is a marked drop into a very lush green valley, with more of the tan-coloured cattle. Ahead on the horizon we could see the rim of blue-wooded hills that we would have to climb over to get back to Vassivière.

In the hamlet of La Villeneuve, the route turns left for Nedde on the D81. The road started to climb almost immediately and quite sharply. This was the haymaking season – it was mid June – and at Chez-Chapelle we passed an old woman seated outside her farmhouse, the evening meal no doubt safely in the oven, as she surveyed at least three generations of her family turning the crop in the field below in the golden evening sun.

Except for a small dip to the Vienne, where was the throaty noise of a multitude of frogs, the trend of the road to Nedde is all uphill: there is a total of 150m to climb. Nedde refreshed us with a couple of Oranginas in a small bar to prepare us for the two or three steep pitches on the road up towards Beaumont-du-Lac.

By now the rim of hills round the lake was a very prominent obstacle, with no obvious way through –

of Chamberet we left the D3, which the D30 had become when it crossed the boundary into Corrèze.

It would be quite possible by continuing through Chamberet to extend the trip to Treignac in the Vézère valley, following the winding and rolling D16, a road we explored a day or two later. There is quite an impressive view of the picturesque tiered town of Treignac as you approach it. The town itself is almost a small resort, with broad open parkland besides its lake and 'beach', north-east of the town on the D940.

Our route, however, took us down on the D132 to a small bridge and then immediately right on the D160, which climbed briskly though alternating

In the square at Faux-la-Montagne.

but at least we could see how far we had left to go. After a short steep section the road joins the D43 just east of Beaumont, and slips through a gap in the hills that we had not been able to spot from lower down. After just under 1km, the route turns left onto the D43^{BIS}, which is a much broader road than the map would suggest, and down to the Lac de Vassivière 'ring-road'. From here there is a gentle climb and descent through aromatic pine plantations back to Auphelle.

Round the Lac de Vassivière

The road round the Lac de Vassivière has become well known to race-following cyclists of recent years

as the scene of some decisive time trial stages of the Tour de France. Our route follows some but not all of the same roads at a decidedly more leisurely pace. We followed the circuit in an anticlockwise direction, but there is obviously no reason why you should not go round it the opposite way as the Tour riders do.

The first part of the route follows the D222 through the pine plantations to the west of the lake. There are views over the water from time to time, with a fine prospect of the wooded islets near this western shore. At the foot of the slope is a shallow reedy pool just off to the right of the road, and we paused for several minutes listening to the frogs calling and answering completely unseen from opposite sides of the water.

At the crossroads here, it is possible by turning left to make an out-and-home detour to the island of Vassivière, where there is a permanent open-air sculpture exhibition in the grounds of the château. The island is reached by a causeway and two bridges: cars are not admitted.

The route follows the road round the lake east to the hamlet of Vauveix, and then turns right on the D34. After a short climb the road comes out into delightful upland meadows, filled with flowers when we passed, and then through thickets of hazel and beech. These give way to open woodland, and soon the road is on a shelf, with extensive views to the left over range after range of very wooded hills. The route turns left at a crossroads, of which the right-hand branch is an untarred track leading to the Calvaire Les Tros Croix and Puy Lagarde.

The left turn leads down a superb, winding forest road that rears and plunges through woodland, eventually to emerge onto the D992 leading to the compact and attractive village of Faux-la-Montagne. This road continues past one or two small lakes, then through a stretch that, when we passed, was ablaze with golden broom flowers, as if to remind us that this was Plantagenet country. Next comes a fairly short climb over to the village of Gentioux-Pigerolles. About 1.5km farther on, the route bears left on the D16 and after a farther 1.5km, in the hamlet of Senoueix, goes left again on the D51.

This very winding and twisting road goes between fields and through woodlands,

Cottage detail at Domps.

with a few short sharp ups and downs. It gives very fine views to the right over the Lac de la Vaud Gelade. The road goes into continuous woodland soon after this, and about 5km farther on comes to the village of Royère-de-Vassivière. The quiet grey-stone village provided a welcome bar and a very agreeable halt sitting outside in the late afternoon sun. There are also a few small shops and a restaurant; you could certainly get most necessities here.

The most pleasant way back to the lakeside from here is to follow the D7 south-west for about 2km, then bear left (at a point where the D7 curves round to the right) over the brow of the hill to the hamlet of Masgrangeas – through a landscape bright with heather and broom when we passed. Soon after Masgrangeas, the route joins the road round the lake, where you turn right. After about 3km of open woodland, the road comes down to the lake shore and then goes over the dam to return, by way of a brief climb and descent, to Auphelle.

Approximate total distances: South to the Vézère 77km; Round the Lac de Vassivière 46km

Maps Michelin 72, panels 19 and 20; IGN 41; IGN 2231 (1:50,000) for the circuit of the lake

Region Limousin

Départements 19-Corrèze, 23-Creuse, 87-Haute Vienne

Accommodation Auphelle, Peyrat-le-Château, Eymoutiers, Treignac, Royère-de-Vassivière, Broussas, Vauveix

Access By road, D979 from Limoges to Eymoutiers, then D940; by rail to Limoges

THE GORGES DE LA DOURBIE AND MONT AIGOUAL

Although not far in a straight line from the Tarn and Jonte gorge routes – in fact you could easily link them – the landscape of this route has quite a different character. Once more geology is the reason: for most of this route the underlying rock is not the limestone of the Tarn but hard granite or metamorphic rocks – affected by heat and pressure from the once-molten granite nearby.

These rocks are not porous in the way that limestone is, nor are they as readily dissolved, so there is much more surface water. Since it is a dominating peak open to moisture-bearing winds from both Atlantic and Mediterranean, Mont Aigoual has a high rainfall – around 225cm each year, which puts it in the same league as Wales or the west of Ireland. Michelin sum the mountain up neatly as 'a gigantic water-tower' and its name means 'watery' or 'rainy' in the local dialect. The high rainfall and the non-porous rock mean that everywhere is intensely green, from the bottoms of the gorges to the top of Mont Aigoual itself. Since soils over these types of rock are generally acidic there is a whole different range of plants from those of the alkaline limestone uplands only a few miles away.

My classification of this route as 'hilly' rather than 'moderate mountain' – although it goes up to Mont Aigoual, the highest point in the southern Cévennes – calls for some explanation. The gradients on this ride are surprisingly gentle, only rarely calling for the smallest chainring. The climb from 600m or so at St Jean-de-Bruel to 1567m at the top of Mont Aigoual for the most part has gradients of no more than 2 to 3 per cent (1-in-50 to 1-in-30). It would make an ideal introduction to mountain riding for a comparative beginner – with the added thrill of getting to the top of the highest point for miles around.

Much of the route lies within the Cévennes National Park. The village of Nant in the valley of the Dourbie, about 30km by road south-east of Millau in the département of the Aveyron, proved to be a good choice as our centre. We found a pleasant farm camping site with a grassy terrace beside the Dourbie at the hamlet of Les Cuns about 3km out of the village.

At this point the river runs through a broad fertile valley, made so productive in earlier times by the labours of the monks of the monastery of Nant that it became known as le Jardin de l'Aveyron (the garden of the Aveyron). Traces of their drainage and irrigation works can still be seen, and the valley remains a centre for growing apples and plums, although the vines of the monks have gone.

The route leaves the main D999 through Nant by a narrow road, just east of the church, signposted to the fourteenth-century Pont de Prade. Just after the fine, curving old bridge the road bends right to follow the right bank of the Dourbie through the fields the monks once tilled. More recently, someone has placed a succession of seats for weary travellers at intervals beside the road. Just as you enter the next village, St Jean-du-Bruel, there is an old humpbacked packhorse bridge across the Dourbie. The rambling village has a range of useful shops and restaurants.

The next stage of the route, up the south-east side of the gorges of the Dourbie, leaves the main D999 at the east end of the village, signposted 'Gorge supérieure de la Dourbie', D114. This proved to be a very quiet road – we saw scarcely half a dozen cars the whole Sunday afternoon. The area is less developed for tourism than the nearby Tarn gorges, with far fewer visitors.

The climbing starts almost at once, with about the steepest gradient of the whole route for a kilometre or so up to the hamlet of Le Viala, where there appeared to be a party involving the whole village. The gorge soon opens up on the left as a wide V-shaped valley, quite different in character from the limestone gorges. The overwhelming greenness is everywhere. The bottom of the valley, beside the tumbling Dourbie, is filled with chestnut trees and conifers, while brilliant patches of yellow broom crown the frequent pinkish rocky outcrops.

The road is very winding, coming out from time to time onto rocky promontories overlooking the ever-deepening valley. It was on this climb, as bees and hover-flies flitted from flower to flower, that we came to appreciate how loud the insect world can be when heard from the silent bicycle. We watched fascinated for several minutes as a couple of hummingbird hawk-moths hovered round some scabious and cornflowers, each skilfully directing its long proboscis into the very bottom of the tiny flowers to tap the nectar.

About half-way up the climb there is disconcertingly a stretch of downhill to the few huddled houses

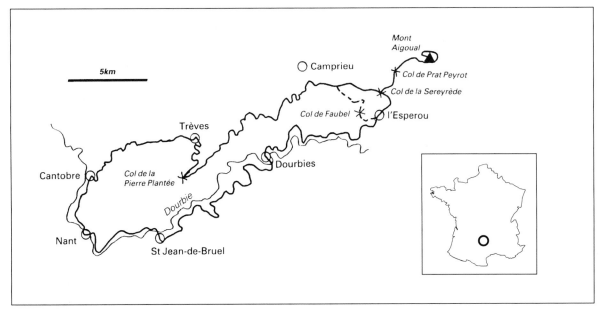

of Les Crozes-Basses, before the gentle climb begins again. This road is a delight – narrow, twisting this way and that, with occasional views down the valley of range upon range of blue hills in the distance. Finally there is a short downhill run to cross the river and then a brief climb into the village of Dourbies.

Turn right onto the D151, which continues to follow the river, this time on the right bank. The river is out of the gorge now, merely nestled at the foot of its little valley, which has become quite pastoral. Everything is still very green: it is a common feature of the hills of southern France that the trees and plants become more northern, more English, as you climb. The ash trees that lined the road from time to time were still in early spring green, while the lush fields led up to beechwoods capping the hills. Familiar flowers such as buttercups and forget-me-nots began to appear in the meadows. At one point cows were splashing through the stream on their way up to the farm, their bells tinkling softly across the valley.

The road continues to rise gently to the junction with the D48. Another 1km brings you to the cross-country ski centre of L'Espérou and a curving climb through pinewoods to the Col de la Sereyrède (1300m). This is the watershed: the streams of the Bonheur and the Dourbie to the west eventually join rivers to the Atlantic, while the Hérault in its impressive gorge to the east flows directly to the Mediterranean. Here you are on the upper slopes of Mont Aigoual and the meteorological observatory at the top can be seen through gaps in the trees.

Until about the 1890s, centuries of felling the beech trees for charcoal-burning and sheep grazing had left Mont Aigoual bare and prone to rapid erosion, floods and landslides during times of heavy rain. The present wooded appearance of the mountain is due to the local head of the Eaux et Forêts, Georges Fabre, who supervised the replanting of mixed woodland to restore its former look. He also established an arboretum on the slopes of the mountain, L'Hort du Dieu, which is reached by a ridable track to the right. Fabre's work is celebrated by a roadside memorial.

The road clings to the flank of the hillside above the Hérault valley, with the turns and twists of the road to Montpellier showing as a jagged zigzag cut through the trees far below. The woodlands, until now mostly beech but here a mixture of cedar and pines, begin to thin out. The gradient steepens a little for the last 2km or so as the road describes almost a complete circle round the hill to reach the top of the mountain.

From the viewing tower with its table d'orientation at the top there is a remarkable panorama. Even if we could not quite see Mont Blanc or the Maladetta on the Spanish border – which it is

Near Nant in the valley of the Dourbie.

claimed are visible on exceptionally clear winter days – the view took in Mont Ventoux to the east and stretched right down to the blue line of the Mediterranean to the south.

There are two routes back down the mountain, but the one we followed on the way up is also the more attractive on the way down. Once at the Col de Sereyrède, you can either turn right directly on the D986 or return through L'Espérou as we did, turning right onto the D986ᴬ to pass over the very pleasant Col de Faubel (1285m). This short climb winds gently up past banks covered in dwarf heathers to come out at an almost Chiltern summit amidst beechwoods.

The D986 and D986ᴬ merge about 3km farther on; after another 2km or so turn left onto the D710. The road is signed to Trèves by way of the Chemin du Suquet. By now it was early evening and we were a little dispirited when the road began to climb once more through the beechwoods. According to all our calculations, not to say hopes, it should have been downhill. It continues to climb – not at all steeply – for about 5km to the foot of the hill spur of Le Suquet.

There had been one or two hints by glimpses through the trees earlier on that the deep cleft of the

Trévezel was opening up to the right, but we were quite unprepared for the view that greeted us as we swept round the first bend of the descent. Below us was the tree-lined gorge, but on the far side was the remarkable round hill on which the tiny village of Comeiras is perched, surrounded by rings of terracing picked out by the low sun.

From here the descent becomes more rapid and exciting until, after a little rise, you reach the D151. Turn right to the Col de la Pierre Plantée, 828m – fortunately a col you reach downhill – and turn right again on the D47 for Trèves. This is a superb downhill stretch, twisting and open – one of the highlights of the whole route. Be sure to look back at the rounded contour of the hillside, with its little rows of poplars placed with supreme artistry.

You enter the attractive village of Trèves by the bridge over the Trèvezel and shortly afterwards bear left down the lower part of the Gorge du Trèvezel on the D157, signposted Millau. This is a fine and almost miniature gorge, with interesting twists and turns on one of which a very small girl was herding goats home for the night as we passed. Oddly, the Trèvezel was quite dry where we crossed it, although there had been plenty of water higher up at Trèves. Since this is about the junction of the granite and

In the valley of the upper Dourbie between Laupies and l'Esperou.

limestone it seems likely that it goes underground for a spell in dry weather.

This little gorge saves one of its best bits until last, the unexpected sight of the village of Cantobre, its houses and church apparently carved from the living rock, right at the end of the valley. The name Cantobre is apt indeed: it derives from an exclamation in the local dialect: *quant obra!* (what a remarkable work!).

Just past Cantobre the road dips to cross the Dourbie and then rejoins the D991 on which you turn left for Nant. Contentedly, if a little wearily, we ate our camp supper watching the sunset first turn the cliffs above Cantobre a deep gold and then a more and more vivid pink. This was a day to savour.

Approximate totale distance   96km
Maps   Michelin 80, panels 15 and 16; IGN 58, 65; also special IGN National Park sheet 354 at 1:100,000
Regions   Midi-Pyrénées, Languedoc-Roussillon
Départements   12-Aveyron, 30-Gard, 48-Lozère
Accommodation   Nant, St Jean-du-Bruel, Dourbies, L'Espérou
Access   By road, N9 to Millau, then D991; by rail to Millau
Restrictions: The highest roads on this route may be obstructed by snow from November to May

MORVAN

The Morvan is in many ways similar to the Haut Limousin, but if the immediate impression of the Limousin was one of greenness, then the first and abiding image of the Morvan is both green and white – the white of the ubiquitous Charollais cattle. Like the Limousin, the Morvan has quite a high rainfall – between 100 and 180cm, depending on altitude, com-

parable with the Welsh borders, or much of Ireland. The summits are said to have rain or snow on half the days of the year. The Morvan is an ancient granite massif, so waters soon gather in the hollows. There are many natural small or moderate-sized pools and several artificial or enlarged lakes.

Something like half of the Morvan is forest. Formerly, beech, oak, hornbeam and birch predominated, but over-felling in earlier centuries left parts bare and barren; these have now been extensively replanted with conifers, particularly in the south. The forest has been worked since at least the tenth century and still is today. We passed many large piles of logs, in places like walls enclosing the road. Much of the wood is destined for charcoal making, which is nowadays an industrial semi-closed distillation, also collecting the useful volatiles from the wood – principally methanol and acetic acid. There

Camping beside the Étang de Goulot at Lormes.

are several large plants in the region.

The cleared agricultural parts of the Morvan are very much bocage, with the little square fields divided by hedges, fences or sometimes rough dry walls of granite blocks. The farming is mixed – in some cases *very* mixed: we saw at one point cows, goats, pigs, turkeys and geese together in one field! But by far the most numerous and most visible, though, are the white Charollais cattle, for Charolles itself is not far away.

The Morvan has never been really prosperous, with its inhabitants often the butt for the wit of the more affluent Burgundians, with their vineyards and fertile valleys. The Morvandiaux have had to make a hard living from a not very yielding soil. At one time even, in the nineteenth century, the region was best known for specializing in the provision of wet-nurses in large numbers for the babies of fashionable Parisiennes. Even now, with tourism expanding, the Morvan remains largely an undiscovered and quiet region – a near paradise for cyclists, in fact!

The routes lie largely in the Morvan Natural Regional Park. For our base for this late September exploration we chose the little town of Lormes, about 30km south of Avallon, and situated on the western edge of the Morvan. The tightly packed town is dominated by its modern church, high on the top of the small hill on whose flank the town is built. From the top there are wide views to the south and west of wooded summits stretching away into the distance. We camped about 1km outside the town, beside the little lake of the Étang du Goulot. Here the early mornings were still and quiet and we had herons and a darting kingfisher as our breakfast companions.

Two routes are described: the first goes east to St Brisson, while the second heads south for the highest parts of the Morvan.

East to St Brisson

There is a quite complicated one-way system in Lormes (which not everybody seems to abide by) but we eventually found our way out east by the D6. After about 2km, the route forks left on the D150, through the hamlet of Sonne and then up through the forest, occasionally passing between walls of piled logs.

The woods appeared very fruitful at that time of year: there was the constant plopping of acorns from above, and it was impossible to tread without crunching them underfoot, while chestnuts abounded. There was also a notable variety of forest smells from the resinous pines and the acid chestnuts.

Once over the brow of the hill, there was a brief view of the Lac de Chaumeçon followed by a quick drop to Plainefas. The route continues over the dam and round by the road that follows the contour of the wooded eastern shore of the lake. Or what would have been the shore: after a dry summer the water level was very low, some 10 to 15m below the mark of the normal shoreline.

From Brassy to Dun-les-Places is very much bocage country. The road is rolling rather than hilly (the climbs in the northern part of the Morvan are steady without being particularly difficult) but for all that the approach to Dun-les-Places, with its broad straight street, is rather like the entry to a remote alpine village. After Duns, you come quite unexpectedly on a very wide road, the D236, which sweeps in a broad curve down to the valley.

From its junction with the D6, where you go right, the road climbs beside the tumbling stream of the Cure, for all the world with its brownish waters, granite boulders and waterfalls like a Welsh or Scottish mountain stream, lined by small beeches and birches. Half-way up the climb, a turning to the left leads to a deer reserve, which has hides from which the animals can be watched.

About 3km after the top of the climb is the Maison du Parc, an information centre for the Regional Natural Park and its activities, set in a walled deer park that you pass on the way down to St Brisson. In the same grounds there is also a Resistance museum – like many not easily penetrated forest areas, the Morvan was very much a Resistance centre from 1940–45. This meant that it was often the scene of brutal reprisals, and several of the villages – notably Montsauche – have been rebuilt after being largely destroyed.

The route forks right at the south end of the village on a narrow, winding road that climbs up into the forest again. Worth noting for a not-so-good day is that there is a picnic shelter at the top. From here the road (D977^{BIS}) sweeps down through woodland and bocage below the village of Gouloux. Just after a long right-hand bend there is a path leading to the waterfall of the Saut de Gouloux.

With the multitude of little climbs and descents you could be forgiven for not thinking so, but the road from here all the way back to Lormes is

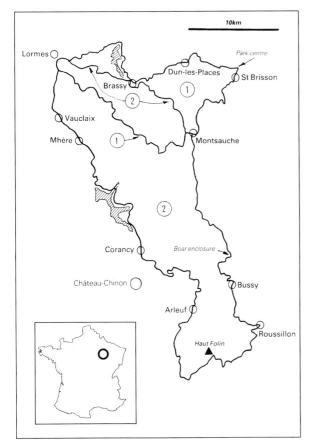

effectively a ridge road. Although it dips to streams on occasion it does not lose a great deal of height overall, and offers views to right and left over the valleys. Just after you fork right for Lormes on the D17 there is a particularly broad view to the west, where we watched the beams of the low sun chasing through the evening clouds before hurrying to beat the fading light back to Lormes, spurred on by the mouth-watering cooking smells hanging in the still evening air as we passed isolated cottages and the occasional hamlet.

South to the Haut Folin

This route leaves Lormes south on the D944. The first stretch is a very pleasant downhill run, which begins through forest and then emerges into bocage country, with every little field seemingly grazed by the white Charollais.

The first village of Vauclaix is marked by a fine steepled church on the hillside above it, on the right of the road. The route continues over the crossroads beyond the village and then forks left after about 1km, by a prominent pine tree. This road is sign-posted to Mhère, which proved to be a pleasantly laid-out village, set around a sunny square.

Here once again a prominent war memorial brought home, as it does in so many small villages of rural France, the tremendous loss of life in the 1914–18 war. Even in a village this size, with perhaps 400 inhabitants today, there are over 60 names on the memorial: virtually a lost generation, and lost in a conflict that must have seemed very far away.

From Mhère the road is very winding and quite up-and-down, through alternating bocage and woodland, as well as several small hamlets. Just after one of these, Liez, the road climbs through some woodland and then after a corner suddenly opens up with a striking panorama over the artificial lake of Pannessière-Chaumard ahead and another smaller one to the west. The gradients on these roads are noticeably steeper than in the northern part of the Morvan.

The route turns left just before the dam at the foot of the lake to follow its picturesque east side. This too is quite a hard little road, winding in and out of the many arms and inlets of the lake, but rewarding with views over the water and open sunny woodland. Once again the water level was very low; only later did we learn that in dry seasons some of these lakes are 'sacrificed' to ensure that the level of the Lac des Settons to the east, developed for water sports, is maintained.

From the head of the lake a relatively easy road leads into Corancy and then straight over the D37 onto the D500. This is a superbly scenic winding road, through grove after grove of fruitful chestnuts, with an impressive view to the west over wooded hills and the valley of the Yonne to Château-Chinon, magnificently sited on its ridge.

In Arleuf, the route turns right on the main D978 and at the end of the village forks left on the D177, another up and down road, through alternating forest and bocage. At Le Châtelet, where you join the valley of the infant Yonne, follow the signs for Haut Folin. The road begins to climb steadily, and about 3km after the hamlet of Les Carnés, the route turns left onto a forest road, signposted Haut Folin. This is quite steep at first but then levels out.

At the end of the forest road, turn left on the

D500, which runs along the Haut Folin ridge. This is the highest part of the Morvan, with Haut Folin itself just edging over the 900m mark. Rather disappointingly there is no viewpoint along the ridge, which is part of a larger plateau only a little lower than the highest point. This was one of the areas denuded of forest in earlier centuries and now extensively planted with pines and spruce.

From the top follow the forest road down to La Croisette. The road surface is very mixed, alternating between immaculate tarmac and some quite holey stretches. At La Croisette bear left on the D179 through the rocky and wooded miniature gorges of the Canche.

At the broad main D978 go almost straight over, left-and-right, to Roussillon-en-Morvan and then left on the outskirts of the village to Le Pommoy. This does not avoid the climb – in fact there is quite a steep pitch up into the forest – but it does avoid making it on the soul-destroying three-lane D978, and offers the bonus of some fine views of the wooded ridge of Haut Folin. From Le Pommoy you inevitably have to follow the main road for a little under 1km before taking the first right turn, D388, signposted Anost. This winding road drops out of the forest into bocage again.

In the hamlet of Bussy, about 5km along this road, the route turns left on a forest road, signposted to the Maquis monument and the Enclos du Sanglier (wild boar enclosure). This narrow road climbs to the monument through open woodland and heath, with extensive views to the south as the road twists and turns. From the monument the road bears right, down a great avenue of conifers, to the D2. It would be possible to reach this point by way of the village of Anost; this would avoid some, but by no means all, of the climbing.

At the D2 junction, on the left, is the wild boar enclosure. A large tract of forest has been fenced off, so that the boar live in natural conditions, although with some obvious restriction on their wanderings. We saw several rooting among the autumn undergrowth, but the scene was largely stolen by a bolder animal who had presumably come to realize that visitors might represent a meal.

The D2 climbs more steadily through the Forêt d'Anost, becoming the D17 as it crosses the boundary back into the département of Nièvre. From here the route is mostly forested to Montsauche-les-Settons. As a variant from the return route of the first loop, bear right on the D235 after climbing the high street of the village, at a wayside cross beside a

Charollais cattle near le Chêne.

Looking westwards from above le Gravet at sunset.

line of trees, through Bonin to Brassy. This is a very attractive little road, less forested than some of the earlier ones. From Brassy, the D6 drops to cross a limb of the Lac de Chaumeçon and then climbs quite firmly to a summit of 624m before the final run down to Lormes.

Approximate total distances   East to St Brisson 74km; South to the Haut Folin 139km
Maps   Michelin 65, panels 16 and 17, and 69, panels 6 and 7; IGN 28 and 36; also special IGN Regional Park sheet 306 at 1:100,000
Region   Burgundy
Départements   58-Nièvre, 71-Saône et Loire
Accommodation   Lormes, Montsauche-les-Settons, Château-Chinon
Access   By road, N6 to Avallon, then D944; by rail to Saulieu, Corbigny
Restrictions   None quoted, but there would seem to be every chance of snow on the Haut Folin from December to at least March

On the Route des Crêtes, Grand Canyon du Verdon.

LE GRAND CANYON DU VERDON

For once there is not a hint of poetic licence, nor of the hyperbole that imagines Switzerland in the low hills of Normandy, in describing the narrow gorge of the middle reaches of this mountain river as the 'Grand Canyon' of the Verdon. Quite simply, it is immense: the deepest canyon in Europe. On the face of it, the route the river takes is utterly perverse, digging deep through a high plateau while there would have been far easier exits through other valleys. Physical geographers suggest that the only explanation must be one of habit: some 30 or 40 million years ago, the Verdon, already an established and firmly flowing river across a limestone plain, merely continued to follow the same course, cutting its bed deeper and deeper as the earth movements that formed the Alps slowly but inexorably lifted the limestone up into an elevated plateau. The result is that the canyon, at its narrowest no wider than six metres at river level, is now an awesome cleft flanked by sheer cliffs up to 700m high. It was not until 1905 that the gorge was first traversed on foot and the low level tourist path – named after Martel, who made that first passage – is still quite a strenuous undertaking. However, three roads, two of them quite recent, now make it possible to cycle a circuit of the rim of the gorge.

Just a few kilometres below the lower end of the gorge lies the dramatically sited village of Moustiers-Ste-Marie, an exquisite tumble of creamy limestone walls and pink roofs beneath a towering cliff. Behind, and high above, the chapel of Notre-Dame de Beauvoir perches in a cleft in the cliff. There has been a chapel on the spot since the fifth century and in mediaeval times it was a noted place of pilgrimage. The name it bore then – Notre Dame des Entreroches ('between the rocks') – describes it far better. We picked Moustiers as our base on our first visit, as do many other people each year, and camped where the southern and northern gorge roads meet. On a subsequent trip we picked La-Palud-sur-Verdon for our two-night stop and it proved an excellent choice.

The route follows an anticlockwise loop, taking in the southern side of the gorge first. This road, not too fancifully named the Corniche Sublime, dates only from 1947 and is a triumph of engineering. The route starts off easily enough, south on the D957, dropping gently to the shores of the Lac de Ste Croix, another recent addition to the landscape formed in 1975 by damming the Verdon. A brief climb over a headland and another drop to cross the Verdon bring you to the start of the gorge road proper, the D19. From the bridge there is a foretaste of what is to come with a view directly up the lower part of the gorge. From the junction the road begins to climb in earnest but relatively steadily in winding loops up to the narrow streets of the village of Aiguines, dominated by its great square château. The picturesque village was once a centre of wood-turning crafts, based on the abundant box trees in the surrounding forests; there is a small museum of wood-turning in the village. The next loop of the road climbs to bring you high above the village roofs with the expanse of the Lac de Ste Croix opening up behind.

About two more kilometres of steady climb through a rocky countryside dotted with low shrubs opens out to yield the first view down into the canyon; this is the Col d'Illoire, 954m. At this point the canyon is quite wooded with the river audible but hardly visible far below, certainly on the misty morning when we were first there. From the col the road drops a little at first and then climbs once more, rather away from the edge of the gorge, in a great horseshoe round the wooded Cirque de Vaumale to reach the highest point on this side of the river, 1,204m. The road on the opposite (north) side of the canyon is 400m lower, so there is a fascinating almost aerial view of the toy cars negotiating the hairpins below.

Back on the south side, there is now rather more woodland as the road falls away gently – with a couple of quite spectacular hairpins at one point – to emerge close to the edge of the cliffs, the Falaises des Cavaliers, here some 300 or 400m above the tumbled bed of the Verdon. Who the knights on horseback were to merit the cliffs taking their name seems to be a mystery, although there is a narrow path leading down into the depths of the canyon.

Looking ahead, the road seems to disappear into the rock and, sure enough, after about 100m of climb there are a couple of tunnels – the Tunnels du Fayet. The walls of the tunnels are pierced, so there is plenty of light, and these holes give spectacular views down the vertical cliff to the river far below, back to the great curve of the Falaises des Cavaliers along which the road passed, and across to the Route des Crêtes on the far side. On the damp April day that we first passed, the tunnel also gave us welcome shelter from a heavy shower that swept a curtain of hail and cold rain across the gorge. We took advantage of the stop and the shelter to have lunch – only to discover that the essential cutlery was back at the camp site. Desperate and hungry cyclists are nothing if not resourceful and tyre-levers were soon cleaned and polished for the job – which may or may not be a useful practical tip.

Once through the tunnels, the road heads inland again in a marvellous freewheeling swoop down to the graceful bridge over the river Artuby, now something of a centre for bungee-jumping, followed by a short climb to the Balcons de la Mescla, some 250m above the swirling confluence of the Artuby and the Verdon. (The Languedoc word *mescla*, meaning a mixing or merging, in this case of waters, crops up in several place names in the region.) From here the road climbs steadily out onto the barer rocky grasslands of the limestone plateau.

About 9km after the Pont d'Artuby, and 3km or so after the highest point on this section, the route leaves the D71 to turn left onto the D90, which plunges swiftly down a twisting little road to the perched village of Trigance, dominated by its sixteenth-century château, now a hotel. Another twisting drop brings you over the stream of the Jabron and up to the D955. Six more kilometres of winding, wooded but fairly level road through a miniature pass lead to the Pont de Soleils, where the route crosses the Verdon to its north bank.

Turn left on the D952. After staying near river level for a short distance this road begins to climb steadily away once more. Close to, the limestone cliffs that had looked quite a uniform warm creamy grey colour from a distance reveal a whole range of subtle warm red, gold and even blue-grey colorations, with – in places – even brighter colours. There are a couple of short tunnels on this stretch

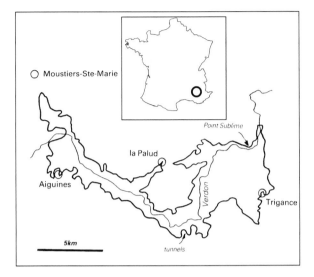

before you reach the path that leads to the viewpoint of the Point Sublime, though as a hungry cyclist you might be more interested in the charms of the Auberge du Point Sublime.

The viewpoint looks out over the impressively narrow eastern entry to the canyon. For a short distance after this the road drops inland, away from the edge of the canyon, to cross the Baou, one of the Verdon's tributaries, tumbling down from the hills to the north. The next 4km are a steady 200m climb up to the village of La Palud-sur-Verdon. About 1.5km before La Palud, the spectacular loop of the Route des Crêtes, D23, turns off to the left.

This 23km circuit, completed only in 1973, climbs round the northern rim of the canyon, at the point where the cliffs are highest, and leads back to La Palud. The start is gentle enough, through lavender fields that betray that this rugged landscape is really part of Provence, then through dwarf woodland. There is quite a bit of climbing involved: the start of the loop is at about 850m, while the highest point is near 1,300m, with a couple of short tunnels near the top. However, the views from the numerous viewpoints make the effort worth while.

From the third of these there is the most dramatic view. East, the narrow entry of the gorge is laid out before you and above it – a feature we had not noticed when we passed under it – the tiny perched village of Rougon, apparently glued to a rock above the Point Sublime. Immediately to the right the vertical wall of the canyon plunges 700m to the valley floor.

The higher viewpoints nearer the top look out across the canyon to the bare rock wall pierced by the square 'windows' of the Tunnels de Fayet on the south side of the ravine. The road, after dropping sharply, climbs back through orchards and lavender fields once more to La Palud.

La Palud-sur-Verdon lies on a small cultivated plateau, quite a contrast to the wild ruggedness all around. It is also by far the largest village on the whole route. The 19km from La Palud back to Moustiers-Ste-Marie are relatively gentle and rolling, with the overall trend downhill once you are over the Col d'Ayen, 1032m and about 3.5km after La Palud. There are several fine viewpoints out over the gradually lowering canyon until you emerge for the last few kilometres into a Provençal landscape of lavender fields and olive groves.

Approximate total distance   126km

Maps   Michelin 81, panels 17 and 18, or 84, panels 6 and 7; IGN 61; also a large-scale strip map of the canyon by A. Monier obtainable locally

Region   Provence-Alpes-Côte d'Azur

Départements   04-Alpes de Haute Provence, 83-Var

Accommodation   Moustiers-Ste-Marie, Trigance, Point Sublime, La Palud-sur-Verdon

Access   By road, D952 to Moustiers, N85 ('Route Napoléon') to Castellane, then D952, or D955 from Draguignan; by rail to Manosque, Draguignan or Les Arcs (junction for Draguignan)

Restrictions   The southern Corniche Sublime and the Route des Crêtes are sometimes blocked by snow from December to March

11

Moderate Mountains

THE LUBÉRON

As you approach from the south or west, the long hazy blue bulk of the Lubéron, south-east of Avignon, dominates the skyline. It is the southernmost of the great limestone ridges of this part of Provence and, although the crest of the western part of the range is only about 700m, it rears over the plains and foothills – dominating them much as Mont Ventoux in its turn dominates the Plateau of Vaucluse to the north.

This part of the world has long been one of our favourites for an early season visit – at Easter or even earlier. In March the weather can be like a warm English May, and the early colour of the almond blossom, together with the leafiness of the evergreen oaks and olives, make early spring one of the best times to explore southern Provence.

One of the attractions of the Lubéron for cyclists is that the ridge road along the Petit Lubéron, the western half, has for some years now been closed to cars, giving over 15km of completely quiet and traffic-free riding on the roof of the world. To get to any roof, though, you have to climb, and the ascent of the western end of the ridge is quite a stiff climb – real low-gear stuff – as you gain about 500m in about 7km, an average of 7 per cent or 1-in-14, with some pitches a good deal steeper, which

Bonnieux, from the upper village.

The village of Roussillon.

The route leaves Bonnieux to the west on the D3, a turn from the lower village leading through a luminous avenue of acacias to a valley of orchards and small fields, followed by a stiff little climb up to the next perched village of Lacoste. Many of the streets in this intricate little place are no more than paths and we very nearly got lost following them. The now ruined château belonged at one time to the de Sade family. The notorious Marquis was lord of the manor here for some thirty years, although he actually spent only his last four years of freedom at Lacoste.

On leaving the village follow the uphill road signposted to the château, bearing left at the top on the D109 towards Ménerbes. This road drops between terraces – probably vineyards now given over to orchards and olives, at the season when we passed a very green valley indeed.

At the crossroads at the foot of the hill, continue almost straight across to climb through yet another acacia avenue into Ménerbes. This – like so many of the other perched villages – has traces of its former

has justified the route's place in the 'moderate mountain' category.

Most of the route lies within the boundaries of the Regional Park of the Lubéron. By way of contrast and easier relief, the second loop of the route visits the colourful village of Roussillon to the north.

We chose as the base for our Easter exploration the perched village of Bonnieux, about half-way up the northern slopes of the ridge. This honey-coloured, attractive and fair-sized village – or villages, since the upper and lower halves are nearly separate – clings tightly to its rocky knoll, rising in tiers of narrow streets and tall houses. From below the slope looks almost too steep to be climbed. Bonnieux has a fair range of shops, hotels and restaurants. An alternative centre and starting point, without much modification of the route, would be the small town of Apt, 12km to the north-east.

The ochre cliffs and quarries at Roussillon.

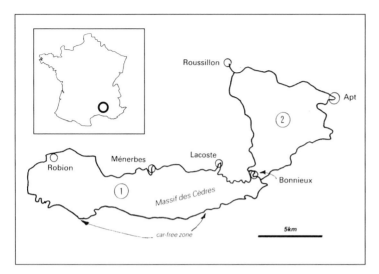

flowing conduit, bringing water from the river Durance to irrigate the dry plain towards Carpentras, which is consequently now a fruitful market gardening area.

Where the D31 makes a staggered left-and-right crossing of the canal, turn left onto a minor road signposted Vidauque. After rather under 1km, the road turns sharply right (the turning to the up-market, second-home village of Vidauque goes left) to begin the Lubéron climb. Note that from here on this is a one-way road so that you should not meet any traffic coming down.

The first kilometre or so is through pine woods – with one very steep section of 16 per cent, 1-in-6. The road then comes out into much barer, open, grey limestone country. The contrast with the greener north face is stark: this is an arid area of low scrub and glaring limestone pavement with a Mediterranean aroma of chalk-loving herbs – mostly thyme and rosemary.

The next part of the climb is hard with a number of short hairpins. On most modern roads the gradient levels out at the bends; on this one it does not, but since the road is one-way you can at least choose to go round the shallower gradient on the outside of the bend. Overall it is quite a tough climb, and at the top of the last large hairpin you have an aerial view of the bends you have traversed. Fine views extend north to Mont Ventoux and to the west along the chain of the Alpilles to the Rhône valley. There is one more steep pitch on the straight climb to the top below the radio mast.

Here the motor road goes straight on – a spectacular descent if you ever have occasion to make it – but to get on to the car-free ridge road you go past the barrier to the left. This road is banned to through motor traffic but you may encounter farm or forestry vehicles on it. It continues to climb from the pass through dwarf evergreen oaks and then out onto real Western-style country of limestone bluffs and weird limestone shapes. You almost expect suntanned heroes on horses to emerge, galloping across the landscape in hot pursuit of villains.

Once more the climb is quite steep in places until you reach the virtual summit on the Hautes Plaines. At the time we passed there were many spring

fortifications, and was bitterly fought over during the sixteenth-century wars of religion, holding out at one stage for a fifteen-month siege.

Leave the village by the D3 down to the junction with the D188. Here the route goes left, following for a stretch the waymarked cycle route linking Apt and Cavaillon (the sign is on the end of a barn and not too obvious when you approach from this direction). This road climbs round through orchards for about 2.5km until, at a right-hand bend, a very narrow road signed as part of the cycle route bears left. Follow this winding and climbing road through woods and orchards to join the D178 just below the imposing ramparts of Oppède-le-Vieux. The road is quite hilly: they obviously expect cyclists not to object to the odd climb or two.

There are very fine views of Oppède as you toil up to it and, looking back, of the ravined northern scarp of the Lubéron. The village, dominated by its stark ruined castle, was for a time virtually derelict but has now become something of a centre for writers and artists.

Continue downhill past the village and then left through Maubec to the main D2. Turn left here: unfortunately it is not possible to avoid about 1.5km of the main road, through the village of Robion. This is the last place with shops or reliable bars, and there is the stiff climb of the Lubéron to follow.

At the west end of the village, turn left on the route (D31) signposted to Taillades. Continue below Taillades and bear round to the left beside the Canal de Carpentras. This is not a navigable canal but a

flowers in evidence – rock roses, a miniature narcissus, dwarf irises and grape hyacinths. In summer, much of this upland is a shimmering sea of soft, long grass waving in the Mediterranean breeze.

Before long the road meets the first of the replanted forest, some pine and some cedar, which line the route for perhaps 6km. There is evidence that cedars grew on the Lubéron 20,000 years ago, and following some centuries of denudation a programme of replanting is under way, using mainly the Atlas cedar from north Africa. The current largest specimens date from the end of the nineteenth century; towards the end of the car-free part, the road passes through what is almost a dark green tunnel of these sombre trees.

At the end of the forest, the road emerges into open heath country, with gorse, broom and dwarf oaks, quite a contrast to the bare and arid slopes at the western end. There are tremendous views to the north over the Vaucluse with the whole of the plateau laid at your feet, together with quite spectacular aerial perspectives of Bonnieux and Lacoste. It is a superb freewheel down to the D36, where you turn left for Bonnieux.

The second, smaller and easier, loop from Bonnieux crosses the valley of the Calavon to the north and pays a visit to the ochre country of Roussillon.

The route leaves Bonnieux up the Lourmarin road (D36) and turns left at the top of the slope on the D232 to the Col du Pointu. This road runs through open heathland, again with gorse, broom and limestone wild flowers, interspersed with patches of dwarf oak.

At the Col du Pointu (499m), turn right again on the D232 to the junction with the D113. The route turns left through avenues of young beech and birch – past the first lavender field we had seen on this route – followed by a fast freewheel down into Apt. Apt is a bustling cathedral town, with a road layout that ought to be easy to follow but is not.

Leave Apt west on the N100 for about 3.5km, and then bear right on the D201 to its junction with the D4. There is a cycle lane on this road as it climbs up through vineyards and olive groves (and into a quite strong mistral if it is blowing). After about 2km the route bears left on the D104 through a pleasant poplar avenue, then climbs steadily up towards Roussillon village.

There are soon signs of red sands in the pinewoods to the right, but this does not prepare you for the brilliant yellows, golds and oranges of the ochre cliffs at Roussillon itself. Quarrying has left the village spectacularly perched on a cliff. Extraction of the ochre, which is used as a pigment, has moved a kilometre or two away, and there is now a trail round the old quarries, off a small dead-end road to the right as you enter the village. It is possible to ride up a farther 200m or so as far as the start of the trail but bikes can really go no farther.

From Roussillon it is a rapid drop on the D108 back down to the valley of the Calavon. Just after you cross the main N100, the road goes over a hump-backed three-arched Roman bridge, the Pont Julien. One of the features of its design is the piercing of the arch supports to allow flood waters to pass without too much resistance; this has obviously worked as it is still there, and in use, after 2000 years. Late twentieth-century traffic lights regulate vehicles across its narrow span. From here it is a relatively gentle climb up through olive groves and small fields back to Bonnieux.

Approximate total distances: The Petit Lubéron 60km; Roussillon 41km
Maps Michelin 81, panels 13 and 14; IGN 60 and 67
Region Provence-Alpes-Côte d'Azur
Départements 84-Vaucluse
Accommodation Bonnieux, Ménerbes, Robion, Apt, Roussillon
Access By road, N100 from Avignon, then D36; by rail to Avignon, Cavaillon; by air to Marseille-Marignane

THE BEAUJOLAIS

Clever marketing and the dubious publicity of the Beaujolais Nouveau dashes in mid November have ensured that the Beaujolais is, to Britons, probably the best-known wine area in France. Many too have read the light-hearted novels of Gabriel Chevalier in which the inhabitants of his not entirely fictional community of Clochemerle live sunburnt lives of village romance and intrigue.

All caricature has to be based on fact, and the wine-growing part of the Beaujolais really is a sun-drenched rolling landscape of vines. But there is more to it than that, and the northern and western

This proved to be a good choice for exploring the north-western route, but we found that we had to move farther south-east to reconnoitre the vignoble rides, and the second two routes start and finish in Quincié-en-Beaujolais. As with all circular trips the starting point is largely a matter of choice, and it would be quite feasible to start and finish all the routes, with no more than minor adjustment, from Beaujeu – the little town that gives the Beaujolais its name.

The Tour of the Five Cols

The route leaves Matour by the D211, which is a turning off the market square in the middle of the village. There is a short drop into the valley, then, as the road begins to climb again, you fork right off the D211 to climb through a wood. Just over the brow of the hill it is best to bear right up a slight slope past a cross; this road then contours round into St Bonnet-des-Bruyères. The left fork would also eventually take you there, but would involve losing some height, followed by extra climbing to recover it.

St Bonnet is a larger settlement than you might expect from the map, with several small shops. From here the route is signposted to Montsols, to begin

part of the area is fine cycling country, too – a land of fertile valleys and forests before you come to the edge of the hills with the vineyards spread below you. The division is geological: the hills are of old crystalline igneous rocks, while the slopes of the southern vineyards are more recent limestones. Subtleties of the soils derived from the older rocks give the wines produced in the different localities their different characteristics.

Although the summits of the Monts du Beaujolais are not very high (only just over 1,000m), and while the highest point on the route is no more than 762m, there are some quite long mountain-style climbs. One or two, on minor roads, are fairly steep, so these routes have – arbitrarily, you might argue – been placed in the 'moderate mountain' rather than the 'hilly' category. You will certainly find some use for those low gears in places.

Since we were travelling from the north, we made our initial base in the village of Matour, which lies at the point where the Beaujolais, the Charollais and the Mâconnais all meet, about 30km west of Mâcon.

St Jacques-des-Arrêts.

Steeple decoration at Germolles-sur-Grosne.

In the valley of the Mauvaise near Emmeringes.

with on the D5, which soon begins to climb gently. Continue straight on at the crossroads of St Bonnet-le-Plat, now on the D52, and at the next junction in pine woods bear left on the D43, still towards Montsols.

From here there is a steady and not at all hard gradient to the first col, the Col du Champ Juin (742m), followed by a fast winding descent down into Montsols. To the left the church of St Christophe-en-Montagne dominates the valley of the Grosne Occidentale, gleaming brilliantly white in the autumn sunshine, while to the right the highest point in the Beaujolais, Mont St Rigaud (1,012m), shows up as a conical peak.

After Montsols – the largest village for some way, and certainly the last with shops – there is a short climb, gaining only about 80m of height, to the next pass, the Col de Crie (622m). Notable at the top is a glass-sided picnic shelter that looked as though it would make quite a cosy stop on a not-too-good day. There is also a comprehensive tourist information board listing local facilities.

The route turns left on the D23, then almost immediately right on the D32, which soon becomes the D18^{E}. This is a very picturesque road with some very good views to the right down a wooded valley,

giving the first glimpses of vines towards Beaujeu. It was while picnicking near here that we realized how mixed the woodland really was, with beech, oak, ash, birch, hazel and larch within a short distance of each other.

After climbing gently the road dips with some very sweeping bends to the eastern branch of the Grosne (the Grosne Orientale), then climbs easily again past the village of Avenas with its picturesque church tucked neatly into the crook of the bend. Next comes the third of the day's cols, the Col du Fût d'Avenas (762m) and just over the top the road begins to sweep down in a series of big loops towards the valley of the Saône.

About 1km after the col there is a viewpoint on the left of the road, known as La Terrasse, opposite a restaurant, giving a remarkable panorama over the vines of the Beaujolais. This edge of the hills marks the transition between the mountain and the wine-growing area. The autumnal day was too misty to see far beyond the Saône, but the table d'orientation suggests that on a clear day you can see away to the east as far as the snow-capped summits of Mont Blanc and the massif of the Pelvoux in the Alps. The villages of the Beaujolais are spread out below, with the twin-towered churches of St Joseph-en-Beaujolais and Régnié against the backdrop of Mont Brouilly particularly prominent among the linear patterns of vines.

Continue down the hill and about 1.5km below the viewpoint, the route turns left on the D18^E. This is a shelf road running between the low scrub on the hill to the left and vineyards to the right, overlooking Chiroubles. It is actually slightly downhill to the next col, the 550m Col de Durbize. (There is a French cycle touring organization known as the Club des Cent Cols – the Club of 100 Cols – with the obvious qualification for membership, though five of the cols have to be over 2000m. If you follow all the routes in this book you will be over half-way to qualifying – see the 'Useful Organizations' section.)

At the five-way crossroads that marks the col we turned left to follow a fine little road that winds in and out of the rows of vines, slightly up and down but not at all tough. The route skirts the next village of Vauxrenard to join the D32 at Les Brigands. This begins a quite serious climb: the slope is steady enough, but it carries on for some way, up past the last of the vineyards and into some pleasant forest to the Col de Fontmartin (640m). The drop into Ouroux is a splendid winding descent in the evening sunlight.

Ouroux is really quite a substantial village, the first since Montsols, with shops and restaurants. From here the route follows the D18 down the valley of the Grosne Orientale through fertile stock-raising country, past the hamlet of St Mamert.

One of the features of the churches in this valley is a gilded decoration of the tiled spires and there is a particularly colourful example at the next village, Germolles-sur-Grosne. The road becomes the D22 for a while after crossing the boundary into Saône-et-Loire, and then the D95 when the D22 branches off towards Tramayes. There is never any doubt, however, as to which is the valley road and you follow it to the outskirts of Pontcharas. There is a mini one-way system round the triangle marked on the map, which you have to follow before turning left to take the rolling road over to St Pierre-le-Vieux.

There is an alternative hillier route, with yet another col, from St Mamert to St Pierre-le-Vieux. This turns off the valley road, the D18, just before it crosses the Grosne Orientale, by the massive cruciform church on its prominent knoll, onto the D22^E. This is quite a resolute climb, although you gain only about 100m, to the Col de la Croix de l'Orme

(491m). Go straight over the crossroads at the top, which is unmarked, down a very steep descent from which there are superb views down into the valley, with the church at Trades in the foreground. It was in this valley, of the Grosne Occidentale, that we saw herons standing motionless in the fields beside the stream.

At the foot of the hill turn left on the D22 for St Christophe-en-Montagne, whose squat and solid tenth-century church is prominent on the hillside from several directions. It is not called 'en-Montagne' for nothing, and once more there is quite a climb up to the village. In St Christophe, turn right on the D52^E, which becomes the D211 at the boundary, down to St Pierre-le-Vieux.

Having arrived by either route, from St Pierre-le-Vieux follow the D45 west. The return to Matour branches off to the right on the D211 at a point where the spire of St Bonnet-les-Bruyères is prominent on the horizon. This road climbs once more – rather more than we needed at that stage of the day – before the welcome drop through the woods and then meadows to Matour.

Two More Cols – and Clochemerle

Quincié-en-Beaujolais is a pleasing warm-stone village set around a plane-shaded square (where the boulangerie/pâtisserie is something rather special). The route leaves the village south-west on the D9, which you leave after rather less than 1km at the top of a slight rise opposite a wayside cross that is not too prominent until you get to it.

The route turns left on a very narrow road that first drops to a copse of willows by a stream and then climbs – really quite steeply, mostly requiring bottom gear – through the vines to join the D72 at a straggle of houses above the village of Marchampt. It was on this road that we spotted a vivid green praying mantis at the roadside. The road itself sits on a little shelf above the vineyards and then climbs, after the last vine has been left behind – they go surprisingly high – into thin mixed woodland up towards the Col de la Croix-Rosier.

There are large clearings in places, with thin scrub and heathland plants, and from one of these towards the top of the climb there is a very fine view into the deep valley of one of the tributaries of the Vauxonne.

From the Col de la Croix-Rosier (721m) there is

no choice but to lose some height, which you do at what seems an alarming rate, down the road towards La Creuse and Le Perréon. After about 1.5km, and actually only 130m lower, there is a junction where we watched a young goatherd marshal her unruly charges onto the open slopes. The route turns right here and now climbs, much more gently this time, through thin woodland and open heath to the Col de Croix Montmain (737m).

The drop from here to Vaux-en-Beaujolais, through ash and chestnuts just beginning to show the tints of autumn, was probably the best on the whole route. It was down here that we surprised a couple of roe deer, which darted away into the undergrowth. After the long hot summer this was a particularly fecund autumn: every tree and shrub seemed to be loaded – rowan and elderberries, rose-hips, sloes with their pale, almost grape-like bloom, bursting chestnuts and the occasional walnut.

Suddenly in mid-swoop the road emerges into open vineyards, with views of the almost etched pattern, blued and softened by the afternoon mist, of lines of vines on the rolling hillsides. Below to the left are the starkly white villages of La Creuse and Le Perréon.

Soon there are signs to remind you that you are nearing the village that Gabriel Chevalier made famous as Clochemerle. Vaux-en-Beaujolais has certainly cashed in on the tales: you can even obtain an authentic Clochemerle Beaujolais, and, naturally, the famous public toilet is preserved (or, rather, appears to have been completely rebuilt) as a shrine or landmark.

The route continues up and down through vines all the way to the perched village of St Etienne-la-Varenne and then down to Odenas on the main D43. Here the route turns left and then right 3km later at La Poyebade to tackle the formidable-looking climb of Mont Brouilly, a great rounded outlier of the mountains, that towers above the vineyards.

In fact, the climb to the 483m summit is not too hard, and there are tremendous views over the whole of the Beaujolais. The chapel on top of Mont Brouilly is the site of a pilgrimage by wine growers on 8 September each year. The road down on the north-east side is rather steeper and rough in places; take care. At the bottom, a left turn past the water tower and through des Samsons brings you back to Quincié-en-Beaujolais.

Beaujolais Villages

This loop can be added to the previous route to make a longer circuit, or tackled separately. In either case, the start is at St Lager, near the foot of Mont Brouilly. From Quincié it means retracing the last few kilometres of the previous route to St Lager, or if descending from Mont Brouilly, turning right at the bottom.

Turn left in St Lager on the D68^E to cross the main D37 at the traffic lights in Cercié. With yet another of those unexplained mysteries of French road numbering, you are now on the D68, which you follow for about 1km, then fork left on the D153 just after a Mercedes service centre, towards Régnié. As you climb through the vines, the twin towers of the church at Régnié-Durette are prominent directly ahead.

On the outskirts of Régnié, at a wayside cross, turn right on the D9. This brings you into Villié-Morgon, following the sign for Centre ville along a fine chestnut avenue that was just turning to a brilliant yellow autumn colour at the time we passed. The village has an attractive centre and to leave it you follow the signs for Fleurie.

The vines of another of the Beaujolais Villages, Chiroubles, climb up the hillside to the left, while ahead lie Fleurie and to the right Moulin-à-Vent. On the still autumn day that we came this way, the smell of fermenting grapes was everywhere.

Although the monoculture of vines predominates, one of the attractive features of this little circuit is the way in which the road goes from time to time through copses, or along tree-lined avenues, weaving round the numerous small streams that run down from the spring-line at the foot of the hills. This end of the vignoble appears much more prosperous than the area round villages such as Vaux-en-Beaujolais farther south, with the neat white houses noticeably more opulent.

About 1km after Chénas, turn left at Les Deschamps on the D68. This stretch just after Deschamps is another pleasant tree-lined road, leading to the junction at Le Fief, where the route turns left on the D26. This, too, starts off lined by trees, this time alignments of poplars beside the small stream that borders the road.

After about 2km the road begins to climb in a series of steps to hoist itself onto a shelf running between the hills and the gentler vine-covered slopes; you are approaching the Col de Durbize (550m) by a rather more strenuous route than on the first tour. From this road there are superb views down onto the villages dotted below.

There is an unexpected parallel here with the crofting communities of western Scotland and Ireland. In both cases a single family can work, and needs for subsistence, a certain area of land, so that the individual houses are spread fairly regularly across the landscape. Here, too, just as in those harsher northern latitudes, the best places to build have been studied over the centuries. The result is a most pleasing harmony between houses and the landscape, with perfect little compositions framed at almost every turn.

From the Col de Durbize, the D26 drops slightly to cross the D18 at the Col du Truges (496m), before embarking on a very winding and up-and-down stretch past the twin-towered church of St Joseph-en-Beaujolais. In addition to the twin towers the church also has decorative tiling on the roofs of its two stumpy spires. The road now opens out to run through the middle of the vineyards – at one place there is even a superfluous signpost pointing to les Vignes – culminating in a dramatic looping drop towards Beaujeu against the backdrop of the blue valley leading up to the 895m summit of Mont Soubrant.

From the outskirts of Beaujeu – an interesting and compact town – it is possible to avoid quite a stretch of the D37 back to Quincié but turning left off it down a minor road signposted to Chapitalle à Panne and Le Grand Cour. After one or two early skirmishes with small industrial estates, this becomes a quiet narrow road running down the valley below the vineyards and beside a disused railway line. At Le Grand Cour continue on this valley road and do not follow the apparently major road up the hillside. The valley road eventually joins the D9 below Régnié. A right turn brings you up to the D37, which you cross in a right-and-left dogleg – by an auberge called Le Raisin du Beaujolais – back to Quincié.

Approximate total distances   Five cols circuit 70km; Clochemerle 53km; Beaujolais villages 59km
Maps   Michelin 69, panel 18, and 73, panels 9 and 10; IGN 43.
Regions   Rhône-Alpes, Burgundy
Départements   69-Rhône, 71-Saône et Loire

Accommodation   Matour, Montsols, Beaujeu, La Terrasse, Quincié-en-Beaujolais, Vaux-en-Beaujolais, Salles, St Lager, Villié-Morgon, Fleurie, Chénas, Julienas, Ouroux
Access   By road, N79 from Mâcon, then D987 to Matour; N6 from Mâcon, then D37 to Beaujeu; by rail to Mâcon, Villefranche-sur-Saône; by air to Lyon-Satelas

THE TARN AND JONTE GORGES

I first visited the Gorges of the Tarn in the late 1960s. It was only my second visit to France, and we swept up nearly the whole gorge from Millau to Ste Enimie in less than a single stifling July day. We were fitter then – and in an impetuously youthful hurry to make our rendezvous with the Tour de France. Although we were awed by the towering rocky prospects, and vowed to return, it was not until we came back to prospect the routes here that I saw the one-sided a view you get by merely following the valley floor. So the routes climb up out of the gorge from time to time, and these climbs are quite long low-gear ones. (This is why I place the routes in the 'moderately mountainous' classification. I am not the only one: when it passes this way, the Tour de France classes several of the climbs as 'first- or second-category'. The rewards are well worth the effort, though.)

This is emphatically limestone country, Jurassic limestone of much the same age as the Cotswolds and North Yorks Moors. As you follow the valley roads you naturally think of the area as gorges hemmed in by hills. However, structurally, it is a great limestone plateau – divided into separate *causses* by the deep channels of the Rivers Tarn and Jonte, and of several lesser streams. The rivers have been aided in their channelling task by the same geological movements fifty or sixty million years ago that raised the Alps and Pyrenees, among others, and led to cracking or faulting of the complex limestone slabs of the causses.

The causses, of which the route crosses two (the Causse Méjean and Causse Noir) are sparsely settled, rolling uplands, covered in woodland, scrub or meadow – an utter contrast to the wooded gorges. In high summer the gorges become very hot; probably May and June, or late September, would be the best times to visit, with the spring and autumn colours a bonus.

The Gorge de la Jonte, from the road from la Caze to Hures-la-Parade.

The Tarn at the Château de la Caze.

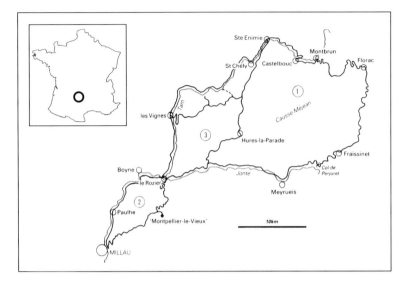

With such an embarrassment of riches one could make up a score of routes, and ten times as many variants. Those we chose are in two loops, with a third as a possible short cut, or giving a chance to follow the central part of the Tarn Gorge.

As the base for our exploration we picked a pleasant little camp site set in a former orchard in the village of Boyne, towards the foot of the main gorge, some 9km up from the N8 Millau–Sévérac trunk road at Aquessac. The pivotal point of the routes, as it were, is the larger village of Le Rozier some 5km farther upstream, where the River Jonte joins the Tarn and where there are bridges over both. It was the beginning of June and agreeably warm.

The Gorges de la Jonte, the Causse Méjean and the Upper Tarn

The first surprise is that Le Rozier has a one-way road system! To enter or leave by the bridge over the Tarn you have to follow the appropriate half of the anticlockwise loop. The straggling village, dominated by its more spectacular neighbour Peyreleau on the other side of the Jonte, has a fair range of shops, the last for quite some distance.

The road up the Jonte, the D996, starts as the main street and soon begins to climb gently east. The road runs some way above the river and before long there are spectacular views down to the tumbling water. This gorge is quite open, with the beige cliffs lying some way back from the small oaks, chestnuts

and occasional pines and birches that cover the gentler slopes of the bottom of the valley. It was below one of the cliffs, north of the road near the Belvedère des Terrasses de Trueil, that we joined for a few minutes a small group of bird-watchers. They had come to admire a soaring and gliding colony of vultures, recently and apparently successfully reintroduced to the area. Looking back down the valley, there is a fine glimpse of Peyreleau perched on its little bluff.

The road winds steadily up the gorge; the gradient is often barely perceptible, but all the way you are gaining height. It was along here that we first noticed the little noise that was to accompany us, on and off, for several days: the flutter of leaves in the roadside plants as lizards that had been basking close to the edge of the road scuttled away to hide. As you climb there is more woodland and the valley begins to close in until you reach the outskirts of the next village, Meyrueis, some 20km after Le Rozier.

Meyrueis is quite a bustling place, if a bit touristy, but certainly the last chance to stock up for 35 hilly kilometres. From Meyrueis there is also a possible out-and-home detour to the Grotte de Dargilan, one of the region's show caves.

About 2km beyond Meyrueis the valley opens up and you emerge onto a much barer, grassier landscape, with flowery meadows. Within a very short space the whole contour of the hillsides changes, becoming much more rolling and rounded, although there are still small natural rock terraces. Beyond the hamlet of Gatuzières, half hidden below the road, the climbing begins in earnest as the road winds up the side of the valley, climbing some 300m in about 5km to the summit of the Col de Perjuret, 1028m.

The run down the other side begins with a broad, open and very exhilarating sweeping run round the interlocking spurs of the hillside, the line of the road ahead traceable on the hillside by a succession of small bushy trees. The road becomes very twisting and the surface, without being rough, is quite wavy in places. Underlining the need for caution is a small piece of cycling history just above Fraissenet-de-Fourques. Inconspicuously marked with a small board is the spot where the French rider Roger Rivière plunged from the road into a little ravine while leading the 1960 Tour de France, breaking his back in the fall and never to race again.

A straighter bit follows, down the valley of the Fraissenet, then the road winds again, still steadily downhill following the River Tarnon, eventually arriving at the small town of Florac. This formally feudal town is tightly packed under the eastern edge of the Causse Méjean, dominated by the dolomite cliffs of Rochefort.

There are two choices here: you can join the main N106 for about 5km, then turn left on the D907[BIS] to follow the River Tarn downstream, or you can take to the hills. If you still have the taste for some more hills, this is the route we would recommend. It is probably the toughest climb on the route, rising nearly 500m in about 5km (10 per cent average), but well worth the effort.

In Florac, turn left in the little square by the war memorial and head up towards the church. At the top end of the square follow the road signposted to the aerodrome and Les Vignes. The climb starts very steeply and the red roofs of Florac rapidly fall away below. The main part of the climb is a 2km shelf clinging to the hillside, beneath the rocky bluffs of the Rocher de Rochefort to the left, with the upper valley of the Tarn far below to the right. The view to the east opens up as you climb, with its rounded hills and forested tops quite reminiscent of mid Wales. Just round the bend that marks the top of the climb there is a dolmen on the right, and you are then on the open causse.

This is a delightful stretch, carpeted with limestone flowers when we passed, with occasional short avenues of ash trees and the ribs of limestone pavements showing here and there through the thin soil. Also shimmering in the strong breeze were great swathes of the fine long silvery grass so characteristic of France's southern limestone hills. This is sheep country, though perhaps less so than the more famous Causse de Larzac to the south-west where the sheep that give the world Roquefort graze. Nevertheless, we saw several herds perhaps a hundred or two strong of the lanky brown sheep that look almost like goats from a distance.

You come after quite a short time to a patch of dwarf conifers where the route turns right on a small road signposted Montbrun. Although whoever draws the green lines beside 'picturesque' roads on

the Michelin map does not think this deserves one, it is a beautiful winding road, largely downhill with open views over the rolling landscape, little patches of maquis with juniper bushes, and more carpets of flowers. When it comes, the descent to Montbrun is quite different from the other routes down to the Tarn – it is a spectacular looping road through almost bare limestone, twisting and turning on its way to the valley bottom.

After Montbrun, continue to the bridge across the Tarn, but instead of crossing it stay on the left bank of the river, on the road signposted to La Chadenède. This delightful little road brings you after 3 or 4km right under the rock and walls of the castle of Castelbouc, a former bandit stronghold that was eventually suppressed by those who, quite understandably, objected to their travel up and down the valley being obstructed. The castle is floodlit on summer evenings. Here the road doubles back to the right over the Tarn to join the main valley road, where you turn left to Ste Enimie.

Enimie was a local saint, a seventh-century Merovingian princess of surpassing beauty, who so disapproved of the baron her father wished her to marry that she developed leprosy, which soon scared off the would-be lover. In a vision she was told to head for this part of the world, the Gévaudan, where a miraculous spring would restore her former beauty. After a long and distressing journey she reached a well known curative spring, but the angel of the vision reappeared and directed her to continue her travels until she reached the deep and wild valley of the Tarn. Here she found her spring and was cured. Every time, though, that she attempted to leave the valley her affliction reappeared and in the end she founded a convent here, spending the rest of her days in saintly works.

In Ste Enimie, now a rather touristy village, the route leaves the valley, turning left over the bridge and beginning a long and steady climb up a fairly straight shelf road that soon yields aerial views of the gorge. At one hairpin bend, after about 5km, there is a really spectacular view of the little village of St Chély-du-Tarn far below, nestled in a sharp bend of the river, and down the gorge to the next great bend, the Cirque de Pougnadoires.

About 3km more of easier climbing brings you to the summit, the 900m Col de Cauperlac (or Coperlac). By now the road is in open upland meadows, full of a mass of colourful – if rather clashing –

The Tarn gorge between les Vignes and le Rozier.

pins beneath enormous vertical, sometimes over-hanging, limestone pinnacles, coming at last to the bridge over the Tarn at Les Vignes. From here the valley road (D907^{BIS}) leads down through several rock arches to Le Rozier.

As we traced the route on that June evening, the mellow light picked out all the crevices and curves of the cliffs high above us, bathing the rock in a light that became more and more golden as the sun sank and the valley's indigo shadow grew.

The Causse Noir

This smaller circuit begins by leaving Le Rozier across the bridge over the River Jonte, signposted to Peyreleau. There is quite a steep pull up from the bridge, passing under the walls of the first few houses, then a very sharp right turn indeed, almost a back double, signposted La Cresse and Millau, on the D187. The road is fairly up and down, but without any severe gradients, following the left bank of the Tarn.

This is cherry country, and the road passes between small fields interspersed with cherry orchards, many of them bright underfoot with yellow rape or red poppies between the trees. In La Cresse continue straight on to the next village, Paulhe. An odd feature here is a narrow section of road in the village controlled by traffic lights that have a fourth phase besides the usual red, yellow and green, reading *troupeaux* – herds of animals crossing! From here, follow the Millau signs, which lead you still along the left bank, well away from the busy N8 on the opposite side of the river. The orchards give way to smallholdings and allotments running down to the now slow-moving Tarn, with fields bright with more poppies on the other side of the road.

On the outskirts of Millau, turn left, for about 50m, on the D991 and then left again on the D110, signposted to Longuiers and Peyreleau as well as a tourist sign to Montpellier-le-Vieux. Note that you are about to embark on a very lonely stretch of road; apart from the auberge at Maubert, there is virtually no habitation on this road for 26km once you have left the last houses of Millau.

This climb begins quite steeply (it is classified by the Tour de France organisers as 'first-category' although it climbs only about 400m in 7km) past almost suburban villas, and then settles down to a

bright red poppies, blue cornflowers and purple vetch when we passed. Although apparently quite a gentle gradient the descent is open and fast and it is all too easy to sweep past the right turn onto the D16. The turning is just before an alignment of trees beside the road. In another 2km the route forks left at a wayside cross, still on the D16, for Les Vignes. The road climbs gently again, through scrub and maquis, clearing now and again into broad meadows. On the sharp bend just before the final slope of the Col de Rieisse, just beyond the hamlet of Rouveret, there is a fine view back over the spire of tiny Rouveret's church towards Mont Lozère and the source of the Tarn.

Just beyond the Col de Rieisse (920m, but not marked on the road) we followed a short detour past the hamlet of Rieisse itself out to the Roc de Hourtous. Here there is another remarkable view down to the narrowest part of the gorge, with the backdrop of the curve of the Cirque des Baumes.

Back on the main route, the road drops gently through more scrub and thin forest until it quite spectacularly reaches the lip of the gorge. This is one of the most dramatic sections of the whole route. The road plunges down the wall of the gorge in long hair-

steady gradient. To begin with there are views over Millau and then the road starts a series of long hair-pin sweeps through thin forest, with fine views back up the Tarn valley from a couple of the bends.

Once again Michelin do not think this road deserves a 'picturesque' green edging after the sum-mit, but we found it delightful, with yellow, blue, cream and purple carpets of low-growing limestone flowers among the squat conifers over almost the whole of the upland route. This is the true Causse Noir: it gets its name from this dark covering of conifers, now much thinned.

At Maubert you can make a short detour to the right to the rocky 'chaos' of Montpellier-le-Vieux. This natural feature is a tumbled mass of weathered limestone shapes, known as it is because locals used to believe it to be the haunted ruins of a former town. We were a little disappointed; although there are a great many of these formations in a very small space we found them less dramatic than many we

The village of Liacous, in the Tarn gorge near le Rozier.

had seen free of charge elsewhere on this and other routes. Whoever coined the fanciful names for the various rock shapes ought to have their poetic licence revoked!

The route back begins as an undulating road similar to the other upland parts, but it suddenly gives way to a tremendous sweeping descent to Peyreleau. Peyreleau is not visible, so close is it under the hillside, and all you can see is Le Rozier far below as a tiny huddle of roofs grouped round a toy church. Then, as you round the last hairpin, there is an almost vertical view of Peyreleau itself. Within moments you are swooping through the narrow streets of the village and back over the bridge to Le Rozier.

The Middle Tarn

This route covers a shorter loop and takes in the middle part of the Tarn Gorge, between Ste Enimie and Les Vignes, which the large circuit misses. It begins by following the River Jonte from Le Rozier as on the first route.

After 7km, at La Caze, turn left onto the small D63 – it is not a very conspicuous turning – signposted to La Parade. The first few hundred metres are quite steep and you rapidly gain height above the valley. There are dramatic views to the right of the upper gorge, with some impressive limestone bluffs in the foreground. Michelin once more do not find it picturesque; we did, with its dramatic rocky defiles and borders of yellow roses, giving way to low conifers, limestone flowers and shrubs.

This part of the Causse Méjean is quite wooded all the way to La Parade. Here there is a reminder of grimmer times with a wartime Resistance memorial (this was one of the Resistance strongholds). There is also – worth noting in such a remote spot – a café with accommodation. Turn left on the D986 to the junction with the D43 at Carnac.

Here you can either go left and take the direct descent to the valley to reach La Malène – or even follow the first tour's route to Les Vignes – or continue straight on, on the D986 over the Col de Cauperlac to go down the road that looks down on St Chély and up which the first tour climbs. (Do not disdain going down roads you have already climbed: they look quite different in the opposite direction and at a different time of day.) This gives the chance to follow the middle 25km of the Tarn gorge – prob-ably the most spectacular and greenest section, with its rearing cliffs, rock arches and neatly placed poplars by the water's edge. These are interspersed with the narrows, where the river rushes as a torrent between rock walls only a short distance apart.

Also interesting are the sites of abandoned villages (and one or two surprisingly not abandoned) on the opposite bank of the river. The only access to them would have been by water or by fording on a horse or mule if the water level were low enough, with a rudimentary rope bridge for supplies. For quite a stretch virtually the whole of the opposite hillside has been laboriously terraced, the work of perhaps a thousand years abandoned by the depopulation the area suffered before tourism began to bring some of the people back. The final 10km from Les Vignes back to Le Rozier are over the same roads as the first route – 10km that easily bear repeating.

Approximate total distances   Jonte, Causse Méjean and upper Tarn 123km; Causse Noir 50km; Middle Tarn 53km
Maps   Michelin 80, panels 4, 5, 6 and 14; IGN 58
Regions   Midi-Pyrénées and Languedoc-Roussillon
Départements   12-Aveyron, 48-Lozère
Accommodation   Boyne, Le Rozier, Les Vignes, La Malène, Ste Enimie, Florac, Meyrueis, Hures-la-Parade, Rivière-sur-Tarn, Aguessac, Millau, Maubert
Access   By road, N9 to Aguessac, then D907; by rail to Millau

THE VERCORS

Seen from the other side of the Rhône valley, particularly late on a sunny afternoon or evening, the enormous limestone cliffs that rear up from the valley to surround the Vercors look like the impregnable ramparts of a gigantic natural castle, and you wonder how anybody can get to the top of them. Over the years, most notably by the Resistance in the Second World War, the natural fortress of this upland region has indeed been put to use.

In form, the Vercors is like an elevated, lop-sided, not particularly smooth and rather tilted limestone saucer, bounded on the north and north-west by the River Isère and to the east by its tributary the Drac. The Drôme marks the southern boundary, and the

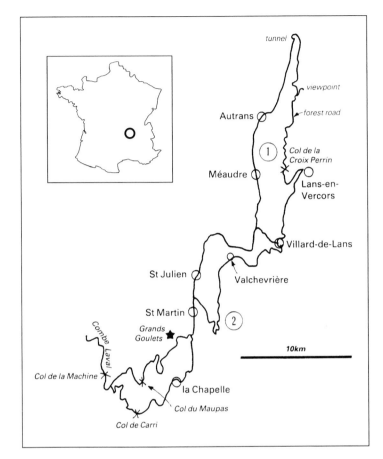

is relatively gentle for such a rugged area. This means that one of the small resort towns such as Villard-de-Lans or Autrans makes a good centre for a moderate stay, with plenty of scope for reasonably energetic but not extreme exploration by bicycle. This part of the Vercors has been relatively unobtrusively developed for winter sports, with a high reputation for the quality of its cross-country skiing.

The routes, which describe a couple of circuits based on Villard-de-Lans, are at the gentler end of my 'moderate mountain' category. This is not how I would classify most of the climbs up the ramparts to reach the Vercors, however, so there are additional notes on two of the climbs up from the valleys outside, the Route des Écouges to the Col de Romèyre from the north, and the Col de Rousset from the south, in the 'High mountain' section which follows this one. Both have climbs of 800 to 850m to justify this classification, even if their summit altitudes are relatively modest. Virtually the whole of the Vercors is now a Regional Natural Park.

Rhône itself lies only a little to the west. The crags that so impress from the north and the west are in fact the lower part of the rim – although still some 1,500m high – and the eastern rim climbs to 2,341m at its highest point. In the middle of the Vercors, the lowest parts are around 700m, while most is around the 1,000m mark. In several places, smaller rivers have cut deep gorges into the limestone, and one of these – the Gorges de la Bourne – offers the only even moderately easy way into the centre.

The Vercors is very green, with its altitude and isolation attracting quite a bit of rainfall. This allows the northern part to have quite lush rolling upland pastures (even boasting their own breed of cattle) and the south to harbour great beech and coniferous forests.

For such an upland region there is an unusual density of minor roads and, apart from the steep slopes of some of the gorges, the inland topography

Pastures and Forests – the Northern Vercors

Villard-de-Lans lies rather over the 1000m mark, so even in early summer nights can be cold. On our mid June visit we found a thin film of ice inside the outer leaf of the tent one morning. The sun soon warmed the world up – we breakfasted in shirt-sleeves – but it was a reminder that with clear skies the daily temperature range in mountain regions can be very wide.

Villard itself is a largely new but relatively restrained resort with most of the facilities you would expect, and lies on a knoll rather above the floor of the long shallow pastoral valley. The pattern of the topography of this part of the Vercors is a series of parallel almost north–south ridges, mostly forested, separated by these gently round-bottomed valleys.

At the foot of the slope from the town, the route turns right on the D531 to follow the valley,

On the forest road from the Col de la Croix Perrin to the Tunnel du Mortier.

accompanied by the infant stream of the Bourne. After about seven fairly flat kilometres, there is a crossroads, and the route turns left on the D106 to begin climbing out of the valley. Almost immediately you are in woodland, mostly beech, as the road curves steadily to the right. The gradient is in the main quite moderate, with only one stretch justifying a Michelin greater-than-5 per cent (1-in-20) arrow. After about 4km the road emerges into a large clearing and levels off: this is the Col de la Croix Perrin, 1,220m. The iron cross that gives it its name is off to the left of the road.

Here the route turns right, along an unsigned forest road. This little road is a delight. After a couple of kilometres of gentle climb, winding through magnificent beechwoods and small clearings that give aerial glimpses of the valley below to the west, the next half dozen kilometres virtually follow the 1,500m contour, faithfully tracing every curve and hollow of the hillside.

Occasionally there are small clearings and it is at one of these that you turn right off the through road up the hillside through a thin pine wood to reach the top of the ridge. It is the only turning, and signed to the Source de la Molière. Here you suddenly emerge over the brow to be faced with a breathtaking view across the valleys of the Drac and Isère to the dramatic snow-capped peaks of the Alpine Écrins massif, dominated by the 4102m Barre des Écrins and the near-4000m peaks of La Meije and Mont Pelvoux. This eastern side of the ridge is an open grassy meadow and in this ideal spot we picnicked in the warm sun, watching the changing pattern of cloud, light and shade on the great hills before us.

Back on the through forest road again, there is a little climb to begin with, then a wonderful steady

Looking across to the Massif des Écrins in the Alps from just below la Molière, off the forest road.

Riding through flower meadows in the valley of the Drevenne, northern Vercors.

freewheel through open forest to the D218. The last couple of hundred metres are a sharp curve down to the left and when you reach the D218 you realize that you have just passed over the entrance of the Tunnel du Mortier, through which the D218 passes. It is worth just going through the tunnel (which is well lit) for the dramatic views across to the Chartreuse massif and down over the outskirts of Grenoble.

From the other, southern, tunnel entrance, the road sweeps down the valley between meadows, flower-filled at that time of year, through the resort villages of Autrans and Méaudre. Beyond Méaudre, where the road has become the D106 once more, the valley closes in to form the narrow wooded Gorges du Méaudret. These join the uppermost reaches of the Gorges du Bourne at Les Jarrands, where you turn left up the last 100m of climb of the now-opening gorge to the upland meadows of Villard-de-Lans.

Cols and Combes – the Southern Vercors

This route leaves Villard-de-Lans by the road signposted to the swimming pool (piscine). At the foot of the hill, go straight over the valley road on the D215$^{C.}$ The road begins to climb almost immediately, through woodland that is quite different from the beech forests of the other route. Here there are resinous pines, interspersed with patches of heath and pockets of hay meadow, brilliantly yellow and purple at that season.

This road leads to one of the more tragic parts of the Vercors, scene of some vicious reprisals for Resistance activities during the Second World War. As a memorial to those who perished, this little road has been laid out with the stations of the cross, culminating in Valchevrière. Each station is marked by a bright and very striking stylised ceramic mosaic illustration set in the rock.

After the last of the hamlets, the road narrows as the pinewoods close in and it was through this resinous tunnel that we climbed to the twelfth station, the tall and slender stainless steel cross of Valchevrière that looks out over the plunging wooded cleft of the Gorges de la Bourne. Below, hidden in the trees, lie the ruins of the hamlet of Valchevrière. Apart from the little chapel, which serves as the last station on the way of the cross, the whole village was set on fire as a reprisal for the tenacity of the Resistance.

From the viewpoint beside the cross, the route turns sharply to the left and continues to climb steadily, with one or two quite sharp pitches, to the 1352m summit. Here the woodland is more mixed, a dappled blend of light and dense shade as we passed. Only a few hundred metres from the top, the road opens out suddenly over a great upland lawn, the vivid green velvet of the meadow luminous against the dark pines.

The road (which became the D221 when it passed into the département of the Drôme at the summit) begins to descend in earnest from here on and suddenly bursts clear of the forest with tremendous views of the little village of St Martin-en-Vercors far below. There is a short stretch of limestone heathland, with close-cropped turf and chalky flowers, before the road comes down to the flower-filled meadows of the valley. Looking back, the impressive cliffs above are crowned by a fringe of woodland.

From the junction at the bottom of the valley it is possible to turn right on the D103 and return direct to Villard-de-Lans, by way of the spectacular part of the Gorges de la Bourne by the Goule Noire. The Goule Noire is one of several points in the gorge where underground streams gush to the surface.

However, we wanted to see two more of the sights of the Vercors before heading back: the Grands Goulets and the Combe Laval. The D103, on which we turned left, runs gently down the valley, past St Martin-en-Vercors and then turns right as the D518 to the hamlet of Les-Barraques-en-Vercors. This is the beginning of the remarkable formation of the Grands Goulets. Here the stream of the Vernaison has cut a narrow passage through the limestone, scarcely wide enough for the road, which shares the space with the torrent. Even in high summer the light barely penetrates as far as the road through the rock fissures and the greenery above. The road has several short tunnels, to emerge perched high above the gorge of the Vernaison.

It would be possible to continue down the valley to Pont-en-Royans and to return to Villard by following the whole length of the Gorges de la Bourne. However, we retraced our steps to Les Barraques and continued on the D518 for about 3km. Here a right turn, unnumbered but signposted to Les Gabriels, leads over the ridge to the next valley, the Combe de l'Oscence. This valley is an utter contrast, cultivated with large fields.

Just after the hamlet of Les Ronnins, the road

surface deteriorates, giving way to about 2km of stony track. This doubles back to the right in a sharp hairpin and climbs quite steeply through the beech and birch woods, becoming much smoother as the gradient eases. The top is the Col de Maupas, 1,124m, where the forest opens out into a clearing that made an ideal lunch spot beside a carpet of spring flowers.

From here the forest road surface progressively improves until it meets the D199, on which you turn right briefly to join the D76 about 1km below the Col de la Machine, 1,011m. Here begins the dramatic valley of the Combe Laval, a symmetrical cliff-edged and V-shaped cut into the plateau, with the road spectacularly perched and tunnelled. There is a viewpoint just after the hotel on the Col de la Machine, where a short scramble brings you out on the very edge of the gorge. It is worth continuing down the road for a way (even though it means losing a bit of height) as far as the last tunnel, about 3km from the Col de la Machine, for the spectacular aerial views over the valley.

The return route involves returning over the Col de la Machine to the point where the outgoing route joined the D76. Here you turn left onto the D199 once more, but instead of turning off on the forest road to the Col de Maupas, bear round to the right to follow the sinuous route through the pine forest to the Col de Carri, 1,202m. From here it is a brisk descent to the D176 and then to La Chapelle-en-Vercors.

In La Chapelle turn right on the D518 and then at the end of the village go straight on where the D518 swings right, on to the D611, which winds down to the valley of the Vernaison. From here, a left turn on the D103 brings you back through St Martin-en-Vercors, St Julien-en-Vercors and so down to the Goule Noire in the Gorges de la Bourne. From here there is a steady climb of about 250m back to Villard-de-Lans.

Approximate total distance   Northern Vercors 65km; Southern Vercors 99km

Maps   Michelin 77, panels 3 and 4; IGN 52; also a special IGN Regional Natural Park sheet 305 at 1:50,000

Region   Rhône-Alpes

Départements   26-Drôme, 38-Isère

Accommodation   Autrans, Méaudre, Villard-de-Lans, Corrençon-en-Vercors, Les-Barraques-en-Vercors

Access   By road, N532 from Valence or Grenoble, then D531; by rail to Valence, Grenoble, Voreppe; by air to Lyon-Satelas or Grenoble-Brézins (the latter is not well served outside the skiing season)

Restrictions   Since the Vercors is a winter sports area, main approach roads are cleared throughout the winter and are likely to be clear quite early in spring, as are some of the approach passes; the Col de la Bataille is officially closed from 15 November to 15 May

12
The High Mountains

The general techniques of mountain riding – both up and down – were covered in the chapter on bicycles and cycling. I have two more warnings to add. The first is that weather can change dramatically and rapidly in mountain regions anywhere. Although you will be travelling on roads and so are unlikely to be left completely stranded, it is essential to have enough warm clothing and waterproofs to be able to cope with any changes. Even on hot sunny days it will be much cooler at the top of a pass than it was when you set out from the valley: a 1°C decrease for each 100m climbed. Remember that you are susceptible to wind chill effects both from winds themselves (which tend to be stronger at altitude) and from the draught of your own freewheeling down long gradients. You may not be following the remote and craggy route of the Alpine climber, but exposure resulting from wind chill made worse by being wet can affect you within minutes. French daily local papers give weather forecasts that include estimates of the zero isotherm – the altitude in metres above which it is likely to be freezing.

Weather can change rapidly in the mountains.

Do not forget that rain at lower levels could well be sleet or snow higher up. Prudence must be your first consideration.

The second warning concerns tackling roads blocked with snow. The approach routes leading to many Alpine and Pyrenean cols may have roadside signs that they are closed (*col fermé*) until they have been cleared of snow and obstructions (such as rock debris) that have accumulated over the winter. In late May or June, and even early July for those over 2500m, many of these roads may well be quite passable by bike, even if you have to scramble through or round the odd snowdrift on a shaded corner. It can

Height of achievement: at the top of Col de l'Iseran.

be great fun and quite an adventure – and of course as a bonus there will be no other traffic at all.

Be cautious, however. Do not attempt to tackle large and possibly unstable masses of snow on steep slopes and do not forget in allowing time that it will be no quicker going down than up if you have to scramble through snow. Snow with a crust from having melted briefly in the sun and then re-frozen can be particularly hard and exhausting work. Walking through snow can make your feet very wet and cold. Once you can ride again, clear all snow from round brake mechanisms before setting off downhill: a continuous stream of very cold melting water onto the rims can make braking performance distinctly unimpressive. Use discretion in tackling any snow-bound crossing and, if in doubt, do not rely on being able to get right over and down the other side. At all times be prepared to turn back if you have to. (Had this book been written a year or two earlier, there would have been no account of the highest road, the Col de Restefond and the Cime de la Bonette. We did

not make it to the top on the first couple of attempts, even though it was mid June.)

Many of the cols described have short tunnels. In almost every case these are short enough for the far end to be quite visible and many are now lit, so there is little hazard. Road surfaces may be less good in a tunnel than outside, so take care, particularly if the tunnel is on a downhill stretch. Noise echoes in a tunnel so do not be alarmed if you hear what sounds like a very heavy vehicle or convoy behind you – it will usually be only a car. We have always found French drivers very considerate with regard to passing us in a tunnel.

Riding on the high roads of the great passes is little short of a spiritual experience. The sense of solitude, the tang of the sharp air, the feelings of elevation and elation, and the awareness of physical achievement all mount as you climb. I hope you find them as inspiring as I do.

Finally, although mountain riding calls for physical effort, provided you follow the advice about

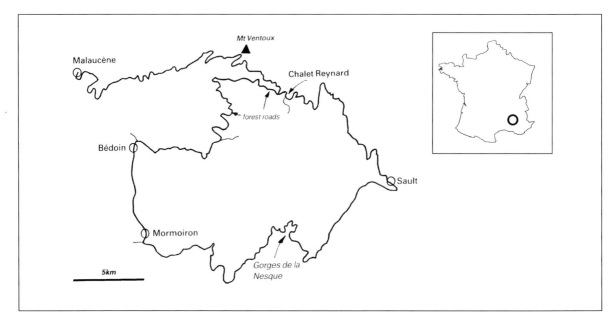

taking it steady in low gears, you do not have to be a dedicated athlete to derive this inspiration from it. One of my greatest cycling heroes is Bernard Migaud from Metz, who climbed his hundredth col to join the Club des Cent Cols, culminating with the 2,770m Col de l'Iseran, in 1983. Following a childhood illness, Bernard Migaud has only one leg.

The routes in this section are rather differently organized from those in the rest of the book. Only one – the Mont Ventoux route – gives an itinerary. The remainder give instead descriptions and illustrations of some of the major passes, and detours and loops that we have found attractive, so that you can incorporate them into your own route. There are so many ways of permutating these cols that trying to combine them, quite artificially, into a single route for each area would be unnecessarily restrictive – and would make for a remarkably tough tour! The cols and detours are listed in alphabetical order, while the sketch map on page 135 shows how the Alpine Cols are placed in relation to each other.

One point that emerged during our researches was the frequency of disagreement on the altitude of a col, with discrepancies common between the roadside plaque, if any, Michelin and IGN. In general, we have followed the precedent of the Club des Cent Cols and quoted IGN figures. Since theirs is the primary survey, these ought to be the most reliable.

MONT VENTOUX

With its top at 1909m, Mont Ventoux is not among the highest mountains; indeed, some of the Alpine roads go several hundred metres higher, to say nothing of the summits. What is particularly spectacular about Mont Ventoux is its position. Mostly surrounded by a plateau some 600 to 700m up, and lying well away from anything of comparable height, the great pale limestone bulk of the mountain dominates the countryside for miles around. Not for nothing is it known as 'Le Géant de Provence' (the giant of Provence). What is also spectacular is the bareness of its upper slopes. From le Chalet-Reynard – a small ski station at 1,419m, where two of the approach roads meet – to the top, the whole upper slope is a limestone scree, a pale pinkish grey but blinding white in the sunlight.

The other attraction of Mont Ventoux is that a road goes virtually to the top, and there are four ways of approaching it. The route as described makes a circuit up the easiest side – the east – and down one of the two hardest, to the south, returning by way of the Gorges de la Nesque. For the sake of completeness the other two possible approaches are covered as well.

Three of the four ascents I have made of this mountain have been at Easter. At that season the top 6km or so of the western approach from Malaucène remains blocked by snow. The road from le Chalet-Reynard to the small ski station of Mont Serein on the other side is officially closed from 15 November to 15 April, but from about mid March the section from le Chalet-Reynard to the top is mostly clear of snow and quite cyclable. Obviously the precise conditions vary from year to year. Early spring can be one of the best seasons to make the climb since the weather is not insufferably hot as it can be on the exposed limestone in summer, and the air is often clearer, giving better views from the top. (But our most recent Easter ascent was through cold, swirling mist – with no view at all!)

The name Ventoux comes from the Provençal word for windy – and the small saddle just below the last few metres of climb to the summit, where there are views to east and west simultaneously, is known as the Col des Tempêtes. The temperature at the top averages 11°C lower than at the bottom, and there are small outcrops of Arctic flowers near the summit, which are said to be at their best in early July. For the cyclist, this temperature difference means having to hand more clothes than you might feel at all reasonable, judging from the temperature when you set out. (One Easter, the day after we had been to the top in bright, clear sunshine, it snowed overnight, which is not what you expect when camping in Provence. Be prepared!)

The most convenient starting point is the small town of Sault, on the Plateau de Vaucluse. One of the advantages of this is that you can see the summit of Mont Ventoux from Sault and get some idea of the weather at the top before you start out. You get glimpses of the top all the way up to Le Chalet-Reynard, after which it is continuously in view. It would also be possible to start from Bédoin, which would mean an afternoon climb of Mont Ventoux, assuming you were doing the whole circuit in one day. In general, Mont Ventoux is best tackled early in the day.

The road from Sault, the D164, starts off a little disconcertingly by going downhill, but it is only for about 1km. Once across the Nesque, here a very small stream, the road begins to climb gently first through cultivated fields and lavender rows, then through limestone heath, a coarse scrub of juniper bushes, box and low chalk-loving plants. It was on this stretch that we watched fascinated on our first trip as an endless head-to-tail string of caterpillars

made their way across the road looking for a new home offering more to eat.

There are occasional patches of thin woodland until at the hamlet of Venosque you pass into more continuous forest, here mostly newly planted pines. The slopes of the mountain were originally naturally wooded until felling in the sixteenth century to supply the shipyards of Toulon cleared much of it. Replanting has been going on since the 1860s, with a mixture of dwarf white oaks, cedars, beeches and pines now stretching up to about 1600m above sea level. There are several points where bends in the road offer clear views out over the trees south over the Plateau of the Vaucluse towards the bulk of the Lubéron.

The climb is steady but not arduous. It is about 20km from Sault to Le Chalet-Reynard, with an overall climb of some 700m, so that the average is only 3 to 4 per cent (1-in-33 to 1-in-25), although there are one or two pitches that merit a Michelin arrow (between 5 and 9 per cent).

At Le Chalet-Reynard the road emerges from the forest and joins the D974 from Bédoin. The bar and restaurant at this junction are the last chance of replenishing drink, apart from a spring on the right of the road about 2km farther on.

From here the road embarks on the remarkable last section of the ascent. It is now completely open, perched on the scree, and climbs in great curves, looping round the small spurs on the flank of the hill, with open views to the left. In sunshine the whiteness of the rock is quite blinding, and on a hot day the reflected heat can be stifling.

The climbing is appreciably harder now, with over 450m to be won in the remaining 6km to the top, an average of 7.5 to 8 per cent, or about 1-in-12. Nevertheless it is mostly quite well graded, with only a couple of noticeably steeper stretches. I have always found it encouraging that the summit, crowned by the observatory and television station, is in sight for virtually the whole climb. To me that means that it is a finite task and you can judge your progress quite accurately.

About 2km below the summit there is a small dark-granite memorial on the scree bank to the right of the road, marking the point where the English racing cyclist Tom Simpson collapsed and subsequently died during a very hot stage of the 1967 Tour de France. It is not always easy to see this tablet from the road, particularly if there is lying snow; it is usually easier to spot it from a little farther up the road.

At the last bend, about 1km before the top, is the Col des Tempêtes, where the view suddenly opens up to the right. When it is clear – which generally means earlier in the day rather than later – it is possible to see the whole western face of the snow-covered Alpine chain, a magnificent panorama.

The last long hairpin brings you round under the walls of the observatory. It is worth going a short distance beyond the top to see the views to the north towards the Vercors and across to the massif of Pelvoux above Grenoble. In season, there is a bar at the top – but do not rely on it at other times.

While it is possible in the absence of snow to continue down the west/north side to Malaucène and complete a circuit via Bédoin, the suggested route retraces towards Le Chalet-Reynard for about 5km. At the junction with a forest road on the right about 1km before Le Chalet-Reynard, turn right.

Mont Ventoux from the Col de Macuègne.

The forest road, which has a somewhat variable but easily ridable surface, contours spectacularly round the hillside, mostly just at the boundary between forest and scree, for about 6km. There are superb views to the left and, every so often, glimpses to the right of the summit, with the dazzle of the limestone making the sky appear a deep cobalt blue.

Then, after a short up-and-down stretch, you rejoin a well surfaced road in an oblique T-junction. Turn acutely left here, to embark on a spectacular winding descent through forest – much of it cedar – to the junction with the D974. Turn right to the attractive large village of Bédoin, with its picturesque little streets and perched church, a number of bars, shops and restaurants.

Leave Bédoin south on the D974, bearing left after 2km on the D14 to Mormoiron. This is cherry orchard country and particularly spectacular in early spring when you may see the snow-capped summit of Mont Ventoux framed in cherry blossom, like an occidental Mt Fuji. Just after Mormoiron the route joins the D942. Turn left through Villes-sur-Auzon to begin the climb through the Gorges de la Nesque. Just after Villes-sur-Auzon do not be sidetracked into taking the D1, which goes off to the left and is the direct route back to Sault.

Most of the climb is quite gentle: the overall rise is about 400m in some 15km, less than 3 per cent, with the steepest parts near the start and end. Once into the gorges proper the road clings to the side of the limestone cleft, high above the blue-misted wooded bottom, giving spectacular views both down and up. It was up here that we met a goatherd in a Citroën 2CV who was trying to trace his small group of animals by listening for their bells on the far side of the gorge – quite possible in the still air, but since they had about fifty square kilometres to roam in, quite a task. We never discovered if he found them!

The most spectacular part of the gorge is after the first of several rock arches, where the road follows a great bend round the Combe de Coste Chaude, leaving the river far below on the right, with the gradient steepening a little in places. At the top of this stretch there is a viewpoint on a rocky ledge, giving fine views up and down the gorge, with the inescapable Mont Ventoux as backdrop to the north-facing view.

Surprisingly, there is some downhill after the viewpoint, through a landscape of almost domestic-looking box shrubs until the road runs close beside the dwindling Nesque. The last 3 or 4km are across the open agricultural lands leading to Sault, which from this direction is prominently perched on its rocky promontory.

There are quite a number of other attractive and less strenuous short circuits possible from Sault, notably to some of the other precariously and picturesquely perched villages in the locality, such as Montbrun-les-Bains and Brantes.

Alternative routes up Mont Ventoux

Even if Mont Ventoux does not qualify as a high mountain, the road from Bédoin to the top via le Chalet-Reynard climbs 1,600m in 22km. This is

Mont Ventoux framed by cherry blossom, from near Mormoiron.

more climbing than in many of the higher Alpine passes, which start off much higher up. About 1,000m of this climb is on a 10km stretch from the little perched village of St Estève to le Chalet-Reynard. This is a hard climb, with an average of 10 per cent (1-in-10) and pitches a good deal steeper. The climb is largely through pine forest, which gives some shade but means that there is little in the way of views. Climbing up the forest road through the Massif des Cèdres (which the route as described comes down) is similarly hard.

The climb from Malaucène, along the northern face, is rather easier, although the total climb is still nearly 1,500m in 21km, an average of about 7 per cent. This road goes up in a series of immense steps, steep pitches being followed by flatter breathing spaces, so that it does not feel too hard. The first part of the ascent is through forest, after which forest and open stretches alternate until the last 3 or 4km through the white limestone scree. As the road is on the north face there is quite a bit of

In the Gorges de la Nesque.

afternoon shade on this climb; when we came up this way, in mid-June, there were even one or two small patches of snow remaining by the roadside near the last bend or two. This is probably the least interesting way up – but it is a tremendous open, well surfaced and fast freewheel down.

Approximate total distance   93km
Maps   Michelin 81, panels 3, 4 13 and 14; IGN 67
Region   Provence-Alpes-Côte d'Azur
Départements   83-Vaucluse
Accommodation   Sault, Chalet-Reynard, Bédoin, Mont Serein, Malaucène
Access   By road, N100 to Apt, then D943; by rail to Orange, Carpentras, Avignon.
Restrictions   The official closure period of the D974 between Mont Serein and Chalet-Reynard is 15 November to 15 April, and during this period other roads may be impassable too; the south-east approach from Chalet-Reynard is often practicable by bicycle well before this, but the other side is not passable until the road is ploughed

COLS AND MOUNTAIN ROADS

Col d'Allos
2,240m, southern Alps

Despite its altitude, the Col d'Allos is not one of the harder climbs when approached from the south. Colmars is already well over 1200m up and the first part of the climb follows the valley of the Verdon, a far smaller stream here than the river it becomes in its Grand Canyon.

The old part of the village of Allos has some fine traditional Alpine houses, a skilful blend of stone and wood – and contrasting with the recent ski developments nearby. We had intended to camp near Allos and, in the absence of any sign of an official site, pitched in a clearing in a little grove beside the Verdon a couple of kilometres up from the village.

From here, the road follows the Verdon up its narrowing valley, through a mixture of pasture and pine wood as far as the ski station of La Foux-d'Allos. So far, even with camping kit, it proved to be a pleasant and quite easy gradient. However, over the last 7km, the road heaves itself up another 500m, in a series of moderately long hairpins, ending with a long last straight stretch on open short-cropped grassland.

This latter is the only stretch that Michelin see fit to accord two chevrons, steeper than 9 per cent (1-in-11). The hairpins alternate between grass-covered banks and outcrops of dark grey schist and slate, so that at one moment you are among spring flowers and the next passing through a rather dour charcoal landscape.

The summit is far from spectacular on this side – it is no more than a shallow grassy cleft – but reserves its surprise for when you breast the crest. Then a great expanse of snow-covered mountain, the Parpaillon, opens up with, nearer at hand, the 2839m Grand Cheval de Bois. At the time of year that we passed, June, there was still quite a bit of snow at the top, although the road was clear and the weather warm. So we did what cyclists usually do, took off our shoes and picnicked in the sun with the peaks of the Parpaillon before us and at our feet the pale Alpine crocuses that seem to spring up just behind the receding edge of the snowdrifts.

The descent towards Barcelonette is superb, beginning with rocky outcrops and tumbling streams. It then passes through pasture with birch and ash, particularly fine in the great loop by the chapel of Les Agneliers.

Maps   Michelin 81, panel 8
Road number   D908
Approximate total climb   1,000m (in direction described)
Linking   Colmars (24km to summit) and Barcelonette (20km to summit)
Closed period   The section from Allos to the Pra Loup junction south of Barcelonette is likely to be blocked by snow from November to May
Region   Provence-Alpes-Côte d'Azur
Départements   04-Alpes-de-Haute-Provence
Accommodation   Colmars, Allos, Barcelonette

Col des Aravis
1,486m, northern Alps

This is as good a col as any to warm up on as you head for the bigger hills. Its 550m or so of climb takes about a gentle 11km, averaging only 5 per cent, and with not many stretches much steeper. Like the Col des Saisies, the next along the road, it is a very pastoral col, climbing largely through meadows and opening out to a great lawn of rolling pasture at the top.

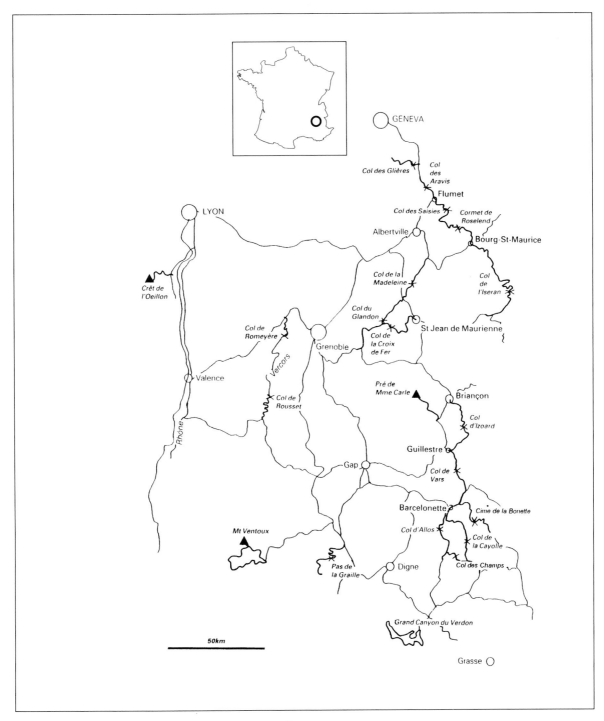

The Alpine and Rhône valley cols and principal linking roads.

The first part leads up from St Jean-de-Sixt to the growing ski resort of La Clusaz, which takes its name from the steep hollow (*cluse* in the local dialect) that the stream of the Nom has carved out for itself. Beyond La Clusaz the road climbs steadily up the side of the valley, on a grassy shelf.

To the right, views open up of the mountains of the Aravis; on the bright September morning that we climbed, patches of mist hung about the middle slopes of the mountains, gradually fading as the heat of the sun drove them off. There is a sequence of three or four hairpins as you approach the summit, and then an open stretch up to the little chapel of St Anne. It is marred only by some rather tatty

Chapel of St Anne at the summit of the Col des Aravis.

souvenir shops opposite. Just over the top there is a very fine view across to Mont Blanc before the gentle winding descent to Flumet.

Maps   Michelin 74, panel 7
Road number   D909
Approximate total climb   550m (in direction described)
Linking   St Jean-de-Sixt (11km to summit) and Flumet (12km to summit)
Closed period   November to April
Region   Rhône-Alpes
Départements   73-Savoie, 74-Haute-Savoie
Accommodation   St Jean-de-Sixt, La Clusaz, Flumet

Cime de la Bonette

2,802m, southern Alps, by way of the Col des Granges Communes or Col de Raspaillon (2,505m) and the Col de la Bonette (2,715m), or by way of the Col de Restefond (2,678m)

Without going so far as to say that this road cheats by going higher than it need to stake its claim as the highest pass in the Alps, the French Club des Cent Cols, in its listing of passes, quotes only the Col de la Bonette at 2,715m, leaving the Col de l'Iseran on its 2,770m perch as the highest 'legitimate' road pass. Indeed, it is arguable that even the Col de la Bonette itself is higher than need be, since the old military road, now a stony track, crosses by the Col de Restefond, a few metres lower still, while the lowest crossing of the ridge in this area is the 2,513m Col de Raspaillon.

With the fluidity of the border between France and Italy and the various dukedoms of the region over the years, this route has been a strategic one since mediaeval times, even though it was no more than a mule track until the 1830s. The modern tarred road is even more recent, construction being carried out only in 1960–64, just a century after Napoleon III had declared it part of an imperial route. There are remains of barracks and military posts at intervals on both sides of the pass.

I had earlier made a couple of attempts to get to the top from the north (Jausiers) side, only to be thwarted by snow too deep even to walk through over the last 6km – and this was mid-June. At last the chance came for us to attempt it from the south, still in mid-June, with no obligation to go right over

In the gorges du Bachelard, Col de la Cayolle.

Near le Villard-des-Arnauds, Col de la Cayolle.

if the north side was impassable. Officially, the pass was still closed.

The first 4.5km stage from St Étienne climbs steadily on the broad D2205 through a larch-lined shallow gorge beside the tumbling Tinée. At Pont Haut, the road turns right and becomes the narrower D64, still climbing relatively steadily, although there are a couple of steeper pitches. Just after one of them, on the right there is the impressive waterfall of the Cascade de Vens, as the stream from the Lac des Vens, high in its mountain cirque plunges to join the Tinée. From here on, the whole of the route lies within the Mercantour National Park, France's newest, created in 1979. By now the larch forest is thinning and the road is bounded by low scrub on the steeper slopes, and by Alpine meadows on the shallower, a riot of colour on our June visit. Just before the few buildings that are La Pra, an impressive view opens up to the south and east of the line of peaks that marks the frontier between France and Italy.

The next section, round the hairpins of the hamlet of Bousiéyas, is appreciably steeper, about 10 or 12 per cent for a couple of kilometres, before the landscape opens out to reveal the vast cirque (glacial combe), in which the infant Tinée rises. From here on you can in fact see the summit as the road sweeps in a great arc, give or take one or two sets of hairpin bends, round the rim of this vast amphitheatre. The grass of the meadows begins to thin out until, by the 2,513m Col de Raspaillon (as it is marked on the wooden signpost beside the road) or Col des Granges Communes (as Michelin have it), there are patches of bare rock and grey scree among the sparse grass and moss. This col marks the saddle where a path leads over the ridge from the valley of the Sagnes, and there are extensive views both to north and south.

From here to the Col de la Bonette it is a steady climb through an increasingly bare landscape; we heard marmots calling here and caught glimpses of them slithering across the rocks. At the col itself, below the little chapel appropriately named Notre Dame du Très Haut (Our Lady of the Very High Place), a short link of road leads to the opposite side of the pass. The route to the summit, however, bears left up the flank of the grey hill for about 800m up a slope that feels – maybe it was the altitude – appreciably steeper than the 10 to 12 per cent it actually is. The 2,802m road summit is marked by a panel let

into a rock, describing the construction of the route. A short scramble up a path brings you to the table d'orientation at the summit, from which there are tremendous views in all directions.

Maps   Michelin 81, panels 8 and 9
Road numbers   D2205, becoming the D64, on southern side; northern side apparently unnumbered (but signposted at junction in Jausiers)
Approximate total climb   1,660m from St Étienne-de-Tinée (in direction described); 1,580m from Jausiers
Linking   Barcelonette and Jausiers (33 and 24km to summit, respectively) and St Étienne-de-Tinée (26km to summit)
Closed period   November to the end of June
Region   Provence-Alpes-Côte d'Azur
Départements   04-Alpes de Haute Provence, 06-Alpes Maritimes
Accommodation   Barcelonette, Jausiers, St Étienne-de-Tinée. Apart from a restaurant at Le Pra and a gîte d'étape at Bousiéyas, both on the south side, and a kiosk at the summit, all of them seasonal, there is nothing in the 50km between Jausiers and St Étienne

Col de la Cayolle
2,327m, southern Alps

This is a col that circumstances forced us to make into an out-and-home day, since we were based in Barcelonette and to make it a circuit would have been well beyond our resources. The route starts quite prosaically on a wide and straight highway, following the valley of the Bachelard. After about 3km it begins to narrow and enters the Gorges du Bachelard.

Never far from the stream, we had more of an impression of ever-present water on this climb than I recollect on any other. After about 6km the river makes a near right-angle bend east, and the road still follows its tumbling progress as it climbs. There are a few hamlets and a fair amount of pasture scattered here and there with minute cultivated fields. On the opposite side of the valley the countless small torrents that plunge down to the Bachelard have cut narrow white ravines in the rock, which stand out against the incredible greenness of the forest and meadow.

A feature of this route is the sequence of quite

spectacular and attractive bridges, and it was beside one of them, just beyond Bayasse that we picnicked. This is where two valleys join; the road up to the Cayolle follows the valley to the right. Straight ahead, the second valley, with no more than a rough track and path, leads up to the Bonette, the highest road in France. From the bridge it was just possible to make out the line of the still snowbound road leading up to the Cime de la Bonette.

For a while the Cayolle road climbs through meadows, with some spectacular patches of gentian, interspersed with cowslips, at the time we passed. There is one passage where the road changes character completely, traversing a scree slope with isolated birch trees before making its final assault in the summit. At that season, June, the road was only just clear of snow and the summit was quite bleak, with icy streams tinkling below the still-deep drifts. There are, however, extensive views over the mountains of Provence to the south to compensate.

Maps   Michelin 81, panels 8 and 9
Road numbers   D902, D2202
Approximate total climb   1,200m (in direction described)
Linking   Barcelonette (30km to summit) and Guillaumes (33km to summit)
Closed period   November to June
Region   Provence-Alpes-Côte d'Azur
Départements   04-Alpes-de-Haute-Provence, 06-Alpes-Maritimes
Accommodation   Barcelonette, Guillaumes

Col des Champs
2,095m, southern Alps

This is a delightful col that is frequently missed by people tackling the better known Cols d'Allos and de la Cayolle on their way from south to north or vice versa. It links the valleys of the Verdon and Var, at the head of which these other two passes lie.

The walled village of Colmars in the valley of the Verdon was at one time the frontier town between France and Savoie, and the fortified surround dates from the war between them at the end of the seventeenth century. Now the village is an intriguing maze of narrow streets and picturesque small squares, each with its fountain. More practically, it also has a delightful small camp site set in a patch of pines.

The road up to the Col de Champs begins just

north of the village as an insignificant-looking junction at the top of a steep pitch on the main D908. The road, the D2, begins to climb in a series of fairly regular hairpins, first through orchards but soon through mixed forest. The gradient is remarkably steady at about 6 to 8 per cent and you soon gain an impressive amount of height, revealed by glimpses back down over Colmars, the pattern of its fortifications very visible. The mixed forest steadily gives way to larches, which themselves become more sparse and interspersed with white limestone scree as you climb. There are several patches where the few larch trees seem to cling to impossible slopes; when we passed there were bright patches of mountain flowers, notably gentians. About 3km before the top the trees finally stop and the last loops of the road before the summit curve in and out of almost bare rock and scree.

The top is, as the name of the col suggests, a vast open upland Alpine meadow, surrounded by sombre grey peaks. The descent swings in great curves through a rocky landscape, where we spent some minutes watching marmots among the rocks, guarding their burrows and warning each other of our approach with sharp squeaking calls. The bare uplands give way to fragrantly herb-covered low scrub and meadows, with frequent fine views of the valley of the Var and the peaks beyond.

Maps   Michelin 81, panels 8 and 9
Road numbers   D2 from west (Colmars) side; D78 from east (St Martin) side
Approximate total climb   860m from Colmars, (in direction described), 1,070m from St Martin
Linking   Colmars (12.5km to summit) and St Martin-d'Entraumes (16.5km to summit)
Closed period   The top part of the col, at least, is likely to be blocked by snow from December to April
Region   Provence-Alpes-Côte d'Azur
Départements   04-Alpes de Haute Provence, 06-Alpes Maritimes
Accommodation   Colmars, Chastelonnette, St Martin

Cirque de Gavarnie
1,570m, Pyrenees

This is an out-and-home route to one of the most striking natural features of the Pyrenees. It is a bit

The almost Scottish upper stages of the Cormet de Roselend.

of a tourist trap in the season – avoid July and August or go early in the day.

From Luz-St-Sauveur, the D921 heads for the hills up the wooded gorge of the Gave (a local word for a torrent) de Gavarnie. Just outside St Luz is the Pont Napoléon, built in 1860, crossing the deep cleft of the Gave in a single arch. From here on, parts of the road are cut into a narrow shelf in the side of the gorge: at times the road winds so abruptly that it is difficult to see any escape.

The gradient on the first part of the valley is quite moderate, up to the pretty village of Gèdre, set in what comes as a pastoral oasis after the more primitive splendours of the gorge, with fields separated by curtains of poplars. The valley closes in again and becomes very rocky after Gèdre.

This very much a glacial valley, with streams from hanging valleys high up the main valley wall cascading down to join the Gave de Gavarnie. The most spectacular of them, on the right after about 2km and a steeper pitch of road, is the Cascade d'Arroude where the Gave d'Aspé tumbles into the valley. The surroundings become a mass of tumbled rocks for the remainder of the road climb.

The village of Gavarnie has become rather a tourist resort, and it is where the surfaced road ends. The traditional (and conventional tourist) way for visitors to get from here up to the cirque is by horse or donkey, and it is with strings of these that the rest of the route has to be shared.

The rock wall of the Cirque de Gavarnie is already partially visible – though you get no feel of its true immensity – as you leave the village along a quite well surfaced but untarred track. This comes out, after following the stream quite closely for a while, into a broad open grassy space, dotted with pine trees.

After about 2.5km, the track enters a wood and becomes very steep and stony, certainly not easily ridable. Indeed, it is questionable whether it is worth taking a bicycle any farther. The path becomes quite twisting as well as narrow farther up so it is probably best to leave bikes, locked of course, at the entrance to the wood.

The climb on foot to the top of the track, the Hôtel du Cirque, is a must. It is only from here that you can appreciate the awe-inspiring scale of the Cirque de Gavarnie. It is a vast semi-circular depression – about 3.5km across – hemmed in by steep cliffs over which streams and melt waters from the snows above tumble, the white of their plumes standing out against the dark rock. The base of the cliffs is a little under 1700m up (the hotel is at 1570m), while the height of the rim ranges from 2800 up to 3248m, so that the sheer wall of the Cirque de Gavarnie rears up by nearly 1500m from the valley floor – an unforgettable sight.

Maps   Michelin 85, panel 18
Road number   D921, then track
Approximate total climb   850m (in direction described)
Linking   Luz St Sauveur (24km to summit) and summit
Closed period   October to April
Region   Midi-Pyrénées
Départements   65-Hautes-Pyrénées
Accommodation   Luz St Sauveur, Gèdre, Gavarnie

Cormet de Roselend

1,968m, northern Alps, by way of the Col de Méraillet (1,605m)

The Aiguilles des Glaciers – the south-western extremities of the Mont Blanc massif – seen up the valley of the Torrent des Glaciers on the descent of the east-ern side of the Cormet de Roselend.

This climb gives you two cols for the price of one, since you pass over the 1605m Col de Méraillet on the way to the top. In fact the wooded hairpins of this first col are quite the hardest part of the climb.

The route leaves Beaufort through the stark V-shaped cleft of the Défilé d'Entreroches, before climbing beside the tumbling waters of the stream that is eventually to become the Doron de Beaufort. The climbing becomes a bit earnest after you pass a small hydroelectric power station, and the road hoists itself up a couple of steep hairpins before settling down to a steadier gradient. Views, except for glimpses down through the trees, are rather restricted on this stretch, since virtually the whole of this part of the climb is through dense pine forest.

Just before the Col de Méraillet, however, the road comes out into the open, with broad views to the left. At the col, where there is a road junction, the route bears sharply left and goes slightly downhill as it circles the waters of the Barrage de Roselend. This is a very attractive lake, for all that it is artificial and relatively recent, with its steep banks dotted with Alpine chalets. Their broad shingled roofs shelter dwelling-house, barn and byre all in the one building, though in many the barn and byre have been converted to extra living-space.

From the bridge at the head of the waters the road begins to climb again, this time through quite different country. This could be Scotland, treeless and grassy, with rounded rocky outcrops, heather and reedy patches. Even the scale of the mountains, relative to the altitude of the road, is Scottish.

The Cormet itself is a wide open savage glen, delicately golden in the late September sunlight when we passed, with shimmering silvery tarns. At the top, the road passes through a rocky cleft and begins the twisting descent to Bourg St Maurice. Do not go down too fast, though, because about 4km from the top there is a spectacular view of the brilliantly white Aiguilles des Glaciers, the glacier-topped southern outlines of Mont Blanc, up a steep valley to the left of the road.

Maps   Michelin 74, panels 17 and 18
Road number   D902
Approximate total climb   1,200m (in direction described)
Linking   Beaufort (12km to Col de Méraillet, 20km to summit) and Bourg-St-Maurice (21km to summit)
Closed period   November to April
Region   Rhône-Alpes
Départements   73-Savoie
Accommodation   Beaufort, Bourg-St-Maurice

Col de la Croix de Fer

2,064m, northern Alps, by way of the Col du Mollard (1,638m)

The Col de la Croix de Fer, between the valleys of the Arc and the Romanche, is one of the most scenic of all the Alpine cols. From St Jean-de-Maurienne in the valley of the Arc there are several variants of routes to the top, and the one given here goes by way of the Col du Mollard (or Molard). This is a delightful road but it adds about 300m of climbing, since the road dips about that much between the two. It is possible to make a circuit from St Jean-de-Maurienne or La Chambre by going up the Col de la Croix de Fer and then down the Col du Glandon (described next) or vice versa; the two cols are only 2.5km apart at the top and only 144m different in altitude.

The route leaves St Jean-de-Maurienne east as if to join the N6 up the valley of the Arc but a left fork on the outskirts of the town, onto the D81 signposted Montricher-Albanne, passes under the main road. About 500m later a right turn on the D80 towards Villargondran begins the climb. There are several delights to this little road. First, while there is no easy way of climbing 800m, this road does its best by going up in about 23 short hairpins so that there is a change of view every few hundred metres, first over a rapidly diminishing St Jean, then impressive panoramas of the peaks of the Vanoise opposite.

On the fine late September day that we made the climb, the views were fringed on this leafy road by the first of the autumn colours on the sycamores and birches. The verges, too, had their share of colour with the pale purple of autumn crocus. The gradient is steady with only two or three short stretches qualifying for a Michelin steeper-than-5-per-cent chevron.

The road eventually emerges above the trees at the hamlet of Albiez-le-Jeune, a collection of Alpine-style chalets. From here to the next village, Albiez-le-Vieux, the road sweeps round in a wide open arc, giving the first views to the left of the dramatic triple peaks of the Aiguilles d'Arves, which are to dominate the landscape for the rest of the climb.

In the centre of Albiez-le-Vieux, a left turn (still on the D80) leads up through chalet-dotted meadows to the Col du Mollard, 1638m. From here, the road swoops downhill quite briskly through Le Mollard and a succession of little hamlets to the dark cleft of the gorge of the Arvan, which it reaches at Pont de Belleville. The route turns left here up the valley, leaving St Jean-d'Arves perched high to the right.

The climb is quite steady up to St Sorlin-d'Arves, then the last tougher stretch begins. From here to the top the road gains 560m in 7.5km, an average of a little over 7 per cent (1-in-14) with a noticeably steeper stretch about half-way up. Despite the ruggedness of the surrounding mountains, the climb – apart from the scale – could almost be Welsh or Pennine. The slopes are grassy, rounded and treeless as the road sweeps up in long hairpins. The view from the top is of range after range of jagged peaks, dominated to the south-east by the three pinnacles of the Aiguilles d'Arves, a magnificent sight.

Maps   Michelin 77, panels 6 and 7
Road numbers   D80, D926
Approximate total climb   1,100m to Col du Mollard, then 700m from Pont de Belleville to Col de la Croix de Fer (in direction described)
Linking   St Jean-de-Maurienne (18km to summit of Col du Mollard, 40km to summit of Col de la Croix de Fer) and Rochetaillée in the Romanche valley (30km to summit of Col de la Croix de Fer)
Closed period   The upper parts of the pass are blocked by snow from November to May
Region   Rhône-Alpes
Départements   73-Savoie (and 38-Isère if descending to Rochetaillée)
Accommodation   St Jean-de-Maurienne, Albiez-le-Jeune, Albiez-le-Vieux, St Sorlin-d'Arves

Col du Glandon
1,924m, northern Alps

This is the twin Col to the Croix de Fer: the heads of the valleys of the two streams, the Glandon and the Arvan, which lead to the two cols from their northern sides are only a few kilometres apart, while a single road leads from the road junction just below the Col du Glandon south-west down the valley of the Eau d'Olle to the valley of the Romanche at Rochetaillée.

It was by this southerly direction that we first approached the Col du Glandon. In this direction it is a steady climb of some 27km, during which, with perhaps a couple of steeper pitches, the road rises about 1200m. In the few years since that first ascent, a large artificial lake has filled a large part of the upper valley.

Knowing only this rather pastoral approach, I found it hard to understand why the Tour de France organisers always grade the Col du Glandon as a tough first-category climb, putting it on a par with some of the real giants. Of recent years, one of the Alpine stages has several times included the Col du Glandon as the second or third climb of the day, between the Col de la Madeleine and the final ascent to the ski resort of Alpe d'Huez. I found the answer when we came to approach it from the north-east. The climb reserves most of its hardest bits for the end (not that the whole of the first part is easy), with about 500m of ascent unevenly distributed over the last 6km.

The lower part of the valley is green and deciduously wooded, interspersed with cultivated fields. Indeed, here the valley seems almost lowland and quite reminiscent in places, with its small and geometrical tree-lined fields, of the bocage country of Normandy. After the village of St Colomban-des-Villards, the landscape becomes more upland; the forest changes from the ash and oak of the lower slopes to pines, while the peaks of the surrounding mountains begin to show above the trees. There are a couple of quite steep pitches on this part of the route, with one fairly short stretch of 13 per cent (1-in-8) just below the hamlet of Léchet.

From here the country opens out as you climb above the tree line, into a wild mixture of rocky outcrops and rough pasture. The final 2km of the climb are up three or four tightly packed hairpins, dominated by the sombre colours of the cliffs of the Aiguilles de l'Argentière, which seem perpetually to be in shadow. From the highest hairpin there are almost aerial views of the road below. Then, as you lift your eyes from the immediate slopes, the view north-east extends back down the straight valley of the Glandon and then up the opposite valley of the Bugeon, which leads to the Col de la Madeleine.

The Aiguilles d' Arves from the Col de La Croix de Fer.

On the last, steep, hairpins of the Col du Glandon

Framed in the blue cleft at the head of the far valley is the distant snow-capped summit of Mont Blanc.

Maps   Michelin 77, panels 6 and 7
Road number   D927
Approximate total climb   1,450m (in direction described)
Linking   La Chambre (22km to summit) and St Jean-de-Maurienne (32km to summit, via the Col de la Croix de Fer) or Rochetaillée (27km to summit)
Closed period   November to the beginning of June
Region   Rhône-Alpes
Départements   73-Savoie
Accommodation   La Chambre, St Colomben-des-Villards, St Sorlin-d'Arves, St Jean-de-Maurienne

Col des Glières

1,425m, northern Alps, by way of the Col du Collet (1,390m)

This was an intriguing climb, partly because it was unexpected. It was the first col we tackled on an Alpine camping tour, starting from Geneva. As far as we could tell from the map it ought to be possible to go right over, making it a convenient short cut from the west to the valley of the Borne, ready to tackle the Col des Aravis the next day. However, the map marks the top 2km as being no more than a path. In the end we need not have worried: it is all eminently ridable.

The route starts in the village of Thorens-Glières and begins to climb almost immediately afterwards, leading gently uphill through pinewoods past the hamlet of Usillon. Then, at a sharp left bend where a dead-end turning goes straight ahead to La Verrerie, the road begins to steepen quite considerably up a series of short hairpins through the forest. Something like 600m of climb is compressed into these last 7km, so that this stretch is quite hard. There are quite fine cameo views of the rocky higher slopes of the valley from some of the hairpin bends before the road eventually emerges into open heathland at the first summit, the Col du Collet (1390m).

This is the beginning of the rolling floor of the pastures of the Plateau de Glières.

This now peaceful open space was the scene of some of the fiercest fighting by the French Resistance in 1944 and much of the plateau is now dedicated as a zone of quiet contemplation, dominated by a huge memorial to the memory of those who lost their lives.

From the Col du Collet the road drops a little to the valley floor before climbing gently again to the Col de Glières itself. At the end of the metalled road the route continues as a broad and hard-surfaced but untarred track, almost level, for some 2km until it rejoins another surfaced road at Chez la Jode. After a farther 2km or so of gentle downhill the road makes a very steep plunging and twisting descent to the valley of the Borne.

Maps   Michelin 74, panels 6 and 7
Road number   D2, then forestry road
Approximate total climb   700m (in direction described)
Linking   Thorens-Glières (11km to summit) and Le Petit-Bornand (15km to summit)
Closed period   None quoted officially but it would seem likely that at least the top part is like-

On the hairpins of the Col du Collet.

ly to be blocked by snow from November to April
Region   Rhône-Alpes
Départements   74-Haute-Savoie
Accommodation   Thorens-Glières, Le Petit-Bornand

Pas de la Graille
1,597m, Provence

The abiding memory of this climb to the summit of the Montagne de Lure in Provence is of heat. The imposing wall of the Montagne de Lure is particularly striking – or daunting – seen from the north. The ridge is an eastward prolongation of Mont Ventoux and the highest point – the Signal de Lure, 1,826m – is less than 100m lower. There the similarity ends, for whereas the upper parts of Mont Ventoux are a desolation of pale limestone scree, the Montagne de Lure is wooded to within a few metres of the top, where a grassy downland takes over.

The climb begins where the D53 turns south from the D946 to cross the stream of the Jabron. The valley is flat-bottomed, with a Provençal landscape of olive groves, almond orchards and lavender fields, with maize here and there. For the first 5 or 6km of the climb, the road through Valbelle and Les Escoffiers follows the valleys of a couple of small streams and is bordered by cultivation.

It was a searing June afternoon when we tackled these slopes. The sun beat down from almost overhead and the light and heat bounced back from the white stones of the road. The little streams were no more than a thin trickle in their large limestone beds. It was some relief to come into the shade of the immense beech forest of La Fayée, but we were even more grateful after a farther 6km or so to find a drinking water source on the left of the road.

The beech forest is quite dense and seemed strangely ominous: there was little or no sound of wildlife or bird song. As the road, already quite winding, comes up to the foot of the wall of rock it embarks on three great hairpin loops, each about 2km long, to hoist itself to the rocky cleft at the apparent top.

Here the forest gives way to a close-cropped and aromatic downland, perfumed by the abundant Provençal herbs. This 'top', although a col, is deceptive and the road continues to climb gently below the grassy ridge of the Signal de Lure to the true summit some 3km farther on. This road is quite open with immense views south over range after range of foothills to the hazy blue line of the Mediterranean.

The highest point on the road is at a sharp left-hand bend, where the hillside plunges away to the right down the valley of a small stream. From here there is an impressive view to the north into the valley of the Jabron and beyond, with the crest of Mont Ventoux to the west at the end of the rising ridge.

The descent to St Étienne is magnificent, through cedars and pines on a beautifully surfaced road with the kilometre bornes ticking away at less than a minute apiece.

Maps   Michelin 81, panel 15
Road numbers   N85, (D53), D946, D53
Approximate total climb   1,100m (in direction described)
Linking   Sisteron (31km to summit) and St Étienne (21km to summit)
Closed period   15 November to 31 May for the whole of the north side and the south side above the ski station
Region   Provence-Alpes-Côte d'Azur
Départements   04-Alpes-de-Haute-Provence
Accommodation   Sisteron, St Étienne

Hourquette d'Ancizan
1,538m, Pyrenees

This is one of the lesser-known central Pyrenean cols, but an utterly delightful one. The better known route from the valley of the Neste, in which Arreau lies, and Ste Marie-de-Campan is by way of the Col d'Aspin. The Aspin, which climbs to 1,489m, is itself a very pleasant climb, showing one of the aspects of southern mountain scenery when it comes under an Atlantic influence, as the western two-thirds of the Pyrenees do. This is that as you climb, so the vegetation becomes more and more characteristic of lower places farther north. So it was that when we crossed the top of the Col d'Aspin on an earlier visit it was through almost Chiltern beechwoods.

The Hourquette d'Ancizan climbs a little higher than the Aspin – to 1,538m – but is a far, far quieter road. It is a lovely climb with a whole variety of aspects; quite steep to begin with as it climbs the side of the glacial valley through mixed forest from Guchan, with aerial views of Guchan and the village of Ancizan. After about 3km, the road reaches the head of the little valley that it has been following and turns sharp right at a bridge, to emerge as a superb narrow shelf road with extensive views backwards towards the high peaks on the Spanish border.

The next stage is through aromatic pinewoods at a steady gradient, and then the road emerges onto almost lawn-like open meadows. This is one of the mountain areas where seasonal migration of live-stock is still practised, and brown cattle, newly brought up from the valley, were grazing on the intense early summer greenness. There are one or two sweeping curves reminiscent of the Peak District, with little rocky outcrops, on this rolling pastoral section.

At the highest point there is a little grassy knoll just off the road to the right that makes an ideal pic-nic spot and offers fine views east over the Neste val-ley. From here the road sweeps down, first through more broad meadows with cows and the clamour of their bells, then into the shade of beechwood to join the D918 near the foot of the Col d'Aspin. Here you can turn left to reach Ste Marie-de-Campan, which lies at the foot of the mighty Col du Tourmalet.

Map   Michelin 85, panel 19
Road number   D113
Approximate total climb   800m (in direction described)
Linking   Guchen or Ancizan (11km to summit) and Ste Marie-de-Campan (19km to summit)
Closed period   December to April
Region   Midi-Pyrénées
Départements   65-Hautes-Pyrénées
Accommodation   Cadéac, Ste-Marie-de-Campan

Col de l'Iseran
2,764m, northern Alps

This is the big one. The 2,802m Cime de la Bonette may sneak a few metres higher, but the long route to the top of the Col de l'Iseran from Bourg St Maurice, or the zigzag up the south wall from the valley of the Arc in the other direction emphasise that this is a giant. Purists argue that this is the highest genuine col in Europe, maintaining that roads that go higher are either dead ends to the tops of mountains (such as the 3,392m Picacho de Veleta in Spain's Sierra Nevada, which does actually continue as an unsur-faced track) or are artificially contrived to go higher than they need (such as the Cime de la Bonette, which loops nearly 100m above the Col de la Bonette).

Whatever the merits of the arguments, the Col de l'Iseran makes a long and hard but extremely rewarding day's work. The road is best tackled in the direction described, north to south, since that yields both the more attractive climb – and the easier, although the term is strictly relative – and the more spectacular descent.

The road, which is the D902 throughout, follows the valley of the infant Isère for much of its length and leaves the main N90 at the small village of Séez, about 3km north-east of Bourg-St-Maurice. Dis-concertingly, in view of what lies ahead, the road starts off with a downhill stretch to the river and then follows it, almost level and mostly through meadows, for some 8km to just below the next vil-lage, Ste-Foy-Tarentaise. A steep double hairpin brings you up to the village, and two more steep pitches follow it, the second just before the first of the eleven short tunnels on the route, just after La Thuile.

By now the road is largely through birch and pine forest, with striking glimpses of the glaciers of Mont Pourri on the opposite side of the valley. The climb is quite unrelenting, with several tougher double-chevron stretches, up to 13 per cent (1-in-8). The last of these brings you up to a dam, the Barrage de Tignes, and the junction for the ski resort of Tignes itself. On the day we tackled it, admittedly with camping gear, the 24km from Bourg-St-Maurice to this point took all morning.

Fortunately the gradient eases off for a spell from here as the road runs beside the artificial Lac du Chevril, with a total of seven tunnels, all lit either naturally or artificially. The road climbs gently away from the head of the lake, followed by a slight drop into Val d'Isère, another ski resort. By this point you have covered rather over half the total climb, leav-ing 930m to be gained in the last 16km to the top.

Val d'Isère is pretty well the last habitation on the route for 30km, and certainly the last of any size. From here the nature of the countryside changes quite abruptly, giving way to an open tumble of rocks and rough pasture. The road still follows the Isère, now quite a small tumbling stream, finally crossing it for the last time at Pont St Charles.

At the bridge the road changes direction and heads west as it zigzags its way up the southern side of the valley, with spectacular views opening up at each bend down the Isère valley, hemmed in by glac-ier-fringed peaks. After passing close to the top

On the middle slopes of the Col de l'Iseran.

The Signal de Mt Iseran from the upper slopes of the Col de l'Iseran.

cable-car station on the Tête du Salaise, the overall direction of the road changes once more, now giving views to the left of the road across a barren rocky valley to the 3,383m Aiguille Pers. Just before the road turns there is a viewpoint a little off the road, known as the Belvedère de la Tarentaise.

The last few hundred metres lead through an utterly desolate and barren landscape to the top of the col, where in summer you may be lucky enough to find the café-restaurant open. The summit of the pass is awesome rather than picturesque, a chaos of jagged peaks and grey rocks, rather emphasized on the last occasion we were there by the gathering September dusk.

The descent towards the valley of the Arc follows a succession of large spectacular bends that cling to the rims of deep clefts in the mountainside. Snow lingers here quite late in the season and I have passed this way in July when the road was a narrow ribbon between 6m snow walls. The first village, Bonneval-sur-Arc, 14km and 1000m below the summit, has hotels, restaurants and a gîte d'étape.

Maps Michelin 74, panels 19 and 20, continued on 77, panel 9

Road number D902
Approximate total climb 1,930m (in direction described)
Linking Bourg-St-Maurice (47km to summit) and Lanslebourg (33km to summit)
Closed period The upper part of the road, between Val d'Isère and Bonneval, is generally blocked by snow from the beginning of November to the beginning of July
Region Rhône-Alpes
Départements 73-Savoie
Accommodation Bourg-St-Maurice, Séez, Ste-Foy-Tarentaise, Val d'Isère, Bonneval-sur-Arc, Bessans, Lanslebourg, Lanslevillard

Col d'Izoard
2,360m, southern Alps

This pass is one of the most memorable of all, with its outstanding feature the striking rocky pinnacles and screes of the Casse Déserte just below the summit. We approached it from the south, since we were based in Guillestre, and this appears to be slightly the better direction.

The route (which is on the D902 throughout)

starts by following the narrow valley of the Guil up the Combe du Queyras. Once you are clear of the first pitch out of Guillestre, this part is quite a gentle climb, through flower-filled meadows and dark pinewoods. About 1km before Château-Queyras, which dominates the skyline to the right for some kilometres, the road to the col doubles back to the left, to head north-west and then north up the valley of the Rivière, climbing a little more resolutely through the village of Arvieux.

Arvieux is an example of the traditional but disappearing style of village of the region, with wooden balconies, some quite ornate, on the broad-roofed houses. The larch shingles that cover the roofs are also a local feature. There are more fine examples of these traditional buildings on the way down the other side of the col, the Chalets d'Izoard, which are inhabited only in summer when the flocks and herds are moved up to their summer pastures.

All the time the road has been climbing, the valley has been closing in and at the hamlet of Brunissard the head of the valley appears blocked by a high, pine-clad wall of rock. The road climbs this in a steep series of wooded hairpins, with the view opening up to give broad panoramas to the east and back down the valley as you climb.

Then comes the surprise of the Casse Déserte: as you round a rocky bend to the right you are suddenly clear of the trees. Ahead is a great curve of the mountain side, with the road clinging to it on an open shelf and passing between jagged pinnacles of rock. The whole hillside is a grey-brown desolate scree, completely devoid of any vegetation. The scale of the rock pinnacles that tower above the road only becomes apparent as you follow the road round the hillside and pass beneath them.

This had been a place that had stirred my imagination ever since I had seen dramatic photographs in French sports magazines of the Tour de France riders in the 1950s, often no more than dots in the vast, empty, dusty double-page landscape. (Somehow, it seemed, it was always an epic side-by-side duel between the two top stars of the day, the rest of the field far, far behind in their dusty wake.) Two plaques on almost the last of the rock pinnacles commemorate two of them, the Italian Fausto Coppi, still to many the *Campionissimo* (champion of champions), and the French rider Louison Bobet, both of whom forged their Tour victories on this very road.

A short steep pitch climbs away from the almost level road of the Casse Déserte to cover the last few

Near Arvieux on the approaches to the Col d'Izoard.

Cyclist brought down to scale: the bizarre landscape of the Casse Déserte, just below the summit of the Col d'Izoard.

hundred metres to the summit, itself rather feature-less, but offering extensive views south and north. The northern side of the col, down to Briançon, is much more verdant, with the bare rock and then small pinewoods soon giving way to rich and open upland pastures.

Since Briançon is some 300m higher than Guillestre, there is rather less downhill on this side than uphill on the other. On the occasion we crossed, this 300m advantage allowed us to make a rapid return down the Durance valley back to our terraced orchard camp site in Guillestre in time to watch the sun set over the Massif de Pelvoux and the Barre des Écrins.

Maps   Michelin 77, panel 18
Road number   D902
Approximate total climb   1,350m (in direction described)
Linking   Guillestre (32km to summit) and Briançon (22km to summit)
Closed period   The pass, or at least the higher parts of it, is usually blocked by snow from October to June
Region   Provence-Alpes-Côte d'Azur
Départements   05-Hautes-Alpes
Accommodation   Guillestre, La-Maison-du-Roy, Château-Queyras, Arvieux, Briançon

Col de la Madeleine
1,993m, northern Alps

The through road over the top of the Col de la Madeleine is relatively recent, having been opened only in 1969. It now provides a very scenic link between the valleys of the Arc and the Isère. We found it quite a tough climb, not so much in having too many steep pitches – although there are one or two – but in being rather relentless in its apparent determination to reach the top. The total ascent of some 1500m in 18km entitles it to be.

The beginning of the climb, from La Chambre up through St Martin-sur-la-Chambre, is quite domestic, winding between cottage gardens and small vineyards. These soon give way to a green country-side of poplars and open pasture – apart from the obvious slope and the glimpses of mountain peaks, almost a lowland landscape. From time to time the road narrows to pass through a short rocky stretch, but for the most part the route is relatively open

with views down to the deepening Bugeon valley to the left and back to the emerging peaks.

Just before St François there is a quite remark-able view to the left across the cleft of the Bugeon of some strangely sculpted earth columns (see the description of the Col de Vars). There is a straggle of new development of ski resorts based on the old villages of St François and Longchamp, which lie in a curved amphitheatre in the hillside, some 1600m up.

The last 400m of climb is by four great hairpin sweeps, about 1–1.5km each, which lift the road rapidly above the valley. By now the countryside is quite open, with rough grass, rocky outcrops and a few swampy patches. As the road climbs, so the views open out, and on the last stretch before the top there is a magnificent view down the steep-sided valley of the Bugeon and then up the valley of the Glandon directly opposite, with the blue cleft of the Col du Glandon visible at the head of the valley. There is a table d'orientation just off the road near the top – and a welcome café. To the north the view is completely dominated by the white bulk of Mont Blanc, which accompanies you nearly the whole way down to the valley of the Isère.

The Madeleine is one of those cols where there appears to be some disagreement about the altitude, different maps quoting 1984 and 1993m, while the sign at the top unequivocally claims 2000m – which might well be true of the top of the sign.

Maps   Michelin 77, panel 7 and 74, panel 17
Road number   D94
Approximate total climb   1,500m (in direction described)
Linking   La Chambre (18km to summit) and N90 (27km to summit)
Closed period   November to the beginning of June
Region   Rhône-Alpes
Départements   73-Savoie
Accommodation   La Chambre, St François, Longchamp, Celliers, Pussy

Crêt de l'Oeillon
1,370m, Mont Pilat, Rhône valley

The main feature of this climb, a pleasant if unex-ceptional wooded ride up the western side of the Rhône valley south of Lyon, is the tremendous views it offers across the Rhône to the complete western wall of the Alps.

Pélussin, the starting point of the route, is a pleasant light limestone village, ablaze with red geraniums when we stayed there on our June visit. The road leaves the village by the main D62, but then bears left after about 2km onto the much smaller D63. Almost immediately the road plunges into oak and beechwoods, and in fact most of the rest of the climb is heavily wooded.

After about 8km there is a temptation to follow the road to Bassin, which looks the obvious route. Do not – it leads directly back down into the valley. Take the right fork, which is still the D63. The woodland on the left of the road begins to thin and through the gaps there are the first of the views over the Rhône. By now on our visit it was mid-morning and the last traces of the mist that had filled the valley from edge to edge earlier in the morning were beginning to burn away.

A farther 2.5km brings you to the road summit of the Col de la Croix de l'Oeillon, 1,234m. However, for the best views turn right onto the road leading up to the television station. At the end of the road a path leads round the enclosure of the TV station, skirting it to the north, and then comes out onto a rocky promontory. From here there is what is probably one of the finest panoramas of the Rhône valley. Beyond the valley in the foreground is displayed the whole of the Alps, dominated by Mont Blanc, visibly head and shoulders above the rest. Beyond the rocky ramparts of the Vercors the peaks of the Écrins – La Meije, Barre des Écrins and Mont Pelvoux – stand out, while it is just possible to make out the distinctive outline of Mont Ventoux to the south.

Maps   Michelin 76, panels 9 and 10, or 77, panel 1
Road number   D63
Approximate total climb   800m (in direction described)
Linking   Pélussin (15km to summit) and Bourg-Argenteuil or St Étienne (20 and 24km to summit respectively)
Closed period   None quoted, probably December to March
Region   Rhône-Alpes
Départements   42-Loire
Accommodation   Pélussin, Bessat, Bourg-Argenteuil

Pré de Madame Carle
1,874m, southern Alps

This is necessarily an out-and-home excursion right into the heart of the Massif des Écrins. The detour begins at the little metal-extracting town of L'Argentière-la-Bessée in the valley of the Durance. We were staying farther south, in Guillestre, which gave us the chance of following the delightful winding road, or combination of roads, up the west bank of the Durance.

From the centre of L'Argentière, the D994[E] follows the valley of the Gyronde, a tumbling tributary of the Durance, up to Vallouise. As the walls of the valley close in, the twin villages of Les Prés and Puy-St-Vincent are prominently perched to the left of the road, high above the dark pines, against a backdrop of the snow-covered summits of the ridges of Mont Pelvoux.

Vallouise is the last village of any size, although there is a string of hamlets farther up the valley forming the Commune of Pelvoux. Like these hamlets, Vallouise has several houses in the Briançon traditional style: these have a stone-built lower storey that houses cattle and horses, above this the wooden-built dwelling quarters and finally, under the ample sloping roof, the barn for storing hay. The houses back onto the hillside, giving ground-level access to all three storeys. Wooden balconies, sometimes quite ornate, form a feature of the dwelling level.

Vallouise is 1,167m up, and up to this point the climbing has been steady, but from the last of the hamlets, Ailefroide, the slope steepens markedly. From Ailefroide the first part of the climb is almost straight, the thinning larches and birches that border the road framing a magnificent view of the twin 3932 and 3946m peaks of Mont Pelvoux. At the time – mid-June – when we climbed this little road we were treated to a superb display of cream and crimson orchids in the clearings bordering the road, just below the steepest section of the climb. Michelin warn of the latter, with three steep-hill chevrons and a 15 per cent (1-in-6) warning.

This is really quite a tough section, but the reward is to come out onto the almost level final stage of the glaciated valley. Here you are above most of the trees, and the landscape is a savage tumble of rocks, with the peaks of the Écrins and their glaciers dominating the view. The road crosses the

Crossing the stream just below the Pré de Mme Carle.

larches – a magical place, and well worth the effort of getting there.

Maps   Michelin 77, panels 17 and 18
Road numbers   D38, D138^A, D994^E, D994^T, D204^T
Approximate total climb   950m (in direction described)
Linking   L'Argentière-la-Bessée (24km to summit) and Pré de Mme Carle (summit)
Closed period   November to May to Ailefroide; October to June for the highest part
Region   Rhône-Alpes
Départements   05-Hautes-Alpes
Accommodation   Ailefroide, St Antoine, Vallouise, L'Argentière-la-Bessée, Guillestre

Col de Romeyère
Route des Écouges, 1,069m, Vercors

The Col de Romeyère itself is not at all spectacular: it is a gentle and almost straight slope through hazel

tumbling milky glacier melt-water by a primitive bridge and heads up the narrow valley to the end of the road, the Pré de Mme Carle.

Despite the name Pré (meadow) the flat floor of the head of the valley is rocky and stony with a few hardy Alpine plants preparing for their brief flowering season. At the time we were there, snow still blocked the way to the final kilometre or so. A quick scramble round the drift brought us out onto clear road once more, quite alone and able to savour the silence of this remote spot – silent, that is, except for the tinkling of the many glacial streams and the occasional creaking that goes with all glaciers as the positions of sun and shadow change. High above, the bright sun picked out the tongues and fissures of the Glacier Blanc and the Glacier Noir, perched high in their hidden valleys. The whole was magnificently set off by the young green of the spring

At the Pré de Mme Carle, with one limb of the Glacier Blanc in the background.

thickets, beechwoods and patches of upland pasture, which merely reaches the top and then goes gently down again. What is really spectacular about this climb is the 700m clamber from St Gervais up the cliff rampart of the Vercors massif. Over the central 6km or so of this stretch the road gains over 550m of height, so that the average is around 9 to 10 per cent. The gradient is far from even, so there are some very tough pitches indeed.

It all starts off gently enough as a winding little road through the orchards of the valley of the Isère, beginning with a sweep to the north, away from the top of the climb. After turning south by two successive sharp bends, the narrow road starts to climb in earnest, through dwarf oak-woods with occasional glimpses across the valley. About 3.5km farther on, with the apparently impenetrable wall of limestone dead ahead, the gradient eases briefly at a point where the stream of the Drévenne cascades impressively down the cliff.

At the bridge the road bends sharply right and begins to scale the cliff in a series of three steep steps. After a sharp left-hand hairpin there are really impressive aerial views of the road you have just come up and the cascade. Part way along this section, where the road is cut out of the cliff, a tunnel leads to the right. Until recently all uphill traffic had to take the 400m tunnel (which

Waterfall of the River Drévenne on the Col de Romeyère.

Below Chameloc on the Col de Rousset.

was unlined, unlit, rough-surfaced, virtually unridable and quite terrifying) but now a dispensation allows cyclists to stay on the outside. This outside road built into the face of the rock is still the downward route for all traffic, so be cautious.

The two branches reunite at a rock arch, from which there are more spectacular views of the start of the cascade. A final relatively short steep pitch leads up to the final gentle ramp to the top of the col.

Map   Michelin 77, panel 4
Road number   D35
Approximate total climb   850m (in direction described)
Linking   St Gervais (13km to summit) and Rencurel (4.5km to summit)
Closed period   Since this is not one of the major access routes to winter sports stations and, farther, is north-facing it is liable to be closed from November to at least April
Region   Rhône-Alpes
Départements   38-Isère
Accommodation   Vinay, Rovon, Rencurel

Col de Rousset
1,254m, Vercors

This is one of the most delightfully compact of all cols – and certainly the most colourful I have ever encountered. I had been intrigued by it ever since I had noted its closely packed coils and turns on the map and had marked it down for a visit. When the time at last came we had only a brief June afternoon available – but, as it turned out, this makes an ideal afternoon out.

From the little wine-producing town of Die in the Drôme valley, the road to the col (the D518) is a turning at the west end of the town. The whole of the first part of the climb, some 9km or so, follows the valley of the Comane stream, and begins by climbing the flank of the little valley, through avenues of pines before emerging onto the rocky heathland that marks the entry into the Vercors Regional Natural Park. At this point you are on quite a ridge with green pastures below, and with the pale limestone cliffs of the Vercors ahead.

A little disconcertingly, the road then dips a little to the small village of Chamaloc but the interruption in the climb is short-lived. Beyond the village the steady climbing resumes (none of it really hard,

which is the pattern for the whole col) through open woodland, mostly dwarf oaks. Here one of the features of the col begins to emerge as more and more laburnum trees line the road, with great cascades of yellow flowers at that time of year.

The final stages of the col, during which the road climbs about 550m in 12km or so, comprise a series of laburnum-fringed legs of increasing length between sharp hairpin bends. The views constantly change, with the southward panorama of blue range after blue range of the Préalpes du Sud opening up with every hairpin. Most dramatic, though, is the changing perspective of the grey and cream-coloured limestone cliffs and turrets above as the road twists and turns between them, gaining height.

The last short leg of the climb finally sweeps round the head of the valley under the sheer wall of the cliff to reach the tunnel that pierces the last few metres of rock. There is a fine viewpoint from a cut-off of the old road just before the tunnel entrance. The tunnel is about 400m long and well lit; it leads through to the Vercors on the other side. At times the weather on the two sides of the tunnel can be utterly contrasting, with the col the boundary between Mediterranean France and the north. The Col de Rousset is reached by a rough path and is about 100m higher than the tunnel at 1,367m.

Map   Michelin 77, panels 13 and 14
Road number   D518
Approximate total climb   800m (in direction described)
Linking   Die (21.5km to summit) and La Chapelle-en-Vercors (18.5km to summit)
Closed period   Although the Col de Rousset is in principle one kept open all year by clearing it of snow within 24 hours of being blocked, it is likely to be open only to vehicles with snow tyres from about December to March; the Col de la Bataille only a few kilometres away in the Vercors and at much the same altitude (although on a rather less important road) is officially closed from November to May
Region   Rhône-Alpes
Départements   26-Drôme
Accommodation   Die, La Chapelle-en-Vercors

Col des Saisies
1,633m, northern Alps

Like the Col des Aravis, the next col along the road

to the north, this pass is quite pastoral at the top and – with its relatively even gradient – not too difficult a climb. In fact, the steeper slopes are near the bottom rather than at the top.

The road sets off out of Flumet with two or three quite resolute hairpins, up towards the dominating silhouette of the Notre Dame de Bellecombe. The next section runs along a shelf road through meadows with increasingly commanding views over the wooded valley of the Nant Rouge. The road dips a little to cross the stream at the head of the valley and then climbs through pine forest interspersed with patches of Alpine pasture.

About 3km short of the summit you emerge above the forest, with broad views of the hills to the north. The countryside is almost like the grassier parts of upland Wales with a broad flat-bottomed valley and flowery meadows. The summit is rather undistinguished, with the rapidly growing little ski resort of Les Saisies spreading its mechanical detritus.

Some 2km beyond the summit it is worth taking the turning to the right, which leads up towards the Signal de Bisanne. This climbs for about 2km through shady and resinous pine forest; avoid the turn to the right that leads up to the Signal itself and another small resort. The left-hand fork begins to descend, and then bursts out onto a tremendous view of the opposite wall of the valley of the Doron-de-Beaufort and the mountains of the Beaufortain. This is a superb freewheel, in long hairpins through upland meadows clinging to the hillside, then through orchards, with changing perspectives of the forests and hills at every turn.

Map   Michelin 74, panels 17 and 18
Road number   D218
Approximate total climb   700m (in direction described)
Linking   Flumet (13km to summit) and Villard-sur Doron or Beaufort (14 and 19km to summit, respectively)
Closed period   November to April
Region   Rhône-Alpes
Départements   73-Savoie
Accommodation   Flumet, Les Saisies, Hauteluce, Beaufort

Col du Tourmalet
2,115m, Pyrenees

The Col du Tourmalet is the highest of the French Pyrenean road cols and features frequently on the route of the Tour de France. Tour stages tend to finish these days in the new ski resorts, which pay handsomely for the privilege of hosting a stage finish, but the classic Pyrenean stage took in the four great cols – Aubisque, Tourmalet, Aspin and Peyresourde – usually on the way from Pau to Luchon or vice versa.

It was on the Tourmalet just after the First World War that one of the legends of the Tour was born. The French rider Eugène Christophe, well placed and with a chance of winning, broke his front forks on the rough road. In those days riders were allowed no outside help, so he scrambled down on foot to the tiny hamlet of Ste Marie-de-Campan, where he commandeered the local forge and re-brazed the forks himself – only to be disqualified later on the grounds that the smith's apprentice had worked the bellows for him.

Ste Marie lies in the valley between the Aspin and the Tourmalet, and the forge is still there. It is about a kilometre down the road towards Campan and Bagnères de Bigorre and must have seemed a dreadful trudge for unlucky Christophe. It is on the right-hand (north-east) side of the road, with a prominent plaque commemorating Christophe's misfortune, and commending his example of *'opiniâtreté'* – a word that conveys far more of his dogged persistence than the dictionary translation of 'stubbornness'. Christophe was never to win the Tour but his exploit passed into legend and he is more famous than many who did succeed.

The Tourmalet is also one of the climbs where the advantage of really low gears came home to me. On my first visit, relatively lightly laden (we were stopping at small hotels) and as a fit 30-year-old, I had to walk one or two of the steeper pitches of the climb. Since my companion was one of the most prolific winners of hill-climb races of his era – and he walked too – I did not feel too bad about it. Nearly twenty years later, with camping kit, but with the appropriate gears, we all rode these steeper bits with relative ease.

The road over the Col du Tourmalet presents two very distinct aspects. The eastern approach that we followed is open, after the wooded parts of the lower reaches, and even here, since the road soon establishes itself on the side of the steep hillside, there are open views away to the right, quite spectacular

On the lower slopes of the Col des Saisies, above Notre Dame de Bellecombe.

On the last hairpins of the Col de Vars with the Parpaillon range in the background.

in places. The western side is much wilder, with deep rocky ravines, and is always to my view much more sombre. However, a former Tour de France rider told me that the west side of the Tourmalet is the fastest descent on the whole race, and I wouldn't argue with that (although on closed roads they do not have to worry about traffic in the resort of Barèges half-way down). It certainly is a tremendously exhilarating freewheel right down to Luz-St-Sauveur.

As already suggested, there are several steep pitches on the eastern climb, mainly near the great loop that the road makes into the hillside about 7km up from Ste Marie-de-Campan. There is one particularly vicious bit, the one that brought us to our feet that first time, in an avalanche gallery just after the main hairpin. The road then climbs through the straggling ski resort of La Mongie before tackling the last few bends through open rocky grassland to the top. The last 3 or 4km often seem to be shrouded in chilling mist, even when the weather is excellent farther down, so that the café at the top can be particularly welcome.

On the north side of the Col de Vars.

Map   Michelin 85, panels 18 and 19
Road number   D918
Approximate total climb   1,250m (in direction described)
Linking   Ste Marie-de-Campan (17km to summit) and Luz-St-Sauveur (18km to summit)
Closed period   November to June
Region   Midi-Pyrénées
Départements   65-Hautes-Pyrénées
Accommodation   Ste-Marie-de-Campan, La Mongie, Barèges, Esquièze, Luz-St-Sauveur

Col de Vars
2,108m, southern Alps

This was a climb we found, approaching from the south and laden with camping gear, to be quite tough in its later stages. The map reveals that two-thirds of the climbing (640m) is indeed concentrated into the last 8km, making an average of 8 per cent (1-in-12), with some legs of the last few hairpins much steeper. The kilometre stones on this climb have the altitudes marked – so at least you can tell how you are progressing – and there are certainly two kilometre stretches with over 140m of climb, 14

per cent or 1-in-7.

The first stage of the route follows the valley of the Ubaye, which is cultivated in parts. After the village of Jausiers, the valley closes in and becomes darkly wooded with pines. Until the end of the nineteenth century, when the road through the part of the Ubaye valley below Barcelonette was cut through, this valley was as easily reached from Italy as from France. This gave some of the narrow passages a certain strategic importance and there are several forts of various eras covering the narrow Pas de Grégoire and Pas de Reyssole.

At the point where the two arms of the Ubaye join, just before the Redoute de Berwick (the Maréchal de Berwick was largely responsible for the valley being ceded to France from Savoie in 1713), the route continues straight on, on the D902, where the D900 bears right for the Col de Larche and the Italian border. A couple of sharp bends bring you up to the attractive village of St Paul, where the road begins to climb in earnest up the grassy side of the valley.

After about 3km there are some earth pillars on the right (marked as *colonnes coiffées* on the map). These are formed when a stratum of soft earthy rock or clay is protected by rocks or boulders on top of it. Particularly in areas that are basically arid but subject to sudden rainstorms from time to time, the block protects the column quite effectively, while the rapidly running water gouges out the channels between. There are some similar columns on the Col de la Madeleine, and a famous and much larger set near Manosque.

The last 4km of climb are – as noted – quite tough, leading up to the tormented and wild rolling rough pasture of the top, dotted with rocky outcrops. An austere little chapel and a monument to the Alpine troops who improved the road over the col between the wars mark the top.

The great joy of the Col de Vars in this direction, though, is the tremendous 1100m 19km descent to Guillestre, with the dramatic glacier-topped jagged peaks of the Massif des Écrins growing nearer at every turn.

Maps   Michelin 77, panel 18, and 81, panel 8
Road numbers   D900, D902
Approximate total climb   1,000m (in direction described)
Linking   Barcelonette (30km to summit) and Guillestre (19km to summit)
Closed period   The col is likely to be blocked by snow between December and April
Region   Provence-Alpes-Côte d'Azur
Départements   04-Alpes-de-Haute-Provence
Accommodation   Barcelonette, Jausiers, La Condamine-Châtelard, St Paul, Les Claux, Ste Marie-de-Vars, Vars, St Marcellin, Guillestre

Useful Books

FRANCE

The tall, thin, green *Michelin Tourist Guides* (Guides de Tourisme) give more detailed information on the regions of France, with a distinct leaning towards the architectural and historical. The series is continually being revised; currently 24 titles in French cover the whole country, region by region. English versions are available for those covering – of the areas relevant to the routes in this book – Brittany, Burgundy, Chateaux of the Loire, Flanders Picardy and the Paris Region, Normandy, and Provence. Also available in English are: Côte Atlantique (only in English), Dordogne, French Riviera, Paris and, I am afraid, Eurodisney.

Other areas available only in French versions but covering other routes in this book are: Alpes du Nord, Alpes du Sud, Berry Limousin, Champagne Ardennes, Gorges du Tarn and Périgord Quercy. Other French-only volumes are: Alsace et Lorraine, Auvergne, Corse, Jura, Poitou Vendée Charentes, Pyrénées Aquitaine, Pyrénées Roussillon and Vallée du Rhône. There are slight differences between the information given in the parallel French and English versions; the French text is usually rather fuller. A further volume in English has recently been added – France – giving an introduction to the geography, history, art and gastronomy of the whole country, plus entries for selected sites. It is intended to complement the detailed regional guides.

Coping with France by Fay Sharman (Basil Blackwell, 1984 – now unfortunately out of print but you may be able to find a library copy) and *Understanding France* by John Harris (Macmillan/Papermac, 1991) are excellent and very detailed introductions to the French way of life and how to approach shops, restaurants, hotels and so on.

Although often thought of only as the bestower of stars and rosettes for luxury and culinary excellence on high-priced establishments, the famous annual red *Guide Michelin* actually includes a wide price range of selected hotels and restaurants in its listings. It also has a large number of town centre plans, keyed to the Michelin 1:200,000 map. The book is a bit too weighty for a pannier or saddlebag, though. In French, with a seven-page introductory section in English.

Also annual, the *Guide des Auberges et Logis de France* lists some 4400 small to moderate-sized and moderately priced family-run hotels, largely in rural, village or small-town locations throughout France. Publishers are the Fédération Nationale des Logis de France, 83 avenue d'Italie, 75013 Paris. In French, with an introduction, giving booking procedures, in English.

Gîtes et refuges en France, by A. and S. Mouraret, is a pretty comprehensive listing of the 2500 or so gîtes d'étape and similar hostel-style overnight halts throughout the country. It is published in France by Éditions Créer; in the UK it is stocked by Stanford's of 12–14 Long Acre, London WC2E 9LP (telephone 0171 836 1321). In French.

A selective gîte d'étape listing for a generously interpreted Alpine area (stretching from Geneva to Nice and Marseille, and as far west as Valence and Avignon) is published as the *Guide des refuges et gîtes des Alpes* by Éditions Glénat of Grenoble; it is distributed in the UK by Cordee, 3a De Montfort Street, Leicester, LE1 7HD. Obviously the listing includes many high-mountain climbers' huts but there are also many within easy reach of cyclable roads. In French.

For campers, the annual *Camping Caravanning France* by Michelin is a valuable listing of a selection

– about one-third – of French camp sites. Although aimed primarily at motor-borne campers, no more than a handful of caravan-only sites are included. The list is particularly useful in indicating where sites may be found in sparsely endowed areas (such as large tracts of northern France) and also where you may expect to find places open outside the summer season. In French, with an explanatory introduction in English, and to be found in most reasonable-sized UK bookshops.

If you wish to take part in organized rides that follow the routes of the classic races, *Classic Cycle Races of Europe* by Rudolf Geser (Springfield Books, 1993) gives information. In English, obviously translated from the original German.

Five very detailed cycling guides to cols in the mountain areas of France, *Atlas des Cols des Alpes du Nord, Alpes du Sud, des Pyrénées, du Massif Central* and *des Vosges-Jura* are published by Éditions Altigraph, BP 1, 49080-Bouchemaine, France; also available via the FFCT (see 'Useful Organizations'). These include profiles, amount of climb and gradient, kilometre by kilometre. There is also a general guide to riding in the mountains, *Guide du Vélo en Montagne*. In French.

BICYCLES

For further information on touring bicycles and their choice and equipment, you can consult *The Cycle Tourer's Handbook* by Tim Hughes (Batsford, 1987, now obtainable only from the CTC Shop and Bicycling Books (see below), *Pedal Power!* by Tim and Roger Hughes (Blandford Press, 1995) and *Touring Bikes: a Practical Guide* by Tony Oliver (The Crowood Press, 1990).

The other standard reference is the rather wider-ranging *Richard's New Bicycle Book* by Richard Ballantine (Pan, 1990). Information leaflets are also available to CTC members from the Club's Technical and Touring Departments (see 'Useful Organizations').

SUPPLIERS

Apart from the CTC Shop, there are several specialist retail suppliers of maps and cycling books:

Bicycling Books, 309/311 Horn Lane, London W3 0BU, telephone 0181 993 3484 (books – mail order and shop sales)

Cordee, 3a De Montfort Street, Leicester LE1 7HD (books, maps and guides – mail order and shop sales)

Map Shop, 4 Court Street, Upton-on-Severn, Worcestershire WR8 0JA, telephone 01684 593146 (maps – mail order and shop sales)

Stanford's, 12–14 Long Acre, London WC2E 9LP, telephone 0171 836 1321 (books, maps and guides – mail order and shop sales)

Travellers' Bookshop, 25 Cecil Court, London WC2N 4EZ, telephone 0171 836 9132 (modern, second-hand and antiquarian travel books, plus some maps – shop sales)

FINDING BOOKS IN LIBRARIES

Most libraries mark and arrange books on their shelves in numerical order according to the Dewey Decimal Classification or a variant of it. The overall classification for France is 914.4, with subdivisions for more detailed sub-classifications – for example, Brittany is 914.41, Normandy 914.42, and Dordogne 914.47.

The numbers for bike books and bike-related books are: 629.2272 Bicycles; 629.231 Bicycle design; 629.28872 Bicycle maintenance and repair; 796.54 Camping; 796.6 Cycling; 796.609 History of cycling. You will find most under 796.6.

Useful Organizations

The principal cycle touring body in the UK is the **Cyclists' Touring Club** (known universally as the CTC) at 69 Meadrow, Godalming, Surrey GU7 3HS, telephone 01483 417217, fax 01483 426994. In addition to offering free third-party insurance and legal aid, the CTC also makes available to members a wealth of technical and travel information through its Technical and Touring Departments. The CTC can arrange travel insurance, while the CTC Shop (same address) has wide stocks of cycling books and maps, including the Michelin 1:200,000 and IGN ranges. These may be bought by callers – whether members or not – during office hours or by mail order.

The nearest thing in France to the CTC is the **Fédération Française de Cyclotourisme,** 8 rue Jean-Marie-Jégo, 75013 Paris. Although it has a few individual members, the FFCT is essentially a federation of cycle touring clubs, grouped under département and regional committees. The FFCT should be able to supply addresses of the regional committees, who can in turn give details of local clubs and their activities. Note that when writing to French voluntary organizations such as the FFCT, it is courteous to send International Reply Coupons (obtainable from post offices) to cover return postage. One coupon covers the cost of sending a simple, minimum-weight 50g letter; two or three coupons should be sent if you expect brochures or leaflets.

For **rail travel** in France, timetables are available, if you apply in person, from the French Railways Office, 179 Piccadilly, London W1V 0AL. They may also be obtained by mail order from European Rail Timetables, 39 Kilton Glade, Worksop, Nottinghamshire S81 0PX.

Details of European Bike Express **coach services** are available from Bolero International Holidays, 31 Baker Street, Middlesbrough TS1 2LF, telephone daytime 01642 240020 or 251440, evening 01642 750077 or 823920, fax 01642 232209.

The organizing body in France for **gîtes ruraux** (self-catering holiday cottages) and **chambres d'hôte** (bed and breakfast) is the Fédération Française des Gîtes Ruraux, 35 rue Godot-de-Mauroy, 75009 Paris. Once again, organization is by département and by region, and the parent organization can supply regional office addresses. The French Tourist Office at 179 Piccadilly, London W1V 0BA can supply, in addition to general information on France and its regions, addresses of regional tourism committees who issue annual lists of hotels.

The two **youth hostel** organizations in France are the FUAJ, 6 rue Mesnil, 75116 Paris; and the LFAJ, 38 boulevard Raspail, 75007 Paris. French hostels are listed in Volume 1 of the annual *International Youth Hostel Handbook,* which is obtainable from YHA Services Ltd, 14 Southampton Street, London WC2E 7HY. The guide, which is in four languages, is updated in March each year. Guides to independent hostels (gîtes d'étape) are listed above in the 'Useful Books' section.

If you would like more information on the two French organizations dealing with **cycling in mountain areas**, L'Ordre des Cols Durs (known in the UK as OCD Cycloclimbing) and the Club des Cent Cols, you can obtain it from the UK representative: John Partington, 20 Spencer Gate, St Albans, Hertfordshire AL1 4AD.

Although rather outside the scope and spirit of this book, a number of bodies and small firms organize cycle tours at all levels in France, often with a following car or luggage transport between overnight stops. The CTC organize a number of

group tours (usually moving-on trips without luggage assistance). These are publicized in an annual Tours Guide, issued as a bound-in supplement to the December issue of the CTC's magazine. You have to become a member to take part.

A number of commercial firms are listed in the Guide, while other cycling magazines produce their own listings, often in late winter issues. The best-known promotions outside these are Suzy Madron's 'Cycling for Softies' tours; these have baggage support and are, as the name implies, usually gentle although there are harder ones ('Cycling for Show-offs'). Cycling for Softies can be contacted at 2–4 Birch Polygon, Rusholme, Manchester M14 6HX, telephone 0161 248 8282.

Glossary of French Road Signs

These are the word signs, official and unofficial, often used with the vertical bar hazard sign, sometimes with others, that you are most likely to meet:

absence de signalisation horizontale   no white lines
absence de signalisation laterale   no road markings
accotements non stablisés   soft verges
affaissement   subsidence
allumez vos codes   put on your sidelights (for lit tunnels)
allumez vos phares   put on your headlights (for tunnels)
attention!   look out, danger

bac   ferry
bande cyclable   cycle lane as part of road
barrières de dégel   frost damage
boue   mud

chantier mobile   moving road-works (usually verge mowing or road resurfacing)
chaussée deformée   wavy or subsiding road surface
chute de pierres   falling stones (below unstable rock hillside or cliff)
circulation interdite   no vehicular traffic
circulez au pas   drive (and ride) at walking pace
col enneigé   col or pass not cleared of snow
col fermé   col or pass closed (because of snow)
col non déneigé   col or pass not cleared of snow
col ouvert   col or pass open
convoi exceptionnel   very large vehicle
couloir cycliste   cycle lane
couloir d'autobus   bus lane
couloir d'avalanche   track that avalanches follow down a hillside
cyclistes interdits de rouler de front   cyclists must not ride two abreast

déviation à 100 m   diversion 100 metres ahead
douane   customs post ahead

éboulement   landslide
élagage   pruning or branch lopping in progress
enneigé   snowbound

fauchage   mowing of road verges in progress
fermé or fermée   closed
feux   traffic lights
feux de signalisation   traffic lights
feux multicolores   traffic lights
fin de chantier   end of road-works
fin de travaux   end of road-works
formellement interdit de   it is strictly forbidden to
fossé   ditch

gravillons   gravel, loose chippings
gué   ford

interdiction de   it is forbidden to
interdit de   it is forbidden to
itineraire conseillée   recommended route

lacets   hairpin bends, sometimes with number of bends indicated
lacets sur 2 km   hairpin bends for 2 kilometres

nappes de brouillard   fog patches
nappes de fumée   smoke patches
nids de poules   potholes
nids de poules en formation   road breaking up into potholes

ouvert or ouverte   open

passage à niveau   level crossing

passage protégé   you have right of way over minor road crossing yours

péage   toll

piste cyclable   cycle path

piste cyclable obligatoire   compulsory cycle path

piste obligatoire pour cyclistes   compulsory cycle path

pont bascule   lifting or bascule bridge

pont mobile   swing bridge

poussière   dust

priorité à droite   give way to traffic from the right

rainurage   installation of drainage channels (see next entry)

rainure   transverse drainage channel, usually with grating

rallentir   slow down

rappel   reminder (usually of repeat speed limit, no overtaking or no parking)

risque de verglas   danger of black ice forming

roulez au pas   drive (and ride) at walking pace

route à péage   toll road

route barrée à 100 m   road closed 100 metres ahead (use your judgement as far as getting through with a bicycle is concerned; it is often less easy to get through with a bike than in the UK where pedestrian access is usually left; major road-works may involve complete rebuilding over sev eral kilometres and you can waste hours; see the introduction to the 'High Mountain' routes with special reference to closed cols)

route en mauvais état   road in bad state of repair

route glissante   slippery road

route glissante par temps de pluie   slippery road in rainy weather

route inondable   road liable to flooding

route inondable par temps de pluie   road liable to flooding in rainy weather

route non déneigée, ni sablée, ni salée   road neither cleared of snow, sanded or salted

route reglementée   road with traffic control (some times one way in opposite directions at different times)

sauf riverains   except for those owning or requiring access to property bordering the road, usually used as a qualification to a general 'no entry' sign to restrict motor traffic on very small roads (I have never known any objection to cyclists using such routes)

serrer à droite or à gauche   filter right or left

sortie d'usine   factory exit

sortie de camions   lorries coming out

sortie de carrière   quarry exit

stationnement alterné jours pairs, jours impairs   parking one side of the road on even dates, on the other side on odd dates (now rare)

stationnement alterné semi-mensuel   parking one side of the road from days 1 to 15, on the other from day 16 to the end of the month

stationnement interdit   no parking

tir de mines   blasting in progress (near quarry or road-works)

travaux   road-works in progress

troupeaux   cattle crossing

verglas   black ice

verglas fréquent   point where ice often forms

virages sur 2 km   bends for 2 kilometres

voie conseillée   recommended lane

Glossary of French Cycle Terms

Words are defined here with their meaning in a cycling context; many have other specific or general meanings. (As a start you can look up *cocotte* and *potence* in an ordinary dictionary.)

If you can manage a little of French, the word *truc* (whatsit, thingummy, gadget) is invaluable for things you do not know the name of but know what they do, have a sample of, or even merely want to put a name to. For example *Je cherche un truc comme ceci*, presenting (probably broken) sample or *Il s'agit d'un truc pour faire...* (It is a gadget to do...) or *Comment s'appelle-t-il, ce truc-ci?* (What is this thing called?). It works – if it did not I would not have been able to buy such things as nylon pot-scourers (which I now know translate as 'plastic knitting').

FRENCH TO ENGLISH

alternateur   dynamo or generator
ampoule   lamp bulb
AR or Ar   rear (common abbreviation)
arrière   rear (as in rear brake)
AV or Av   front (common abbreviation)
avant   front (as in front brake)
axe carré, fixation sur   square taper fixing for cranks on bottom-bracket axle
axe du moyeu   hub spindle
axe du pédalier   bottom-bracket axle

base or base arrière   chainstay
bavette or bavette de garde-boue   mud-flap
bécane   bike (a slang word somewhere between the pejorative and the affectionate)
bicyclette   bicycle
bidon   bottle

billes   balls in ball-bearing
blouson thermique   thermal jacket
boulon   bolt
boulon à six pans creux   socket-head bolt (Allen key fitting)
boyau   tubular (racing) tyre
braquet   slang term for gear ratio, expressed as 46 × 16 (chainwheel and sprocket)

câble   cable
câble de dérailleur   gear cable
câble de frein   brake cable
cadre   frame
cale-chaussure   shoe-plate (or cleat of clipless pedal)
cale-pied   toe-clip
casque   helmet
cassé or cassée   broken
cataphote   reflector
chaîne   chain
chambre à air   inner tube
chape   range of adjustment of derailleur gear
chappe (du pneu)   tread (of tyre)
cintre   handlebar bend
clavette   cotter pin
clé à rayons   spoke nipple key
clé à six pans   Allen key
clé anglaise   adjustable spanner
clé de 10mm   10mm spanner
clé hexagonale   Allen key
cliquet   pawl (of freewheel)
cocotte   brake-lever hood (slang)
collant   tights
collant à bretelles amovibles   bib-tights
colle pour la réparation des pneus   rubber solution
compteur cycle   cycle computer
cone   cone of bearing

couronne   sprocket of free-wheel
courroie de cale-pied   toe-strap
crevaison   puncture
cuissard   skin-shorts
cuvette   cup of ball bearing

DEL   LED
démonte-pneu   tyre lever
denture   number of teeth (of freewheel or chain
   wheel)
dérailleur   gear mechanism
dérive-chaîne   chain rivet extractor
développement   gear ratio (measured as distance
   travelled in metres per pedal turn)
diode électroluminescente   light-emitting diode
diode électroluminescente de forte puissance
   super-luminescent light-emitting diode

écrou   nut
en panne   broken down
entretoise   bridge between seat stays or chainstays
étrier   brake stirrup or brake arms

feu rouge arrière   red rear lamp
filetage   screw-thread
fixation à six pans creux   Allen key fixing
flasque   hub flange
fond de jante   rim-tape
fourche avant   front forks
frein   brake
frein à tirage central   centre-pull brake
frein à tirage lateral   side-pull brake
frein cantilever   cantilever brake

galets   derailleur pulleys
garde-boue   mudguard
gonfler les pneus   to pump up the tyres
graisse   grease
guidon   handlebar

halogène   halogen
hauban arrière   seat stay
huile   oil

jante   rim
jeu de direction   steering head bearing or headset
joue   flange of hub

K-Way   waterproof jacket (a trade name now used
   generically)

machin   thingummy or whatsit
maillon   link (of chain)
manette   lever (of gear or quick-release mechanism)
manivelle   crank
moyeu   hub
moyeu à blocage rapide   quick-release hub

panne   breakdown
pas   pitch (of thread)
patin de frein   brake-block or pad
patte de dérailleur   rear gear hanger
pattes de fourche   fork-ends
pédale   pedal
pédale automatique   cleat-fixing pedal
pédalier   bottom bracket assembly
phare   headlamp
pile   battery
plateau de pédalier   chainwheel
pneu   tyre
pneumatique   wired-on tyre
poignée de frein   brake lever
pointage   size (as in size of toe-clip)
pompe   pump
poncho   cape
porte-bagages   bag support
porte-bidon   bottle cage
porte-sac   bag carrier
potence du guidon   handlebar stem

raccord   lug (of frame)
rayon   spoke
réglage   adjustment
régler   to adjust
ressort   spring
rondelle   washer
roue   wheel
roue-libre   freewheel
roue-libre à cassette   freehub or cassette hub
roulement   bearing
roulement à aiguilles   needle roller bearing
roulement à billes   ball bearing
roulement annulaire   annular (sealed) bearing
rustines   tube patches (the trade mark of the best
   known French make, used generically)

sacoche   bag
sacoche de guidon   handlebar bag
selle   saddle
serrage   tightness (as in bolts)
serrer   to tighten

silex flint
soudé or soudée brazed-on
surbaissé or surbaissée low-mounted (as with pannier bags)

têtes de rayons spoke nipples
tige de selle seat-pillar or saddle-pillar
timbre-avertisseur bicycle bell
tournevis screwdriver
tresse tape
tresse auto-collante sticky tape
tringle de garde-boue mudguard stay
tringle de pneu tyre wire
tringle souple plastic edge-wire of foldable tyre
truc thingummy, whatsit or gadget
tube tube (of frame)
tube de base chainstay
tube de direction head tube
tube de selle seat tube
tube diagonal down tube
tube horizontal top tube

valve valve
vélo bike
vélo tous terrains or vélo tout terrain mountain bike
vérifier to check (condition or adjustment)
voilé or voilée buckled or out of true
VTT mountain bike

ENGLISH TO FRENCH

adjust *régler*
adjustable spanner *clé anglaise*
adjustment range (of derailleur gear) *chape*
Allen key *clé Allen, clé hexagonale or clé à six pans*
Allen key fitting *fixation à six pans creux*
alloy (light) *alliage léger*
aluminium alloy *alliage d'aluminium*
ATB or all-terrain bike *VTT or vélo tous terrains*

bag *sacoche*
ball bearing (assembly) *roulement à billes*
balls in ball bearing *billes*
battery (primary) *pile*
battery (rechargeable) *accumulateur*
bearing *roulement*
bell *timbre-avertisseur*

bib-tights *collant à bretelles amovibles*
bicycle *bicyclette* (more formal than vélo, as with bicycle and bike in English)
bike *vélo or bécane* (the latter affectionate but disparaging)
bolt *boulon*
bottle *bidon*
bottle-cage *porte-bidon*
bottom bracket *pédalier* (complete assembly)
bottom bracket axle *axe de pédalier*
bottom bracket cups *cuves de pédalier* (note that French cups do not fit English frames)
brake *frein*
brake arm *étrier*
brake block *patin de frein*
brake cable *câble de frein*
brake lever *poignée de frein*
brake lever hood *'cocotte'*
brake stirrup *étrier*
brake (cantilever) *frein cantilever*
brake (centre-pull) *frein à tirage central*
brake (side-pull) *frein à tirage lateral*
brazed on *soudé or soudée*
broken *cassé or cassée*
broken down *en panne*
buckled wheel *roue voilée*
bulb *ampoule*

cable *câble*
cantilever brake *frein cantilever*
cape *poncho* (not really the same garment)
carrier *porte-sacoche or porte-bagages*
cassette hub *roue-libre à cassette*
centre-pull brake *frein à tirage central*
chain *chaîne*
chain link *maillon*
chain rivet extractor *dérive-chaîne*
chainstay *base arrière*
chainwheel *plateau de pédalier*
check *vérifier*
checkpoint *contrôle*
cone (of bearing) *cone*
cotter pin *clavette* (French pins do not usually fit English cranks)
crank *manivelle*
crossbar *tube horizontal*
cycle computer *compteur cycle*

down tube *tube diagonal*
dynamo *alternateur*

flint *silex*
fork-end *patte*

forks   *fourche*
frame   *cadre*
freehub or cassette hub   *roue-libre à cassette*
freewheel   *roue-libre*
front   *avant* (often abbreviated *AV* or *Av)*
front forks   *fourche avant*

gadget   *truc*
gear (mechanism)   *dérailleur*
gear (ratio)   *braquet or développement*
gear cable   *câble de dérailleur*
gear hanger (rear)   *patte de dérailleur*
gear lever   *manette*
gear tension pulleys   *galets*
grease   *graisse*

halogen   *halogène*
handlebar (assembly)   *guidon*
handlebar (bend)   *cintre*
handlebar bag   *sacoche de guidon*
handlebar stem   *potence*
handlebar tape   *tresse pour guidon*
head tube   *tube de direction*
headlamp   *phare*
headset   *jeu de direction*
helmet   *casque*
hub   *moyeu*
hub flange   *flasque or joue*
hub spindle   *axe de moyeu*

inner tube   *chambre à air*

leather   *cuir*
LED   *DEL*
lever (brake)   *poignée*
lever (gear or quick-release)   *manette*
lever (tyre)   *démonte-pneu*
light alloy   *alliage léger or alliage d'aluminium*
light-emitting diode   *diode électroluminescente*
loosen   *déserrer*
low-mounted (as in pannier bags)   *surbaissé or surbaissée*
lug   *raccord*

mountain bike   *VTT or véo tous terrains*
mud-flap   *bavette de garde-boue*
mudguard   *garde-boue*
mudguard stay   *tringle de garde-boue*

nut   *écrou*

oil   *huile*

pannier   *grande sacoche*
pannier carrier   *porte-sacoche*

pannier rack   *porte-bagages*
patches (for inner tube)   *rustines*
pawl (of freewheel)   *cliquet*
pedal   *pédale*
pitch (of screw-thread)   *pas*
Presta valve   *valve presta*
pump   *pompe*
pump up   *gonfler*
puncture   *crevaison*

quick-release hub   *moyeu à blocage rapide*

rear   *arrière* (often abbreviated to *AR* or *Ar)*
rear lamp   *feu arrière*
reflector   *cataphote*
rim   *jante*
rim-tape   *fond de jante*
rivet extractor (chain)   *dérive-chaîne*
rubber solution   *colle pour la réparation des pneus*
   or *colle pour rustines*

saddle   *selle*
saddle-pillar   *tige de selle*
Schraeder valve   *valve schraeder*
screw-thread   *filetage*
screwdriver   *tournevis*
seat tube   *tube de selle*
seat-pillar   *tige de selle*
seat-stay   *hauban arrière*
shoe-plate   *cale-chaussure*
side-pull brake   *frein à tirage latéral*
size (of clothing)   *taille*
size (of frame)   *hauteur*
size (of toe-clip or shoe)   *pointage*
skin-shorts   *cuissard*
spanner   *clé*
spoke   *rayon* (lengths and diameters are quoted in
   millimetres)
spoke nipple   *tête de rayon*
spoke nipple key   *cléà rayons*
spring   *ressort*
sprocket (of freewheel)   *couronne*
squared-taper (cotterless) fitting   *fixation à axe
   carré or fixation sur axe carré*
steel   *acier*
steering (head)   *direction or jeu de direction*
stem (of handlebar)   *potence*
sticky tape   *tresse autocollante*
super-luminescent light-emitting diode   *diode
   électroluminescente de forte puissance*

tape   *tresse*
thermal top or jacket   *blouson thermique*
thingummy   *truc*
thorn   *épine*

tighten   *serrer*
tightness   *serrage*
tights   *collant*
toe-clip   *cale-pied*
toe-strap   *courroie de cale-pied*
tooth (of sprocket or chainwheel)   *dent*
top tube   *tube horizontal*
tread (of tyre)   *chappe*
tube (of frame)   *tube*
tube (of tyre)   *chambre à air*
tubular (racing) tyre   *boyau*
tyre (foldable)   *pneu à tringles souples*
tyre (tubular)   *boyau*

tyre (wired-on)   *pneu*
tyre lever   *démonte-pneu*
tyre wire   *tringle de pneu*

valve   *valve*
valve, Presta   *valve presta*
valve, Schraeder   *valve schraeder*

washer   *rondelle*
whatsit   *truc*
wheel   *roue*
wing-nut   *écrou papillon*

Place Names Index

Abbaye St Michel (nr Prades), 16
Administrative regions (map), 8
Administrative regions:
  Alsace, 10
  Aquitaine, 15
  Auvergne, 14
  Basse-Normandie, 9
  Bourgogne (Burgundy), 12
  Bretagne (Brittany), 11
  Centre, 11
  Champagne-Ardenne, 10
  Corse (Corsica), 18
  Franche-Comté, 13
  Haute-Normandie, 9
  Ile-de-France, 10
  Languedoc-Roussillon, 16
  Limousin, 14
  Lorraine, 10
  Midi-Pyrénées, 16
  Nord-Pas-de-Calais, 8
  Pays de la Loire, 11
  Picardie, 8
  Poitou-Charentes, 14
  Provence-Alpes-Côte d'Azur, 17
  Région Parisienne, 10
  Rhône-Alpes, 15
Aigoual, Mont (route), 98–101
Aiguilles d'Arves, 142, 143
Aiguilles de l'Argentière, 143
Aiguilles des Glaciers, 142
Aiguines, 106
Ailefroide, 151
Albiez-le-Jeune and -le-Vieux,
  142
Allos, 134
Alpes Mancelles (route), 76–79
Alpilles (route), 71–73
Alpine cols (map), 135
Ancizan, 146
Anse de Vauville, 65
Anse du Brick, 66
Anse St Martin, 65
Apt, 111

Aqueducs de Barbegal, 73
Ardèche, River, 13, 15
Arles, 74
Arleuf, 103
Arvieux, 149
Auderville, 65
Auignac, Ile d', 69
Auphelle, 94
Authie, River, 61
Autrans, 126
Avaloirs, Mont de, 76, 78
Avenas, 113
Avenay-Val-d'Or, 90
Averton, 79
Avoine, 83
Ax-les-Thermes, 16
Azay-le-Rideau, 80

Bagat-en-Quercy, 88
Balcons de la Mescla, 106
Ballon d'Alsace, 11
Barcelonette, 134, 138
Barèges, 157
Barfleur, 66
Barguelonne, River, 87, 89
Bayeux, 9
Beaufort, 142, 155
Beaujeu, 116
Beaujolais, 13, (route), 111–116
Beaumont (Manche), 65
Beaumont-du-Lac, 95
Bédoin, 132, 133
Beurainville, 61
Biville, 65
Blayon, 89
Bonaguil, 88
Bonin, 105
Bonneval-sur-Arc, 148
Bonnieux, 109
Bordeaux, 15
Bouloc, 87
Boulogne, Forêt de, 62
Boulogne-sur-Mer, 59

Boulvé, 87
Bourbourg, 66
Bourg-Argenteuil, 151
Bourg-St-Maurice, 142, 147
Bourne, River and Gorges, 124,
  126, 127
Bousiéyas, 138
Boyne, 118
Brantes-la-Jolie, 133
Brassy, 102, 105
Bréca, 70
Briançon (Hautes-Alpes), 150
Briançon (nr Chinon), 85
Brière (route), 67–71
Bussy (Morvan), 104
Bussy-Fontaines, 84

Camargue (route), 74–76
Camer, 68
Camerun, 68
Camiers, 60
Canal du Midi, 44
Canche, Gorges de la, 104
Canche, River (Pas de Calais), 61
Candes, 83
Canigou, Pic du, 17
Cantobre, 101
Cap Lévy, 66
Carnac (Brittany), 11
Carnac (Tarn), 122
Casse Déserte (Col d'Izoard), 149
Castelbouc, 119
Castelfranc, 88
Castelnau-Montratier, 86
Causse Méjean, 119, 122
Causse Noir, 121
Cazes-Mondenard, 87
Cazillac, 88
Cercié, 115
Chalet-Reynard, le, 131
Chamaloc, 154
Chamberet, 95
Champfrémont, 78

Champigny, 83
Champillon, 93
Chapelle-des-Marais, la, 70
Chartreuse, 15
Château de la Caze, 117
Château-Queyras, 149
Châtelet, le, 103
Chaudes-Aigues, 14
Chaumuzy, 92
Cheillé, 85
Chénas, 115
Cher, River, 82
Cherbourg, 63, 64
Chigny-les-Roses, 92
Chinon, 84
Chiroubles, 115
'Christophe's forge' (Ste Marie-de-Campan), 155
'Chute de Rivière' (1960 Tour de France), 119
Cime de la Bonette, 136
Cinto, Monte, 18
Cirque de Gavarnie, 139, 141
'Clochemerle' (Vaux-en-Beaujolais), 115
Cognac, 14
Cols: these are listed in the order,
Col d', Col de (including de la),
Col des, Col du
Col d'Allos, 134
Col d'Ayen, 107
Col d'Illoire, 106
Col d'Izoard, 148
Col de Carri, 127
Col de Cauperlac (or Coperlac), 119, 122
Col de Crie, 113
Col de Croix-Montmain, 115
Col de Durbize, 114, 116
Col de Faubel, 100
Col de Fontmartin, 114
Col de Frères, 16
Col de Guardia, 18
Col de l'Iseran, 129, 147
Col de la Bonette, 136
Col de la Cayolle, 138
Col de la Crêt de la Neige, 13
Col de la Croix de l'Orme, 114
Col de la Croix de Fer, 142
Col de la Croix de l'Oeillon, 151
Col de la Croix Morand, 14
Col de la Croix Perrin, 124
Col de la Croix Robert, 14
Col de la Croix-Rosier, 114
Col de la Machine, 127

Col de la Madeleine, 150
Col de la Pierre Plantée, 100
Col de Macuègne, 52, 132
Col de Maupas, 127
Col de Méraillet, 142
Col de Parpaillon, 43
Col de Perjuret, 118
Col de Prat Peyrot, 99
Col de Raspaillon, 138
Col de Redondet, 14
Col de Restefond, 127
Col de Rieisse, 119
Col de Romeyère, 152
Col de Rousset, 154
Col de Sereyrède, 99, 100
Col de St Sulpice, 76, 79
Col de Truges, 116
Col de Vars, 157
Col de Vergio, 18
Col des Aravis, 134
Col des Champs, 139
Col des Glières, 145
Col des Granges Communes, 138
Col des Saisies, 154, 155
Col des Tempêtes, 131, 132
Col du Champ Juin, 113
Col du Collet, 145
Col du Fût d'Avenas, 113
Col du Glandon, 143
Col du Mollard (or Molard), 142, 143
Col du Pointu, 111
Col du Tourmalet, 16, 155
Colmars, 134, 139
Combe Laval, 126
Comeiras, 100
Concourson-sur-Layon, 84
Corancy, 103
Cormet de Roselend, 141, 142
Corniche du Pail, 79
Corsica, 18
Cotentin (route), 62-66
Cotentin, 9
Courchamps, 83
Course, 62
Course, River, 61
Cravant-les-Côteaux, 85
Crémarest, 62
Crêt d'Oeillon, 150
Crêt de la Neige, 13
Croisette, la, 103
Crossac, 69
Crozes-Basses, les, 99
Cuchery, 92
Cumières, 92

Damery, 93
Daudet's windmill, Fontvieille, 71
Dénezé-sous-Doué, 83
Départements:
01-Ain, 15
02-Aisne, 8
03-Allier, 14
04-Alpes-de-Haute-Provence, 17
05-Hautes-Alpes, 17
06-Alpes-Maritimes, 17
07-Ardèche, 15
08-Ardennes, 10
09-Ariège, 16
10-Aube, 10
11-Aude, 16
12-Aveyron, 16
13-Bouches-du-Rhône, 17
14-Calvados, 9
15-Cantal, 14
16-Charente, 14
17-Charente-Maritime, 14
18-Cher, 11
19-Corrèze, 14
2A-Corse-du-Sud, 18
2B-Haute-Corse, 18
21-Côte-d'Or, 12
22-Côtes-du-Nord, 11
23-Creuse, 14
24-Dordogne, 15
25-Doubs, 13
26-Drôme, 15
27-Eure, 9
28-Eure-et-Loir, 11
29-Finistère, 11
30-Gard, 16
31-Haute-Garonne, 16
32-Gers, 16
33-Gironde, 15
34-Hérault, 16
35-Ille-et-Villaine, 11
36-Indre, 11
37-Indre-et-Loire, 11
38-Isère, 15
39-Jura, 13
40-Landes, 15
41-Loir-et-Cher, 11
42-Loire, 15
43-Haute-Loire, 14
44-Loire-Atlantique, 11
45-Loiret, 11
46-Lot, 16
47-Lot-et-Garonne, 15
48-Lozère, 16
49-Maine-et-Loire, 11

50-Manche, 9
51-Marne, 10
52-Haute Marne, 10
53-Mayenne, 11
54-Meurthe-et-Moselle, 10
55-Meuse, 10
56-Morbihan, 11
57-Moselle, 10
58-Nièvre, 12
59-Nord,
60-Oise, 8
61-Orne, 9
62-Pas-de-Calais, 8
63-Puy-de-Dôme, 14
64-Pyrénées-Atlantiques, 15
65-Hautes-Pyrénées, 16
66-Pyrénées-Orientales, 16
67-Bas-Rhin, 10
68-Haut-Rhin, 10
69-Rhône, 15
70-Haute-Saône, 13
71-Saône-et-Loire, 12
72-Sarthe, 11
73-Savoie, 15
74-Haute-Savoie 15
75-Paris, 10
76-Seine-Maritime, 9
77-Seine-et-Marne, 10
78-Yvelines, 10
79-Deux-Sèvres, 14
80-Somme, 8
81-Tarn, 16
82-Tarn-et-Garonne, 16
83-Var, 17
84-Vaucluse, 17
85-Vendée, 11
86-Vienne, 14
87-Haute-Vienne, 14
88-Vosges, 10
89-Yonne, 12
90-Territoire-de-Belfort, 13
91-Essonne, 10
92-Hauts-de-Seine, 10
93-Seine-St-Denis, 10
94-Val-de-Marne, 10
95-Val d'Oise, 10
Deschamps, les, 115
Desvres, 62
Desvres, Forêt de, 62
Devinière, la, 84
Die, 154
Digue de la Mer, 75
Dizy, 93
Domps, 95
Dordogne, River, 15

Dourbie, Gorges de (route), 98–101
Dourbies, 99
Drôme, River, 122
Druye, 80, 82
Dun-les-Places, 102
Durance, River, 40, 151
Duravel, 88

Ecalgrain, Baie de, 65
Embry, 61
Emmeringes, 113
Enquin-sur-Ballons, 62
Epernay, 90
Epieds, 84
Equieudreville, 63
Estrée, 61
Etang de Fangassier, 75
Etang de Galabert, 75
Etang de la Dame, 75
Etang de Vaccarès, 74, 75
Etang du Defais, 77
Etang du Goulot, 102
Eymoutiers, 94

Faubel, Col de, 100
Faux de Verzy, 91
Faux-la-Montagne, 97
Fedrun, Ile de, 68
Fermanville, 66
Fleury-la-Rivière, 92
Florac, 119
Florressas, 87
Flumet, 136, 155
Fontainebleau, Forest of, 9
Fontvieille, 71
Forêt d'Anost, 104
Forêt de Boulogne, 62
Forêt de Chinon, 85
Forêt de Multonne, 78
Forêt de Pail, 79
Forêt de Sillé, 77
Forges, 83
Fossés Blancs, les, 68
Fraissenet-de-Fourques, 118
Frayssinat-le-Gélat, 88
Frencq, 60
Frères, Col de, 16

Gèdre, 140
Gentioux-Pigerolles, 97
Germaine, 90
Germolles-sur-Grosne, 113, 114
Glaciers Blanc et Noir, 152
Gorges de la Nesque, 133

Gorges de la Dourbie and Mont Aigoual (route), 98–101
Gorges du Bachelard, 137, 138
Gorges du Méaudret, 126
Gorges du Tarn et Jonte (route), 116–122
Goule Noire, 126
Gouloux, 102
Grand Ballon, 11
Grand Canyon du Verdon (route), 105–107
Grand Goulets, 126
Grand Romeu, 74, 76
Grande Brière (route) 67–71
Grenoble, 15
Gréville-Hague, 64
Grosne, Rivers, 113, 114
Guardia, Col de, 18
Guchan, 146
Guillaumes, 139
Guillestre, 148, 158

Halinghen, 60
Hameau-de-la-Mer, 64
Hardelot, Forêt de, 60
Haut Folin, 103
Haut Limousin (route), 93–97
Haut Pays d'Artois (route), 59–62
Haut Pichot, 60
Hautvillers, 93
Hénoville, 61, 62
Herbignac, 70
Herpinière, Moulin de, 83
Hesdineuil-lès-Boulogne, 60
Historical provinces (map), 9
Hourquette d'Ancizan, 146
Hucqueliers, 62
Huismes, 83

Ile-Martin, 83
Indre, River, 80, 82
Isère, River, 122

Jausiers, 138, 157
Jonte and Tarn Gorges (route), 116–122
Jura, 12, 13

Kerbourg, 71
Kerhinet, 69, 70

In deciding to classify places under l', la or le we have followed local usage as to whether or not the definite article is used as an inseparable part of the name. Others appear with the article after the name.

l'Argentière-la-Bessée, 115
l'Espérou, 99
la Caze, 122
la Chambre, 145, 150
la Chapelle-aux-Naux, 82
la Chapelle-en-Vercors, 127
la Clusaz, 134
la Cresse, 120
la Fosse (underground village), 83
la Malène, 122
la Palud-sur-Verdon, 107
la Parade, 122
la Roche, 65
la Terrasse (near Beaujeu), 113
la Turballe, 70
la Verrerie, 145
Lac de Chaumeçon, 102
Lac de Ste Croix, 106
Lac de Vassivière, 94, 96
Lacelle, 95
Lacoste, 109
Landemer, 64
Landes, 15
Lauzerte, 87, 89
le Chêne, 104
le Fief, 115
le Gravet, 104
le Hâble, 65
le Portel, 60
le Puy (near Chinon), 85
le-Puy-Notre-Dame, 84
Lerné, 84
le Rozier, 118
les Jarrands, 126
les Saisies, 155
les Vignes (Tarn), 120, 122
les-Barraques-en-Vercors, 126
les-Baux-de-Provence, 71
les-Verchers-sur-Layon, 84
Liacous, 121
Limousin, Haut (route), 93–97
Loire, River, 80
Loire valley (route), 79–85
Longchamp, 150
Longvillers, 61
Lormes, 102
Lot, River, 88
Louresse, 84
Louvois, 91
Lubéron (route), 108–111
Ludes, 92

Luz-St-Sauveur, 140, 157
Luzech, 88

Mailly-Champagne, 92
Maladetta, 16
Malaucène, 133
Maninghem, 62
Marais Breton, 14
Marais Poitevin, 14
Marchampt, 114
Marenla, 61
Mareuil-sur-Ay, 90
Marles-sur-Canche, 61
Marne, River, 90
Masgrangeas, 97
Massif Central, 14, 15
Massif des Cèdres, 133
Massif des Ecrins, 151, 158
Matour, 112
Maubec, 110
Maubert, 121
Méaudre, 126
Ménerbes, 109
Méron, 84
Meyrueis, 118
Mhère, 103
Millau, 120
Moirmoiron, 132
Mont Blanc, 14, 136, 150
Mont Brouilly, 115
Mont-St-Jean, 77
Mont St Michel, 9
Mont St Rigaud, 113
Mont Ventoux, 53 (route), 120–134
Montagne de Lure, 145
Montagne de Reims, 56, (route), 90–93
Montbrun (Tarn), 119
Montbrun-les-Bains, 133
Montchenot, 92
Montcuq, 87
Montfort, 83
Montpellier-le-Vieux, 121
Montreuil, 61
Montreuil-Bellay, 84
Montsauche, 102
Montsauche-les-Settons, 104
Montsols, 113
Montsoreau, 83
Morvan, 13, (route), 101–105
Moustiers-Ste-Marie, 105
Multonne, Forêt de, 78
Mutigny, 90, 92

Nant, 98
Nedde, 95
Nesque, River and Gorges, 131, 132
Neufchâtel-Hardelot, 60
Neuville-au-Larris, le, 92
Neuville-sous-Montreuil, 61
Nîmes, 17
Normandy, 9
Notre Dame de Bellecombe, 156

Odenas, 115
Offin, 61
Oppède-le-Vieux, 110
Orcourt, 92
Ouroux, 114

Pannessière-Chaumard, Lac de, 103
Paradou, 73
Pas de la Graille, 146
Pas de Peyrol, 14
Paulhe, 120
Pélussin, 151
Pelvoux, Commune de and Mont, 151
Petit Ballon, 11
Petit-Bornand, le, 145
Petit Lubéron, 108, 110
Petite Brière, 69
Peyrat-le-Château, 94
Peyreleau, 118
Peyrol, Pas de, 14
Pierre Fendue, la, 70
Plainefas, 102
Point Sublime (Grand Canyon du Verdon), 107
Pomarède, 88
Pommoy, le, 104
Pont-à-Mousson, 19
Pont d'Arc, 13
Pont d'Artuby, 106
Pont-de-Briques, 59
Pontcharas, 114
Pont du Gard, 17
Port Racine, 65
Pourcy, 92
Poyebade, la, 115
Prayssac, 88
Pré de Madame Carle, 151, 152
Préalpes du Sud, 17
Provinces, historical, 9
Puy de Sancy, 14
Puy Mary, 14
Puy-de-Dôme, 14

Quercy, 16, (route), 86–89
Querqueville, 64
Quillan, 16
Quimiac, 70
Quincié-en-Beaujolais, 114

Rambouillet, Forest of, 9
Ranrouet, Château de, 70
Redondet, Col de, 14
Régnié, 114, 115
Régnié-Durette, 115
Reims, 10
Reims, Montagne de, 10, (route)
    90–93
Rencurel, 154
Renievast, 66
Rhône, River, 74
Rilly-la-Montagne, 92
Rimboval, 61
Robion, 110
Roc de Hourtous, 120
Roc Trévezel, 11
Rochemenier (underground
    village), 83
Rochetaillée, 145
Roiffé, 84
Rougon, 107
Rousillon (region), 17
Roussillon (near Apt), 109, 111
Roussillon-en-Morvan, 104
Route des Crêtes (Grand Canyon
    du Verdon), 107
Routes (map), 57
Royère-de-Vassivière, 97
Rozé, 69

Saillé, 70
St Aubin-le-Désert, 79
St Bonnet-des-Bruyères, 112
St Bonnet-le-Plat, 113
St Brisson, 102
St Cénéri-le-Gérei, 78
St Chély-du-Tarn, 119
St Christophe-en-Montagne, 114
St Colomban-des-Villards, 143
St Cyr-en-Bourg, 83
St Estève, 133
St Etienne (near Sisteron), 145
St Etienne, 19
St Etienne-de-Tinée, 138
St Etienne-la-Varenne, 115
St François, 150
St Georges-le-Gaultier, 78
St Georges-sur-Layon, 84
St Germain-de-Coulamer, 79

St Germain-des-Vaux, 65
St Gervais, 153
St Hilaire-les-Courbes, 95
St Jacques-des-Arrêts, 112
St Jean-d'Arves, 143
St Jean-de-Bruel, 98
St Jean-de-Maurienne, 142, 145
St Jean-de-Sixt, 134
St Joachim, 69
St Joseph-en-Beaujolais, 113, 116
St Julien-en-Vercors, 127
St Just-sur-Dive, 83
St Lager, 115
St Léonard (Pas de Calais), 60
St Léonard-des-Bois, 78
St Lyphard, 68
St Malo-de-Guersac, 68
St Mamert, 114
St Martin-des-Entraumes, 139
St Martin-en-Vercors, 126
St Martin-le-Gréard, 66
St Martin-le-Redon, 88
St Martin-sur-la-Chambre, 150
St Molf, 70
St Paul (Col de Vars), 157
St Paul-le-Gaultier, 78
St Pierre-des-Nids, 78
St Pierre-le-Vieux (Beaujolais),
    114
St Sulpice, Col de, 76, 79
St Vaast-la-Hougue, 66
St Vincent-Rive-d'Olt, 88
Ste Enimie, 119
Ste Foy-Tarentaise, 147
Ste Marie-de-Campan, 147, 155,
    157
Ste Reine-de-Bretagne, 69
Stes Maries-de-la-Mer, 75
Saire, Val de, 66
Saix, 84
Samsons, des, 115
Sandun, 70
Sarthe, River, 76
Sault, 131
Sauzet, 88
Savigny, 83
Séez, 147
Seine, River, valley of, 10
Sereyrède, Col de, 99, 100
Sermiers, 92
Sillé-le-Guillaume, 77
Simpson memorial (Mont
    Ventoux), 131
Sisteron, 145
Souzay, 83

Sylvéréal, 75

Tarn and Jonte Gorges, 8,
    (route), 116–122
Teurthéville, 66
Thèze, River, 88
Thorens–Glières, 145
Tourmalet, Col du, 16
Treignac, 95
Trèves, 100
Trévezel, River and Gorge, 100
Trigance, 106

Ussé, 82

Val d'Enfer, 72
Val d'Isère, 147
Valbelle, 145
Valchevrière, 126
Vallouise, 151
Vassivière, Ile de, 97
Vassivière, Lac de, 94, 96
Vasteville, 65
Vauclaix, 103
Vauremont, 91
Vauveix, 97
Vauville, 65
Vaux-en-Beaujolais, 115
Vauxrenard, 114
Venosque, 131
Vercors, 15, (route), 122–127
Verdon, Grand Canyon du
    (route), 105–107
Verdun, 10
Vergio, Col de, 18
Verzenay, 91
Verzy, 91
Vézère, River, 94, 95
Vienne, River, 83, 85, 94
Villaine-les-Rochers, 83
Villaines-la-Juhel, 79
Villandry, 82
Villard-de-Lans, 123, 126
Villard-des-Arnauds, le, 137
Ville-en-Selve, 91
Villers-Allerand, 92
Villes-sur-Auzon, 132
Villié-Morgon, 115
Vire-sur-Lot, 87
Vosges, 10

Widehem, 60

Subject Index

Accident procedures, 23
Administration, 7
Administrative regions, 8–18
Air services, 27
    prohibited items, 27
Auberges, 30
Auberges de Jeunesse (youth
    hostels), 31

Banks, 19
Bars, 35
Bed-and-breakfast (chambres
    d'hôte), 31
Bike books, 160
Bike hire, 27
Bike shops, 22
Bike spares, 54-56
Bikes
    for touring in France, 37
    on air services, 27
    on Channel Tunnel services, 26
    coach service, 29
    on French trains, 26
Books, cycling, 160
    suppliers, 160
Bornes de kilometrage, 45, 47
Bottom bracket fittings, 56
Bread, types and names of
    loaves, 20–21

Cafés, 35
Camping, 31–33
    guides, 159
Carrying luggage, 41
Cave dwellings, 83, 84
Chambres d'hôte, 31
Channel Tunnel rail services, 24
Classic road races, 51
Climbing techniques, 39
Clothing, 52–54
Club des Cent Cols, 161
Code de la route, 43
Cold, clothing for, 53

Colonnes coiffées, 150, 157
Cranks, 55
Credit cards, 19
Critériums (cycle races), 51
Cross-Channel ferries, 24
CTC, 161
Currency, 19
Cycle lighting regulations, 44
Cycle racing, watching, 50
Cycle terms
    English to French, 167–169
    French to English, 165–167
'Cycling for Softies' (organized
    tours), 162
Cycling on right of road, 42
Cyclists' Touring Club, 161

D-roads, 42
Descending mountain roads, 40

Earth pillars, 150, 157
Eating out, 34–36
Emergencies, 23
Eurocheques, 19
European Bike Express coach
    service, 29

Fédération Française de
    Cyclotourisme, 161
Ferries, cross-Channel, 24
FFCT, 161
Forest roads, 43
Freewheels, 55
French language, 18

Gearing of bicycle, 38
Gears, 38
Gîte guides, 159
Gîte organizations, 161
Gîtes d'étape, 31
Gîtes ruraux, 30

Heat, clothing for, 53–54

Hire of bicycles, 27
Hostelleries, 30
Hostels, independent (gîtes
    d'étape), 31
Hostels, youth, 31
Hotels, 30

IGN maps, 49
Independent hostels (gîtes
    d'étape), 31
Insurance, travel, 23

Kilometre stones, information
    on, 43, 45, 47

Language, 18
Libraries, finding cycling books
    in, 160
Logis, 30
Luggage carrying, 41

Maps, 47–49
    suppliers, 160
Markets, 22
Medical procedures, 23
Metric system, 20
Michelin maps, 47–49
Michelin tourist guides, 159
Money, 19
Mountain cycling techniques, 38
Mountain guides, 160
Mountain-bike races, 51

N-roads, 42

Ordre des Cols Durs, 161
Organizations, useful, 161–162

Passports, 24
Pedals, 55
Pensions, 30
Priorities, road, 46
Provinces, traditional, 9

Rail timetables, 161
  bikes by, 26
Randonnées, 51
Randonnées permanentes, 52
Regions, adminsitrative, 8–18
Restaurants, 34
Road classification, 42–43
Road priorities, 46
Road signs, 44–46
  glossary of, 163
Roadside emergencies, 23
Routes départementales
  (D-roads), 42
Routes forestières, 43
Routes nationales (N-roads), 42
Routes *see* place names index

Routes stratégiques, 43
Rule of the road, 42, 43

Seasons, best, 7
Shops, 20–22
Shorts, cycling, 53
Signposting, 46
Sunburn, prevention of, 54

Telephones, 22
Tour de France, 50
Touring bikes, 37
Tourist information centres
  (Syndicats d'Initiative), 30
Traditional provinces, 9
Traffic light sequence, 46

Trains, French (SNCF), 26
Tyres, 55
  sizes, 55

Using low gears, 39

Visas (for non-EU travellers), 24
Volume measures, 20

Watching cycle racing, 50
Water, drinking, 54
Weather, 7

Youth hostels, 31
  organizations, 161